What the Future Holds

What the Future Holds

Insights from Social Science

edited by Richard N. Cooper and Richard Layard

The MIT Press
Cambridge, Massachusetts
London, England

This book was set in Bembo in 3B2 by Asco Typesetters, Hong Kong.
Printed and bound in the United States of America.

Library of Congress Cataloging-in-Publication Data

What the future holds : insights from social science / edited by Richard N. Cooper and Richard Layard.
    p.   cm.
  Includes bibliographical references and index.
  ISBN 0-262-03294-5 (hc : alk. paper)
  1. Social prediction. 2. Forecasting. I. Cooper, Richard N. II. Layard, P. R. G. (P. Richard G.)
HM901 .W53   2002
303.49—dc21   2001032976

Contents

1   Introduction   1
Richard N. Cooper and Richard Layard

2   The River and the Billiard Ball: History, Innovation, and the
Future   17
Peter Schwartz

3   The Future of Population   29
Joel E. Cohen

4   The Future of Energy from the Perspective of the Social
Sciences   77
Clark C. Abt

5   Modeling Climate Change Impacts and Their Related
Uncertainties   123
Stephen H. Schneider

6   The World of Work in the New Millennium   157
Richard B. Freeman

7   Threats to Future Effectiveness of Monetary Policy   179
Benjamin M. Friedman

8   The Architecture of Government in the Twenty-First
Century   209
Timothy Besley

9   The Cybernetic Society: Western Future Studies of the 1960s
and 1970s and Their Predictions for the Year 2000   233
Alexander Schmidt-Gernig

Contributors   261
Index   263

1

Introduction

Richard N. Cooper and Richard Layard

Most human decisions involve making judgments about the future. When people think about a course of study, they form a view of what job opportunities it might lead to. When deciding where to buy a house, they forecast how life in different neighborhoods might develop. When planning a family, they make guesses about their future level of economic security.

Businesses too must make judgments about the future whenever investments are made. Should an oil company build a new refinery, and if so when? It depends on the future demand for gasoline, and on the world price of oil—in two or ten years' time.

Similar problems face other industries. What will be the demand for air travel a decade from now? What kinds of aircraft will be required? Both Boeing and Airbus forecast that demand will grow about 4.5 percent a year for the next decade (which does not mean the forecast will be correct), but they differ sharply over the character of demand. Airbus is betting that the main growth will be in travel between major airport hubs, while Boeing believes it will be to secondary destinations.

Government too has to forecast. The U.S. Navy orders ships today that will make up the fleet twenty years from now. What will the world be like then, and what ships will be most appropriate for that world? Or what about policy toward climate change? Continued "business as usual" in the growing use of fossil fuels will increase further carbon dioxide concentrations in the atmosphere, which in turn will affect the earth's climate. How seriously? Should we act urgently today to limit emissions?

Organized society cannot avoid thinking about the future and trying to discover as much as possible what it will be like. Knowledge is power, and knowledge of the future gives power to influence it. If you can foresee the future, you can make money, you can win wars, and you can improve society. So from the beginning of time man has examined entrails and consulted oracles to know what destiny held in store.

The oracles of today are science, which generates the new technology, and social science, which evaluates its impact upon human society. But the art of forecasting is still in its infancy. Egregious errors are made everyday. In 1980, IBM forecast the total sales of personal computers at 280,000—so few that they subcontracted the software to Bill Gates and the chips to Intel. Actual sales have been one hundred times higher, at 30 million. The fortune lost to IBM went to Microsoft and Intel. Wars too have happened due to forecasting errors. In 1914 Germany forecast that, if she invaded Belgium, Britain would remain neutral.

Forecasts go wrong because forecasting is so difficult. Two possible conclusions can be drawn. According to one school of thought, the likelihood of error is so great that no respectable person would become involved. On this view, academics should stay well away from the future—rather as, until recently, they were advised to stay away from the present.

This view is quite untenable. For the actions of every one of us are driven by some picture of the future. If that picture is wrong, we can make dreadful mistakes. But many of the more obvious mistakes could be avoided by systematic study. As with the study of the present, systematic analysis of the future leads to clearer understanding.

Predictions and Scenarios

The study of history and the interpretation of events goes back at least 2500 years, both in the eastern Mediterranean and in early China. Historians today differ sharply over what exactly should be the role of a good historian—simply to tell a story well and accurately, or to go further and draw general "lessons" from the historical record for the present and future. Social scientists do not have the luxury of such a debate: their objective is to generalize about human behavior. If social science claims to "explain" the past, it must be saying two things. First, the constellation of events up to time T determined what happened from time T onward. Second, we can analyze the events up to time T in a way that "predicts" the subsequent events.

But, if we can make that "prediction" of past events, we must be able to use the same framework to predict future events. A social scientist cannot claim to explain the past and deny that she or he has anything to say about the future. As Milton Friedman insisted in his *Essays in Positive Economics* (1953), the chief test of a scientific theory is its ability to predict.

Even so, predicting the future is decidedly more difficult than explaining the past. Change results from a mixture of general and specific factors. One could predict some important features of Britain's industrial revolution from the ready availability of coal, the depletion of forests, the accumulation of capital through foreign trade, and so on. But the explanation would be incomplete without including Watt's specific invention of the steam engine. Even if we could not fully explain that invention, we should want to include it in our overall historical prediction of what followed.

But when we turn to the future we cannot know the specific new knowledge that will be discovered (though for a decade or so ahead we may have some good general ideas). This removes one important prop from our ability to think about change.

A similar problem relates to political events. The history of Europe was transformed by a Corsican officer who happened to be stationed in Paris in 1795. No one forecasting in 1790 could have predicted Bonaparte's future role, but when we look back it was decisive. Similarly with respect to Adolph Hitler in 1923, or the discovery in 1948 of the semiconducting properties of silicon and related substances. Looking ahead, our uncertainty about these specific features means that it is much easier to forecast general social and technological trends than it is to forecast specific political or technical events.

All predictions are of course uncertain since we could never know all the factors at work nor the exact process through which they have their effects. This is obviously true of the future, but it is equally true of the past. When a historian tells you that X caused Y, he cannot possibly mean that from knowing X you would have been certain that Y would follow. All predisposing circumstances give rise to a range of possible outcomes. That is how forecasts should be expressed.

Some planners go further and shun the word forecasting altogether. According to them the future is so difficult to descry that we can only offer various scenarios of what might happen. This process of scenario building was developed at Shell by Pierre Wack and his successor Peter Schwartz. It can serve a crucial function in forcing decision makers to consider seriously those possible futures, which, though not the most likely, could easily happen and (if they did happen) introduce a quite new ball game. For example in 1982 Schwartz speculated that oil prices might fall to $16 a barrel and in consequence Shell was ready should it happen, as it did three years later.

Scenario builders do not usually attach explicit probabilities to the different scenarios. But there are at least some implicit ranges of probability. In principle the number of possible scenarios is infinite. In selecting four or five, the scenario builder is implicitly choosing those that are most significant. But he is also insisting that the range of possible outcomes is often very wide—and becomes wider the further we peer into the future.

For a small firm the use of prediction is to forecast what the market will be like, which is essentially independent of what the firm does. But for a government (or even a large firm) the aim is to forecast what will happen in response to what the government (or firm) does. Thus the decision maker wants to know the probability of different outcomes for each of the policy options it is considering. It can then select the policy option that offers the highest expected level of social welfare or profit (or whatever else the decision maker wants to maximize).

The Role of Social Science

The various possible outcomes are of great importance to the general public. But there is remarkably little systematic public discussion of these issues. From around 1950 to around 1980, there was substantial discussion, stimulated originally by the work of the Twentieth Century Fund and other nonprofit organizations in the United States, and later by the Club of Rome (see chapter 9). But since 1980 most crystal gazing has been undertaken in private for private corporations. Academics have been loath to get involved. This is a tragedy for democratic debate and for the refinement of methods, which is almost always best done in the clear light of day.

The purpose of this book is to encourage more academic research and more public debate. If social scientists thought harder about the future, this would make them focus their research into the present and past more fruitfully, with more attention to the key predictors of change.

All of the social sciences have their own contribution to make. Economists have for many years offered short-term forecasts, of growing sophistication and accuracy (McNees 1992). But their longer term musings have generally focused on broad aggregates of income levels and energy use, and less on the microstructure of the economy or on patterns of working life. The great strength of economics is its concept of market equilibrium and of adjustment to shocks. Economics is thus especially strong in analyzing variables that tend to cycle around an equilibrium.

Sociologists and social psychologists by contrast are interested in permanent and irreversible changes. While economists and political scientists tend to assume certain enduring elements in human nature and in social arrangements, sociologists are looking for what is new. They are interested in the impact of new social values—for example regarding the economic role of women, which appears to have undergone a durable change. The tension between these two perspectives (economic and sociological) is potentially fruitful for the understanding of change.

And then there are the natural scientists and engineers who generate the new technology. The U.S. research community has been much more successful in promoting interaction between science and social science than is common in Europe. This may be because more people move between the disciplines themselves. (The authors of the next four chapters all began as scientists.)

How Do We Predict?

How do we think about the future? The simplest "forecast" is to assume that tomorrow will be like today: for any variables of interest y, we assume $y_{t+1} = y_t$. This turns out to be the best prediction for market interest rates or exchange rates in the short run, since any other forecast would lead to an instantaneous change in the current rate. We predict that the sun will come up tomorrow, as it did today. If y is the time of sunrise, however, close observation suggests some drift, so that $y_{t+1} = y_t + at$ would be a more accurate forecast, where a is the daily drift in time of sunrise. This prediction would, however, produce increasingly greater errors, as the seasons advance. Further careful observation over several years would suggest that $y_{t+1} = y_t + a \sin(t/91)$ would be a superior forecast. Indeed, the annual periodicity of dawn was one of mankind's earliest empirical observations, and accurate forecasts. Only later, with Ptolemy, was a systematic "explanation" offered, and that turned out to be incorrect. Copernicus offered a more nearly correct explanation, with his "model" of the solar system, based on rotation of the earth around its axis combined with its revolution around the sun. Kepler refined the predictions, and Newton provided a deeper explanation with his laws of motion.

Simple (arithmetic or geometric) extrapolation or periodicity may offer useful predictions for many phenomena, at least over relatively short periods of time, where the definition of "short" depends on the subject at hand. However, we know, or at least we believe, that many phenomena, for example the rate of economic growth, depend on other variables, for example the rate of investment, which in turn may depend on (and help to determine) the rate of interest. Some of these determining variables may be subject to conscious human control, for example the rate of taxation on new investment. Thus the prediction takes the form $y_t = f(x_t, x_{t-1}, \ldots, p_t)$, where $f(\ldots)$ means "depends on" in some specified way, the xs are present and past values of determining variables whose future values we must predict if we want to predict y_{t+1}, and the p's are variables that are subject to individual human or organizational decisions or to public policy.

Even if we are very good at specifying the model, depicted here by $f(\ldots)$, we will never have the ability to predict everything, or even many things with high accuracy. We have learned from "chaos theory" that complex systems, of which human society is surely an example, are impossible to predict accurately beyond the relatively near future because their evolution is extremely sensitive to exact values of the determining variables. Yet the precision with which we can know the "initial conditions"—as Cohen demonstrates in chapter 3, with respect to the existing population of any territory, much less the world—is in practice limited. In addition, every earthly society is subject to perturbations from outside, either by nature (e.g., volcanic eruptions) or by neighboring societies, that might in time greatly deflect the initially predicted evolution.

Despite these limitations, we do want to know what the future will bring. Many decisions today depend on some view of the future, and that fact has spawned an industry of consultants who offer views about the future. Simplicity and comprehensibility are virtues, unless they lead us into deep error. Some consultants develop their views of the future explicitly and formally—elaborations of the approaches suggested above.

Others rely on their expert judgment. But except for those who operate on intuition alone, or have discovered new ways of soothsaying, they implicitly rely on the formal approaches as well. Nonspecialists can rely on the testimony of experts, as in the Delphi technique, which essentially averages the quantitative predictions of experts, possibly allowing for revised opinion after learning the opinion of other experts.

The conference (held in Oxford in July 1999) that gave rise to this book was convened to address how we might think intelligently about the future. Rather than focusing on the methodology of futurology, however, we decided to ask some well-known specialists to write about the future, drawing on their expertise. Then we could discover what method each used to address issues of the future. In the remainder of this introductory chapter we offer brief summaries of the subsequent chapters, and comment on the approach that each author took.

Scenarios

Chapter 2 by Peter Schwartz insists that point predictions are often not useful, and may actually mislead decision makers, whether in business or in government. Precisely because of the unpredictability of the future, decision makers should be prepared for a variety of contingencies, some of which, if unprepared for, could be devastating to the objectives of those responsible for decisions. Thus Schwartz specializes in the production of "scenarios," alternative futures within a given domain. All of them should be plausible even if they are somewhat remote in likelihood: some possible futures could make a huge difference to the well-being of the organization in question, and it should be prepared to cope even with these remote possibilities. Of course, to be plausible scenarios must have their roots in the present, or represent patterns that have been observed elsewhere that could conceivably apply to the domain under examination. The process of formulating and examining alternative scenarios itself involves broadening one's horizon from the routinely predictable and represents a useful exercise in relevant learning. An example of scenario building in practice can be found in Schwartz's 2000 book (written with James Ogilvey), *China's Futures: Scenarios for the World's Fastest Growing Economy, Ecology, and Society*, where three radically different but internally consistent China's are sketched for the year 2022, covering a prosperous, increasingly democratic China; a plutocratic, highly fragmented China; and a China rescued from pervasive corruption by an authoritarian, repressive general who, incidentally, absorbed some of Russia's Far East into an enlarged China. None of these scenarios may materialize, but they bound a possible range that businesses and governments alike should consider in framing their approaches to China.

Population

Demographic developments are perhaps among the most underused determining factors (one of the xs in the equation above) for the evolution of economy and society. People alive today will inexorably age over time; those who turn fifteen in 2015 have all been born already. People go through a natural life cycle of infancy, adolescence, young (possibly fecund) adulthood, maturity, and old age, with implications in any given social setting for educational requirements, consumption (and savings) behavior, labor force participation, and many other factors. Much information about the next few decades is thus contained in today's population and age profile. Still, long-term demographic forecasts can be in serious error, as was the celebrated Twentieth Century Fund (Dewhurst and Associates 1955) forecast in the early 1950s that the world's population by 2000 would be 3.6 billion. The estimated actual population was 6.1 billion, a figure that would have astounded social scientists a half-century ago, implying a forecast error in excess of 300 percent! Demographers usually divide populations into age cohorts, and then impute existing or extrapolated mortality and natality rates to each cohort; from these assumptions they can build a profile of the population ten, twenty, or even fifty years from now.

In chapter 3 Joel Cohen documents just how fragile population projections are, and indeed how uncertain estimates of existing population may be. Mortality, while relatively predictable in the medium run, has declined significantly more rapidly than was estimated two, four, or especially six decades ago; by comparison natality remains something of a mystery, with substantial increases and declines that forecasters have missed entirely.

In the very long run the growth in population is likely to be close to zero, as it was throughout most of mankind's history; the twentieth century marks a major exception. But we do not know the ultimate base from which this near-to-zero growth will proceed. However, one can place plausible bounds on the size and characteristics of the world population over the coming century: it is sure to increase, but at least for the next half-century at a decreasing rate; it will age; and it will become increasingly urban. By 2050 world population is likely to range between 8 billion and 12 billion, up from 3 billion in 1960. Cohen engages in reasoned speculation about some of the consequences of these developments, especially the changing attitudes and role of women, the pressures for migration, the adaptation of agriculture and extension of aquaculture, the value placed on nature, and the value placed on more detailed information about the earth's ecology and geophysical characteristics. As population growth slows in developing countries, the perceived value of a human being is likely to grow, as it did following the population crash in fourteenth-century Europe. That in turn may accelerate the diffusion of civil, political, and social rights.

Energy

One of the important foundations of modern society—some would say the most important material base—is the consumption of inanimate energy, especially fossil fuels, a consumption whose rate has grown sharply with economic development and industrialization. Yet such consumption has a number of undesirable side effects—from local air pollution to acid rain to gouged landscapes to possible changes in the global climate. In chapter 4 Clark Abt reviews a number of past forecasts of total energy and oil consumption, and finds that they were typically wide of the mark—although some overestimated and others underestimated relative to the final outcome. Mainline forecasts for the early twenty-first century suggest a world still heavily dependent on fossil fuels, and a growing dependence on them in today's relatively poor countries.

Abt sketches some of the alternative, technically available sources of energy, which could propel modernization forward in poor parts of the world without many of the unwanted side effects, and in some cases without some of the expensive infrastructure. His approach represents a *possible* and in his view more desirable future in the domain of energy. But human behavior is largely inertial in the absence of compelling reasons for change. Thus achieving preferable outcomes requires not only heightened awareness of the favorable alternatives to fossil fuels, but also the creation of incentives (e.g., through taxation and regulation) for millions of households and firms—the real decision makers—to adopt the improved technologies. Abt's approach represents a variant on the identification of scenarios. If a best prediction looks unattractive, choose an alternative scenario, which of course must be feasible, and identify the conditions for its realization.

Climate Change

One of the undesirable side effects from heavy use of fossil fuels may be significant change in the global climate. The emission of carbon dioxide (from coal and oil) and other so-called greenhouse gases has "thickened" the blanket provided by the earth's atmosphere, leading to a gradual warming of the earth's surface. This warming, in turn, may alter the amount and pattern of rainfall, the frequency and magnitude of storms, and the levels and currents of the oceans. That the concentration of carbon dioxide in the atmosphere since the beginning of the industrial revolution two centuries ago has risen significantly is not in doubt. But the future implications of this continuing rise, as coal and oil are burned in ever greater amounts, remain a source of considerable uncertainty.

In chapter 5 Stephen Schneider discusses what we know about these complicated processes, and how we know it. The technique in this instance is to build complex mathematical models of the earth's climate, called general climate models (GCMs), which reflect basic principles of physics and are fitted to historical data. These models are then "shocked" with a steady increase in atmospheric carbon dioxide, as from growing emissions from fossil fuels. The next century of climate is then simulated by computer to discover what might happen to surface temperature, precipitation, wind velocity, and other variables of interest. These simulations provide the basis for making predictions about future climate change, contingent on continued high emissions of carbon dioxide. Schneider distinguishes what we know with high confidence from what we are still trying to discover through ongoing research, and some of the reasons for the many remaining uncertainties. Individual scientists believe their results with varying degrees of certitude, and the results of polled expert opinion are also reported and discussed, another technique for making judgments about the future.

Scientific discovery and forecasts of the future, even when held with high confidence, do not automatically translate into requirements for public policy. That depends on assessments of the social impacts of the forecast climate change, on the costs and benefits of taking particular actions to reduce net greenhouse gas emissions into the atmosphere, and on the values and preferences of publics around the world with respect to likely or possible non-economic as well as economic consequences of forecast climate change. Schneider also briefly addresses these issues.

Work

Will information and communications technology lead to an increasingly atomistic economy in which workers have increasingly short-term relationships with their employers, and firms become increasingly fragmented? As Richard Freeman points out in chapter 6, the alleged trend toward shorter jobs is based on slender evidence to date. In many cases the trend is toward greater engagement of workers with their employers, as specific human capital becomes more important. Similarly, though smaller firms employ a growing fraction of the workforce, so at the other end of the spectrum do larger ones, whose brands span the globe. Human beings will use the Internet for those purposes that suit them, but they will not allow it to cut them off from ordinary forms of collective human action.

Freeman points out the widespread forecast in rich countries of job availability, by industry and skill level, and discusses the relatively primitive methodology for making such "forecasts," ignoring as they typically do economic feedbacks from the marketplace on wages and other terms of employment. But they are significantly better than simple extrapolation of job growth for particular classes of workers, such as seriously embarrassed the National Science Foundation with respect to future U.S. need for scientists and engineers.

Freeman identifies six qualitative trends in the workplace, and speculates on the nature of future employment in Europe and the United States. The trends involve increased employment of women in higher-paying jobs, the increase in average skill and age of workers, the global shift in world labor force toward countries that today are considered "developing," the shift in manufacturing employment to these countries and continuing decline of manufacturing employment (but not necessarily output) in rich countries, the growth in employment in health care and personal services, and the near universal use of information technology at the workplace and in the market. The impact of these trends on labor contracts, unionism, wage inequality, leisure, wage formation, and on the nature of the workplace is not as straightforward as many analysts have suggested, leaving lots of room both for variety and for continued debate over the practical significance of the trends.

Money

Advances in computational and communications technology among other things are making it easier and less costly to make payments electronically. It is possible to imagine a world, as Benjamin Friedman does in chapter 7, in which almost all payments in advanced societies are made in this way, and balances or lines of credit are extended by many commercial institutions other than traditional banks. It is not only possible to imagine such a world; it may represent a good prediction of what the world will be like in a decade or two, if past technological advances can be confidently projected into the future, along with continuing reduction in the costs of electronic (or, increasingly, photonic) transactions.

But current national monetary management depends intimately on the ability of each national central bank to control the amount of reserve credit held by commercial banks, which in turn (with less certainty) determines the amount of credit available to firms and households. Enlarging the bases by which credit is extended and means of payment are created, including increasingly overseas transactions, may eventually undermine the ability of central banks to steer the economy through monetary policy, and indeed even raise questions about the stability of the national price level. While this possibility is not predicted with high probability, and indeed has been seriously contested by other economists (for instance Charles Goodhart in the July 2000 issue of *International Finance*), it poses a sufficiently radical change in current conventional ways of framing policy as to provoke reflection on possible alternative ways to manage the economy. Here we see the extrapolation of technological trends, combined with assumptions about human response to cheaper or more convenient ways to carry out their activities, blended with expert imagination to forecast an unanticipated and possibly undesirable outcome.

Government

This brings us to the impact of technological change upon political life. At the international level, the globalization of economic life means that an increasing number of problems can only be dealt with by international collaboration or international institutions (see chapter 8, by Timothy Besley). Obvious examples include problems of climate change and transboundary pollution, of financial stability, of trade policy, of labor migration, and of capital mobility. Increasing interdependence in all these dimensions makes it desirable that more decisions are taken collectively, at a supranational level. Whether this will actually occur is less certain, but political pressures for governments to realize their stated objectives make it highly likely to happen, baring some disaster that rekindles nationalism in the major countries of the world. At the same time, as power goes upward beyond the nation-state, regions may feel confident enough to claw down for themselves some of the remaining functions now performed by the nation state, and which can as easily be addressed at the subnational level. Thus the logic of greater economic interdependence may move us toward a more diffuse structuring of political authority.

Besley's approach to the future is thus to identify the key functions expected of government, to suggest that technological developments will alter the characteristics of those functions, and to predict that in time the structure of government will inevitably adapt to those changes, without however specifying how long the process will take. Concretely, as the activities of people impinge increasingly on others outside their national jurisdiction, pressures will arise for greater international cooperation, and even for delegating limited powers to supranational bodies. The European Union offers a contemporary example of this process at work. Improvements in communication introduce new methods for assuring political accountability, which could also diminish the importance of the nation–state.

Modern Futurology

In chapter 9 Alexander Schmidt-Gernig places "futurology" into its intellectual and historical context. Men have sought to foretell the future for millennia—the oldest known Chinese writing is on "oracle bones" of the thirteenth century B.C., and our word "delphic" derives from the ancient Greek oracles of Delphi. But a new "systems" approach to futurology emerged in the 1960s, drawing inspiration from Norbert Wiener's study of "cybernetics": the science of communication and control in both inanimate and animate systems. Schmidt-Gernig characterizes three broad schools or movements of the 1960s and early 1970s. The first focused primarily on technical achievements, methods of production, and the nature of the workplace; the second on relations among states and the nature of political relations and decision making; the third on pressures on resources and the environment, and on social relations among individuals and groups of people. In brief oversimplification, the first tended to project by the year 2000 a world of great achievement and high well-being, the second an erosion of the role of the nation-state, and the third a world of resource exhaustion, ecological disaster, and widespread human disaffection. All three schools shared a common analytical assumption, namely that technology drives change, not only in producing new goods and services and in altering methods of production, but also in institutional arrangements and even social norms and cultural values.

Some of the forecasts for 2000 were remarkably prescient. In their list of 100 technological achievements, for instance, Kahn and Wiener in 1967 identified the widespread use of computers (not only in the workplace but also in the home, communicating with the outside world and offering vast new opportunities for home education), the broadcast from satellites to homes, multiple applications of lasers, new techniques of birth control, and increases in life expectancy. Others, however, were far from the mark (although they may still come to pass in a more distant future), such as the construction of large artificial moons, control of weather, interplanetary travel to extraterrestrial cities, and genetic control over the basic constitution of individuals. In particular, futurologists of a quarter century ago tended to exaggerate the malleability of social institutions and cultural values.

To forecast disasters correctly is extremely difficult. The postwar period produced many forecasts of disasters that did not occur, such as nuclear war and an end to economic growth caused by shortages of energy. Both of these forecasts, however, may have served a useful purpose in stimulating human response precisely to avoid the predicted outcome. Thus not all forecasts that prove to be "incorrect" are without social value; on the contrary, one purpose of forecasting, and of scenario building, is to identify unwanted or undesirable outcomes long enough in advance and with sufficient persuasiveness to lead to evasive social action.

Social science has only begun to address itself to the problems of forecasting the medium run. In economics much was learned about the economy through efforts to make short-term forecasts. Similarly, much could be learned about society, economics, and politics by trying to make forecasts of the medium term. Academics do not like doing this, because they would so often be wrong. But mankind would be much better off if we could improve the number of accurate forecasts by even a small percentage. And if, in consequence, we developed better models of social processes, we could better forecast which policies would improve the world.

References

Dewhurst, J. Frederic, and Associates. 1955. *America's Needs and Resources: A New Survey*. New York: Twentieth Century Fund.

Friedman, Milton. 1953. *Essays in Positive Economics*. Chicago: University of Chicago Press.

Kahn, Herman, and Anthony J. Wiener. 1967. *The Year 2000: A Framework for Speculation on the Next Thirty-Three Years*. New York: Macmillan.

McNees, Stephen K. 1992. "How Large Are Economic Forecast Errors?" *New England Economic Review* (July/August).

Ogilvey, James A., and Peter Schwartz. 2000. *China's Futures: Scenarios for the World's Fastest Growing Economy, Ecology, and Society*. San Francisco: Jossey-Bass.

2

The River and the Billiard Ball: History, Innovation, and the Future

Peter Schwartz

What is the right metaphor for the flow of time? Does time flow more like the turbulent river in which Heracleitus said you could not step twice? Or does it unfurl more like the mechanical universe of Newton's billiard balls? Does new knowledge make unpredictability fundamental as Paul Valery argued or is it merely a function of our ignorance? Prediction is only a matter of getting smarter and more knowledgeable. Are the lessons of yesterday a reasonable guide to tomorrow? These questions lie at the center of any attempt to anticipate the future. How one answers them will determine one's approach to foresight.

The key judgment anyone wishing to anticipate the future needs to make is whether the future is essentially similar to the past. This is obviously a question of domain and intellectual orientation. Are we interested in the future of traffic congestion on a given bit of highway or are we thinking about the future of the U.K. economy? In the former case it is likely that recent history will be a good guide to the future. Mathematical models will usually work reliably. In the case of the U.K. economy, sometimes history is a good guide and sometimes it isn't. U.K. exchange rate policy based on the rules of the game before the Euro-era was one thing. History may not serve one as well in making policy in the new world of the Euro. The methodologies of anticipation are dependent upon the answers to these questions.

What is the realm of inquiry? Is it narrow, simple, and stable or is it broad, complex, and volatile? If the dynamics of the relevant system are well bounded, fairly stable, and simple, then forecasting may be a reasonable goal. Expert judgment and rigorous mathematical models can be useful in that environment. In either case it is history that is shaping the forecast. The expert forms his judgment on the basis of his historical

experience. The model is based on historical relationships. The fundamental questions are the validity of the model and the quality of the data.

Essentially every forecasting method is based on some form of historical analysis. Daniel Patrick Moynihan in his days as a social scientist,
before becoming a U.S. senator, made one of the better forecasts of this
sort. In the late 1960s he rightly forecast that the rate of violent crime
would decline in the early 1980s no matter what our criminal justice
policy was. He observed that since young men committed most violent
crimes and that their number would inevitably be declining by the early
1980s, the crime statistics would inevitably follow the demographic
numbers downward. (Of course, the rules of the system were about to
change with the advent of the crack epidemic leading to an explosion of
violent crime caused by a dramatic increase in the financial incentives.)

Improving all of the conventional forecasting approaches essentially
relies on improving the quality of expert judgment, the quality of one's
model, or the quality of one's data. The simplest method for improving
expert judgment is simply to find a better expert. But there are more
methodical ways.

The Delphi method is a widely used technique for improving the
quality of expert judgment. It assumes that a large number of experts are
better than one, and that if you give them feedback in multiple iterations
of polling they will learn and improve their forecasts. Questions are put
to a panel of experts who are given the results of the first round of
questions as a way of sharpening the results of the next round. Several
iterations of forecasts should, in theory, lead to some degree of conver-
gence. Because outlier results are rejected, it tends to converge on a "no
surprises," conventional view of the future. By definition it will fail in
situations of high uncertainty and complexity.

Improving models has been the area of forecasting that has drawn
the most effort. Research has focused on the underlying theory, the
forms of models, and the mathematical capabilities of models. Advances
in computer technology have allowed ever more sophisticated, data-rich,
and complex models to be run fairly easily. As mathematics has advanced, new forms of models have also been possible. The mathematics
of chaos, along with massively parallel computers, has led to very complex models that are capable of dealing with nonlinear data-rich phenomena. A good example is modeling and predicting turbulent flow in
a fluid. Once mathematically impossible, the new models can literally

forecast the positions of small bundles of molecules in a fluid, treating them like Newtonian objects leading to very precise models of turbulent flow.

All such models rely on the assumption that the most important variables can be precisely specified and that the premises underlying the model do not change in any fundamental way. Unfortunately, in most important realms of forecasting, neither of these assumptions is likely to hold. Variables such as culture, values, beliefs, and behavior have proven to be very difficult to rigorously and precisely specify. They are not objective like the inflation rate. Human consciousness enters into all of these variables and, as a result, makes them self-referential and vulnerable to surprising shifts. Culture shapes values and beliefs, which shape what we selectively pay attention to, and reinforces culture and values.

The assumptions underlying models are also vulnerable to surprising and sudden shifts. The oil shocks of the 1970s threw most economic models out the window. The Phillips curve, linking unemployment and inflation, predicted that when inflation rose, unemployment would fall. Inflation results from growth in excess of the real potential of the economy. So high growth leads to tight labor markets, high wage growth, and high inflation. But a reallocation of global energy income toward OPEC led to inflation, low growth, and rising unemployment. Stagflation entered the economic vocabulary in the 1970s. In the 1990s the economists were fooled again. They could not imagine that productivity gains from new technology could be so large as to restore a high growth, low inflation environment. Fortunately, the chairman of the Federal Reserve, Alan Greenspan, was not too much a prisoner of the models. He kept searching for hints that the rules might be changing and managed the U.S. monetary policy accordingly.

As I noted earlier, the intellectual orientation of the forecaster also influences the choice of the model. There seem to be two very different kinds of intellectual mindsets. One sees the world as mechanistic and reductionist. A forecast should lead to a correct prediction. The intellectual problem is simply one of better models and better data. These forecasters will invest all their energy and effort in refining and elaborating their models and the pursuit of more data. This is the route to the *right* answer. The other intellectual orientation sees the world as intrinsically complex, holistic, and indeterminate. For those who follow this orientation, learning and better decisions are the goals not better prediction. The intellectual problem is gaining insight into the elements, structures, and dynamics of the relevant systems.

Now, as a practical matter, we are constantly forming historical analogies and acting on them. In most aspects of day-to-day life this presents little problem. However, in hugely consequential decisions with long-time constants, getting the historical model right can be critical, even a matter of life and death. And it is in just those decisive moments where we run into a fundamental epistemological flaw in all historical analogies of any complexity. As with the future there are alternative pasts. For every significant historical event there are multiple significantly different histories.

As I write this paper, for example, two of the most widely read and discussed histories view the same event through very different eyes. Niall Ferguson's insightful, provocative, and elegant *The Pity of War* and John Keegan's engaging and lucid *The First World War* see a different war and draw different historical lessons from that event. This is not because one is a good historian and the other a poor one. They ask different questions, bound the temporal domain differently, use different tools, and seek different purposes, so it is little surprise that they come to unique conclusions. It is fair to say that Keegan's is the more conventional of the two, which fits his intellectual disposition and history. And it is little surprise that Ferguson's would be more challenging, as he has pioneered a more innovative approach to history in the contemporary revival of the use of counterfactual histories.

These distinctions have consequence, for example, when we draw such conclusions as Saddam or Milosovich is like Hitler. Such an historical analogy gives weight to a policy of massive response in favor of a morally superior position. There is an implied counterfactual forecast in these analogies. If we do not act to stop these evil geniuses now there will be terrible consequences later. We have, in other contexts, classified men of similar evil as less important. For example, Idi Amin. What is the right historical context for understanding Saddam? Does he resemble Hitler or dozens of other minor dictators who have engaged in border wars in recent years?

So, when the central question for the forecaster becomes which of the competing historical models is a more useful guide to the future, the problem gets more interesting. Rigorous multiple interpretations are needed when the realm of inquiry is complex, with fuzzy boundaries, with not well understood or defined variables and dynamics. In short, if a single history is not necessarily the best guide to the future, what do we do? How we incorporate the "novel" in forecasts is the hardest problem we face in anticipating the future. The problem is complicated by the fact that there are two very different types of novelty. The sources of novelty are either exogenous or endogenous to a system; they arise surprisingly from outside or they are the result of the internal dynamics of the system itself.

The purely exogenous surprise is the most difficult to anticipate and deal with. An asteroid collision from deep space and the emergence of an evil genius like Hitler are good examples. In the case of the asteroid we know it has happened before and might again, we just don't know when and with what consequences. In the case of Hitler, the traumas of Germany might have been anticipated, but the capacity of one unique individual to exploit those miseries to such horrible ends was an unpredictable surprise. One can be systematic in the search for such surprises, but in the end it is mainly a matter of imagination. Though once such a potential surprise is identified one can be fairly rigorous in assessing its plausibility and significance.

The more interesting and common surprises are those that arise endogenously from the internal dynamics of the relevant system. This is the natural result of the stochastic outcome of concatenating events. Minor events trigger small branches in the flow of history. Chaos theory is an example of this kind of dynamic. Think of the growth of a tree as it expands in an ever more elaborate nimbus of branches. The interesting question is always "What are the important and interesting major branches?" Such major branches are usually the result of the accumulation of major endogenous events.

A good example was the oil shock of 1973. Part of the story lay in the oil policies of the United States, which simultaneously encouraged unconstrained demand by keeping prices down and discouraged supply by constraining oil development. This meant that U.S. oil imports rose dramatically around 1970. The other part of the story lay in the increasing nationalization of oil reserves in the OPEC nations. The Yom Kippur War was the trigger that determined the timing of the oil shock, but it was possible because of the dynamics of the international supply and demand system. My predecessors at Royal Dutch/Shell used that understanding to develop several scenarios of an impending oil shock, each of which differed in the trigger and timing. Only one of the scenarios avoided a price explosion and it seemed the least likely.

Experience with scenarios as a tool of anticipation indicates that they can be a powerful aid in seeing the big surprises long before they happen. Successfully using scenarios to anticipate the novel, first requires defining the boundaries of the system properly—otherwise the change appears exogenous and unpredictable. In the oil example above, looking only at national dynamics in say the United States or Japan would not have led to the right conclusions. Successful scenarios are usually the result of in-depth research into the nature of the system, and a rigorous, systematic process for exploring the alternatives. Many different approaches have been used to develop scenarios, but all of them are a combination of serious research, systematic processes, and imagination.

Scenarios as a forecasting tool can be seen as a systematic response to the problems and virtues of historical models. For example, useful scenarios will often incorporate the results of historical mathematical models run with alternative assumptions. Good scenarios, however, are not built on one model run three times. This is sensitivity analysis. Rather they are based on three different models embodying three distinct interpretations of history. Predictive forecasting is almost impossible where the problem forces us to deal with complex interactions of incommensurate driving forces and events. Alternative scenarios are built on such complex dynamics of driving forces and events systematically explored for plausibility and relevance. The boundaries of the relevant are neither objective nor arbitrary. They are defined by the relevant question. While the approach is systematic, it does not pretend to the rigor of mathematical forecasting. Imagination and stretching conceptual boundaries are essential in developing good scenarios, hence the craft is as much an art as it is a science.

The Shell 1984 scenarios that anticipated the fall of the Soviet Union and the end of the Cold War reflected these lessons from forecasting. They began with the question of whether there was a plausible end to the Cold War in the near future. That future was defined as the lifetime of the contracts for the new natural gas fields of the North Sea that were in competition with Soviet gas in the European market. A conventional economic model showed the Soviet economy moving forward at a tolerable pace. Thus there was little motive for radical change. A model we built, however, showed a contradiction between the energy and the economic numbers. The alternative model showed a Soviet Union on the verge of economic collapse facing a certain economic crisis. The question then became what would be the outcomes of such an inevitable crisis. The conventional historical interpretation suggested a renewal of even more stringent authoritarian methods of control, a scenario we called the New Stalinism or Fortress Russia. The plausibility of an alternative scenario of radical reform required finding an historical analogy of major reform from within in another communist system. The experience of introducing market reforms in Hungary became that model and led to a scenario we called Devolution or the Greening of Russia. In this scenario the Berlin Wall fell and the Cold War ended by 1990, with the Soviet Union breaking up soon thereafter.

Scientific and technological advances as sources of the novel pose unique problems for forecasting. There is a long and successful record of fairly rigorous mathematical tools being used in forecasting the performance of well-known technologies—miles per gallon of an internal combustion engine or mips of a mainframe computer. Again true novelty poses the greatest difficulties. One kind of problem arises when we want to see the big breaks in technology; the shift to electric vehicles or the births of the microchip and the personal computer, for example. A second and more difficult problem arises when the technological advance is based on fundamental advances in science—molecular biology and the resulting new therapies, for example. Is it possible to anticipate such leaps in basic science as well as technology?

Thus there are three classes of uncertainty resulting from advances in science and technology.

1. The technology is known but the application is uncertain. Today we can see that the Internet will be very important, but we are not sure of how fast and what specific ways it will transform the economy.

2. The science is known but the technology is uncertain. How fast will the fuel cell achieve cost and reliability levels needed for commercialization?

3. There are signals of change but the science is uncertain. What will be possible when the human genome is understood?

Major jumps in scientific insight are usually the result of some combination of new conceptual/mathematical tools, new experimental tools, and anomalous data. For example, the birth of both general relativity and quantum theory were the result of all three. Today, we are again ripe for a major leap in physical theory.

Among the lessons of the twentieth century in physics is that either relativity is right or quantum theory is right but not both. We have recently discovered that the neutrino, whose definition is that it has zero mass, now seems to have mass, however slight. It turns out that the universe may be expanding at an accelerating rate rather than at a stable or decelerating rate. Planetary solar systems seem to be common. Life might have existed once on our nearest planetary neighbor. Anomalies are cropping up all over. New tools are abundant from super computers to new kinds of telescopes to scanning tunneling microscopes. The result of all of these forces for change might merely be an incremental advance in physics. Another scenario might be a more radical leap akin to relativity. Super string theory might be just such a leap, but there are other competing theories that lead to other scenarios at the frontier of knowledge. A similar set of arguments can be made for advances in biology and chemistry.

Do these scientific scenarios lead, in turn, to technological scenarios? The current ideas and anomalies in physics do suggest what is possible and what is not. For example, there is little reason to believe in faster-than-light travel or instantaneous matter transportation. But there are hints that communicating faster than light, finding life elsewhere in the universe, or discovering the secret to antigravity might not be impossible. While it requires a great leap of imagination to imagine worlds of radical change where such advances are real, it is not plausible to put meaningful time or probability parameters on such scenarios. They are mainly useful only in guiding basic research at the frontier.

Looking ahead we can see important scientific and technological scenarios based on all three kinds of uncertainty.

1. One of the most important economic uncertainties of our time is whether the Internet will trigger a global wave of growth that will lift all boats into prosperity or cause only a few to rise to the crest while most remain in the trough. The wave may even prove to be only a ripple. The technology is well known, but its application is quite uncertain.

2. Over the past twenty years advances in genetics and molecular biology have revolutionized our understanding and capabilities of biological systems. Our scientific understanding has leapt ahead. What we will able

and allowed to do with it, however, is not at all clear. Will the advances lead to widely available cures for the mass or a better lifestyle for the well off? Will we cure disease or create disease-resistant organisms? Will deliberate misuse or accidental harm dominate over the benefits of bio-technology? And there are many more uncertainties.

We have the science in hand for a practical fuel cell. Most of the uncertainties involve engineering. Can we make it cheap and reliable enough to replace today's mobile and stationary power sources? If the answer is "yes" the result may be a green energy revolution. "No" may mean a much more polluted environment.

3. Nanotechnology is the dream of building devices from the atom up. An advance of this proportion would transform human life. But here even the science is uncertain. There are strong hints in new tools such as the atomic force microscope, early success in microelectromechanical machines (mems), and existence proofs in biological systems that nano-technology might not be a distant dream. Indeed not only is it plausible but we can map out several plausible scenarios for getting there from here. We come down from the top from mems to nanotech. This would imply a more mechanical nature to the technology. An alternative sce-nario path would come in from the side, from the worlds of molecular biology. In that case nanotech might resemble organisms.

The broad wave of technological innovation now underway may allow prosperity and a sustainable environment to go hand in hand. In-formation technology is making us more efficient, fuel cells lead to clean cars, and biotech and nanotech lead to ultra-efficient industrial processes. As the new technologies become embedded in how we do nearly everything, we will be able to do vastly more with much less ecological impact. Or varying degrees of failure and malign motives could combine into a scenario of a wealthy few and a poor desperate mass, in a toxic world driven by high-tech conflict. The advance of science and tech-nology does not automatically create a more benign scenario. They merely create the potential for such scenarios to be plausible.

As the relevant domains of forecasting have become more complex and susceptible to the novel, the methodologies of forecasting have also had to evolve. The pace, breadth, and depth of innovation are driving a transformation of economic and social life as profound as the industrial revolution but in a collapsed time frame and on a global scale. We have moved from a world where prediction was a reasonable goal of fore-casting to one where the value is mainly in what we can learn. Devel-oping and thinking through the consequences of surprising but plausible scenarios has proven to be the most useful tool for dealing with a world saturated with novelty. Scenarios are a reasonably systematic tool for a world where the value of history is balanced against the impact of innovation.

So what do you do if prediction is impossible? Of what value is forecasting if uncertainty is profound and essentially irreducible? Per-ceptive anticipation can prepare the mind's eye to recognize significant changes in a timely way. Many early adopters of the Internet saw the meaning of the World Wide Web, and the development of browsers turned that early perception into some of the quickest fortunes in his-tory. Taking a long view can aid in identifying and developing new competencies needed to assure long-term survival. Good scenarios can be a powerful tool in bounding and managing risk. The goal becomes making the most adaptive decisions in a timely fashion rather than get-ting the future right.

In a time rich with discontinuities, a central question becomes how much should one believe a forecast or any scenario of the future. How much can one base decisions and actions upon that view? From a meth-odological point of view there are at least three different approaches to creating the suspension of disbelief needed to take on radical new ideas. The first and most obvious is simply in-depth research supporting one's scenarios. Beyond that is the use of what we call "learning journeys." Put most simply, getting out and seeing things. This is especially effective because a group of decision makers will have shared experiences. Third is the power of simulation. This can range from simple but interactive models all the way to sophisticated forms of virtual reality.

A function of the belief formation process is assessing the balance of risks. The fundamental question is one of regret. What is the cost of being wrong? Is it a fatal error? Can you recover from the error? How costly is the insurance or hedge? Is it an opportunity you would pro-foundly regret failing to grasp?

In the end, it is decision and action that matter. But what does one do in the face of profound uncertainty? If one's belief is low, risks are low, and costs are high, then the primary initial action may simply be watching the situation. If you believe you can actually change the out-come in your favor and the risks are low, then affirmative action may be the right approach. If the belief in the scenario remains low but con-sequences high, then creating future options is the right tack. Finally, if one believes in the discontinuity and there are large consequences then preemptive action may be warranted. Useful anticipation can endow the decision maker with confidence in the face of risk. Denying risk is mere bravado. But having considered the possibilities and being prepared to respond is simply how one must live now.

3

The Future of Population

Joel E. Cohen

I propose to survey the main changes in the human population in the twentieth century and to look ahead to changes in the human population of the twenty-first century. Human populations interact strongly with their economies, environments, and cultures. I will touch on these interactions historically and prospectively.

To build modesty, I will consider the task of anticipating in 1900 the course of population in the twentieth century. Thus humbled, I will sketch one of the many possible worlds of the twenty-first century. Human choices will influence the human future.

This limited survey will concentrate on global description, though local and regional differences in populations, economies, environments, and cultures are important and often have consequences globally. Although the science of populations, including but not limited to demography, has advanced more in the twentieth century than in all previous centuries, this survey will omit the progress of the scientific study of populations.

Major Population Changes in the Twentieth Century

The twentieth century is likely to be unique in all of human history as the only century in which the earth's human population nearly quadrupled. The Earth's human population numbered between 1.6 billion and 1.7 billion around 1900. It numbered around 6.1 billion in 2000 (table 3.1). Looking backward from 1999's population of 6 billion, the most recent doubling of the human population took only 40 years. Never before the second half of the twentieth century (except possibly in the garden of Eden) had any human being lived through a doubling of

Table 3.1
Quantitative indicators of population, economics, the environment, and culture in 1900, 1950, 2000, 2050, and 2100.

Variable	Unit	1900	1950	2000	2050	2100	Notes
Population							
Aggregate population							
Population size	billion people	1.65	2.5	6.1	8.9	10.4	1
Low estimate	billion people				7.2	5.6	2
High estimate	billion people				10.8	17.5	3
Annual increment	million people	10	47	78	33	8	4
Population growth rate	%/year	0.61	1.88	1.28	0.37	0.08	5
Doubling time	years	114	37	54	187	901	6
Distribution of population							
% in "more developed" regions	% of people		32	20	13		7
U.S. population	million people	76	151	281	450	575	8
India population	billion people	0.24	0.36	1	1.53	1.62	9
China population	billion people	0.4	0.56	1.3	1.5	1.5	10
% of people in cities	%	13	30	47	61		11
Urban population	billion people	0.21	0.75	2.87	5.43		12
Urban centers of ≥10 million	number	0	1	20			13
% urban pop. in urban centers ≥ 10 million	% of people	0	1.6	9.6			14
Age structure							
Median age	years		24	26	38	40	15
Children (% <15)	%		34	30	20		16
Older persons (% 60+)	%		8	10	22		17

	Units						Ref.
Mortality and fertility							
Life expectancy at birth	years (M + F)	30	46.5	66.5	76	81.7	18
Total fertility rate	children per woman		5	2.7	2		19
Environment							
Population density	persons/sq. km.	12	19	45	66	77	20
Population per permanent cropland	persons/ha	1.2	1.9	4.5	6.6	7.7	21
Atmospheric C emissions per person	tons C/year/person	0.3	0.7	1.2	(0.22, 0.33)	(0.15, 0.45)	22
Atmospheric C emissions	billion tons C/year	0.5	1.8	7.3	2.4	2.5	23
World water withdrawals	1000 km^3/year	0.5	1.3	(3.3, 4)			24
Nitrogen released in NO$_x$ from fossil fuel combustion	million tons N per year	1.2	6.1	25			25
Nitrate mass fraction in ice	parts per billion	45	55	120			26
U.S. lead production	KtPb/yr	450	1100	1250			27
Net primary production	GtC/yr	46	47	52	62	74	28
CO$_2$ partial pressure	Pa	29	30	(34, 36.5)	48	70	29
Global average temperature	deg. C. annual	13.75	13.95	14.35			30
Land temperature	deg. C. annual	12.2	12.3	12.9	14	16.2	31
Economy							
GDP per person	1990 Geary Khamis dollars	$1,263	$2,138	$5,204			32
Size of the world economy	trillion (10^{12}) 1990 Geary Khamis dollars	$2.08	$5.35	$31.74			33
Culture							
U.S. persons per Senator	million people	0.84	1.57	2.75	4.50	5.75	34
U.S. persons per Representative	million people	0.19	0.34	0.63	1.03	1.32	35

Table 3.1 (continued)
Quantitative indicators of population, economics, the environment, and culture in 1900, 1950, 2000, 2050, and 2100.

Variable	Unit	1900	1950	2000	2050	2100	Notes
Primary education							
Northwestern Europe, N. America, Anglo Pacific	primary gross enrollment ratio (PGER)	72	107	103			36
Latin America, Caribbean	PGER	30	84	101			37
East Asia	PGER	21	94	110			38
Southeast Asia	PGER	4	71	104			39
Sub-Saharan Africa	PGER	16	54	85			40

Notes.
1. United Nations Population Division, briefing packet, 1998 revision, 14; Year 2100: *World Population Projections to 2150.*
2. Ibid.
3. Ibid.
4. Years 1950–2050: United Nations Population Division, *World Population Prospects: The 1998 Revision,* 2. Year 1900: United Nations Population Division, briefing packet, 1998 revision, 14. Year 2100: *World Population Projections to 2150.*
5. Computed from population size and annual increment.
6. Computed from growth rate.
7. United Nations Population Division, briefing packet, 1998 revision, 4.
8. Years 1900, 1950: U.S. Bureau of the Census, *Historical Statistics of the U.S., Colonial Times to 1970: Part 1,* 8, series A2. Year 2000: based on first results of Census 2000 at http://www.census.gov/main/www/cen2000.html. Years 2050, 2100, median of four "combined scenarios" from Dennis A. Ahlburg, and James W. Vaupel, 1990, "Alternative Projections of the U.S. Population," *Demography* 27(4): 639–652. Year 2100 figure is estimate for 2080.
9. United Nations Population Division, briefing packet, 1998 revision, 3. *World Population Projections to 2150,* 29. For 1900: Angus Maddison, *Monitoring the World Economy 1820–1992* (Paris: OECD, 1995), 114.
10. Ibid.

11. Year 1900: Brian J. L. Berry, "Urbanization" Pp. 103–119 (110, figure 7.8) in B. L. Turner et al., 1990, *The Earth as Transformed by Human Action*, Cambridge: Cambridge University Press. Year 1950: United Nations Population Division, *World Urbanization Prospects: The 1996 Revision*, 1 May 1997, 12. Year 2050: figure pertains to 2030; 13. Year 2000: *World Resources 1998–1999*, 274.

12. Calculated from percent of people in cities and total global population size.

13. United Nations Population Division, *World Urbanization Prospects: The 1996 Revision*, 1 May 1997, 103.

14. Ibid.

15. United Nations Population Division, briefing packet, 1998 revision, 27.

16. Ibid., 26.

17. Ibid.

18. United Nations Population Division, *World Population Prospects: The 1998 Revision*, 2. *World Population Projection to 2150*, 6, table 3. For 1900: Individual country life expectancies given by Angus Maddison, *Monitoring the World Economy 1820–1992*, 27, range from twenty-four years for India (low) to fifty-six years for Sweden (high) among twelve countries for which estimates are available. Global estimate of thirty years is from Samuel H. Preston (personal communication, April 1999).

19. For 1950–2050: United Nations Population Division, *World Population Prospects: The 1998 Revision*, 2.

20. Ibid. Estimates from population size for other dates.

21. Assumes 10 percent of all land can be used for permanent crops. One square kilometer equals 100 hectares.

22. Robert Engelman, *Profiles in Carbon: An Update on Population, Consumption, and Carbon Dioxide Emissions* (Washington, D.C.: Population Action International, 1998), 18, figure 6. Years 2050, 2100: estimated allowable emissions per person with high or low future population growth.

23. C emissions per person times total population. Years 2050, 2100: estimated allowable emissions per person with high or low future population growth.

24. 3.3 in 2000: *World Resources 1998–99*, (Oxford: World Resources Institute, Oxford University Press, 1998), 304. 4.4 in 2000: Sandra L. Postel, Gretchen C. Daily, Paul R. Ehrlich, 1996, "Human Appropriation of Renewable Fresh Water," *Science* 271: 785–788. Other figures: Peter H. Gleick, "The World's Water 1998–1999," graphed in *New York Times*, 8 December 1998, p. 7 of special section "The Natural World."

25. J. F. Muller, 1992, "Geographical Distribution and Seasonal Variation of Surface Emissions and Deposition Velocities of Atmospheric Trace Gases," *Journal of Geophysical Research* 97: 3787–3804. For 1900 and 1950: personal communication from J. F. Muller via Elisabeth A. Holland (2 April 1999). For 2000: extrapolation from estimates up to 1990.

Table 3.1 (continued)

26. Robert U. Ayres, William H. Schlesinger, Robert H. Socolow, "Human Impacts on the Carbon and Nitrogen Cycles," in *Industrial Ecology and Global Change* (New York: Cambridge University Press, 1994), 121–155. Page 126, figure 2, ice pack in South Greenland.

27. Robert Socolow and Valerie Thomas 1997. "The Industrial Ecology of Lead and Electric Vehicles," *Journal of Industrial Ecology* 1(1): 13–36. Page 23, figure 3, including primary and secondary production and net imports.

28. F. I. Woodward, M. R. Lomas, R. A. Betts, 1998, "Vegetation–Climate Feedbacks in a Greenhouse World." *Philosophical Transactions of the Royal Society of London B* 353: 29–39. Page 36, figure 10, simulations allowing feedback of vegetation on atmospheric CO2 partial pressure and temperature.

29. Ibid. Page 36, figure 9, simulations allowing feedback of vegetation on atmospheric CO2 partial pressure and temperature. High estimate for year 2000: J. A. Raven, 1998, "Extrapolating Feedback Processes from the Present to the Past," *Philosophical Transactions of the Royal Society of London B* 353: 19–28, 22, table 1.

30. Office of Science and Technology Policy, Executive Office of the President 1997, *Climate Change: State of Knowledge*, 7, figure 7, derived from data of Hansen et al. 1995, Goddard Institute for Space Studies.

31. Woodward, "Vegetation–Climate Feedbacks," 29–39. Page 36, figure 9, simulations allowing feedback of vegetation on atmospheric CO2 partial pressure and temperature.

32. Maddison, *Monitoring*, 228. Year 2000 figure is GDP per person for 1990.

33. GDP/person times population size. Year 2000 figure uses 1990 GDP per person.

34. Number of states and representatives in 1900 and 1950 from: U.S. Bureau of the Census, *Historical Statistics of the U.S., Colonial Times to 1970: Part 2*, 1084, series Y216–217. Numbers of senators and representatives are assumed to remain fixed at 100 and 435, respectively, from 2000 onward.

35. Ibid.

36. James H. Williams, "The Diffusion of the Modern School," in *International Handbook of Education and Development: Preparing Schools, Students, and Nations for the Twenty-First Century* ed. William K. Cummings and Noel F. McGinn (New York, Tokyo: Pergamon, Elsevier Science, 1997), 119–136, 122, table 6.2. Year 2000 gives 1960 data. Year 1950 gives 1960 data. Year 2000 gives 1988 data.

37. Ibid.
38. Ibid.
39. Ibid.
40. Ibid.

the human population. Now everyone who is 40 years old or older has seen the earth's population double.

Some commentators who would minimize concerns about rapid population growth have suggested in the popular press that rapid population growth is, or will shortly be, over (Crossette 1997; Eberstadt 1997a, b; Laing 1997; Wattenberg 1997). Contrary to these suggestions, rapid global population growth continues (Gelbard and Haub 1998). This growth is driven principally by continuing high fertility in many developing countries. In a few countries that had high fertility in the recent past and presently have low fertility (such as China, Taiwan, Thailand, and South Korea), rapid growth in numbers is also driven by the very high proportion of young people.

To put present population growth in perspective, note that in 1900 the annual increment to global population size was 10 million people, with a growth rate of about 0.6 percent per year (table 3.1). In 1999 the estimated annual increment of population is about 78 million people per year (nearly 8 times larger), and the estimated annual rate of growth is approximately 1.3 percent per year (more than twice as large). For the less developed regions as a whole (about 80 percent of the world's population), the average woman would have 3.3 children in a lifetime at the estimated 1998 age-specific fertility rates (Population Reference Bureau 1998). If China were excluded from the less developed regions, the average number of children per woman at current fertility rates would be 3.8, sufficient to double a population in about 35 years. Announcing the end of the population explosion seems premature at best, deceptive at worst.

The extraordinarily rapid population growth of the twentieth century, especially in developing regions, produced a very high fraction of young people. During population growth, more people are added to a population (as infants) than die (generally as older people), so the proportion of young people increases. Contrast the age structure of the rapidly growing populations in regions called "less developed" by the United Nations Population Division (all regions of Africa, Latin America and the Caribbean, Melanesia, Micronesia, Polynesia, and Asia except Japan) with the age structure of the so-called more developed regions (North America, Japan, Europe, Australia, and New Zealand). In the less developed regions, the median age dropped from 21.3 years in 1950 to 19.0 years in 1970, then slowly rose to 23.2 years in 1995. By the end of the century, even after a third of a century of falling population growth rates, half the people in the less developed regions were less than 23 years old. By contrast, in the more developed regions, the median age rose steadily from 28.6 years in 1950 to 35.9 years in 1995 (United Nations Population Division 1999).

Rapid population growth also brought a very rapid movement of people from rural to urban areas. While the absolute size of the global population increased 3.8-fold during the century, the percentage of the population living in cities increased 3.6-fold (from 13 percent to 47 percent), resulting in a nearly 14-fold increase in the number of people living in urban areas (from perhaps 210 million in 1900 to nearly 2.9 billion in 2000).

The past half-century saw another major demographic event that is also without precedent in human history. Around 1965–1970, the global population growth rate reached an all-time high of 2.0 percent or 2.1 percent per year, and then declined by at least one-third to 1.3 percent or 1.4 percent (the higher estimates in both cases are given by Population Reference Bureau 1998, the lower by United Nations 1999). In the fourteenth century, the population growth rate fell because of increased deaths from plagues, war, and famine. By contrast, in the twentieth century, apart from the catastrophic effects of AIDS across the middle of Africa and the collapse of the economy of the former Soviet Union, life expectancies have increased almost everywhere, indicating overall better human health (Preston 1995). These increases in life expectancy are largely attributable to improvements in sanitation, diet, reductions of environmental hazards, behavior, and, to a limited extent, improvements in medical care. Unlike the fourteenth century, the fall in the population growth rate since 1965 has been caused largely by voluntary reductions in fertility, and the most important reductions have come in the poor countries, where a majority of the world's people lived and live. A detailed understanding of what drives major changes in fertility remains beyond the grasp of the social sciences.

Fertility is often measured by the period total fertility rate (TFR), which is the number of children a woman would have in the course of her entire lifetime if, at each age, she had the fertility rate that women of that age have in the current period. For the world as a whole, the TFR fell from approximately 5 in 1950 to 2.7 at the end of the century. This striking reduction in fertility is the nub of fact behind the premature claim that the population explosion is over. The claim is premature because, in demographic terms, a TFR of 2.7 children per woman is much higher than the replacement level TFR of 2.0 or 2.1 children per woman. (To dramatize the demographic impact of differences in TFR of less than one child per woman, compare the 1998 high-variant and low-variant projections of the United Nations. If the TFR falls to 2.51 children per woman, the population by 2050 is estimated to be 10.67 billion. If the TFR falls to 1.56 children per woman, the population projected for 2050 is 7.34 billion. The difference in fertility over most of the period up to 2050 is smaller than the difference of 0.95 children per woman reached by 2050, yet the difference in population size in 2050 is 3.3 billion people, according to these projections.)

While 44 percent of the world's population lives in countries where the level of fertility is below the replacement level, what counts for global population growth is how far below replacement the low-fertility countries are, compared to how far above replacement the high-fertility countries are (in addition to the young age structure of countries that recently had high fertility). The balance of those distances below and above replacement, weighted by the relative sizes of the populations in low-fertility and high-fertility regions, determines whether global fertility levels lie above or below the replacement level. At the end of the twentieth century, the balance of high and low fertility still favors a rapidly rising population.

Both the speed of population growth since World War II and the dramatic fall in global fertility since 1965 are without precedent. The timing and magnitude of both events were not predicted by anyone. Why these colossal failures of prediction?

One may think about population as one vertex of a symmetrical pyramid in which the other vertices are the environment, economics, and culture (Cohen 1995). Any corner can go on top. One reason (though perhaps not the only reason) that no one foresaw the rapid rise in population after World War II and the fall in fertility starting around 1965 is that our scientific understanding did not, and still does not, encompass these four dimensions. Thinking in terms of this pyramid provides a checklist of crucial dimensions, though it will not eliminate uncertainty about the future.

Related Changes in the Twentieth Century in Economics

Economic growth during the twentieth century has more than quadrupled the average gross domestic product (GDP) per person, from less than $1,300 to about $5,200 (table 3.1). As population size nearly quadrupled during the century, the world's GDP grew roughly 16-fold. The GDP has serious limitations as a measure of economic well-being. To an important extent, the process of economic development substitutes market production for domestic production (Keyfitz 1993): eating in a restaurant replaces cooking at home; paying for childcare replaces parental rearing of children. Hence the GDP rises faster than real (including domestic) production. The GDP also includes commercial gains from market activities but neglects their drawing-down of environmental and social capital (Daly and Cobb 1989). Though the numbers that economists use to measure economic growth have uncertain interpretations as indicators of welfare, it seems clear that economic well-being has improved for many people during the twentieth century.

Not all the world's people shared in this dramatic improvement in average incomes. Between 1870 and 1985, the ratio of incomes per person in the richest countries to incomes per person in the poorest countries increased 6-fold, while the average absolute income gap between the richest and poorest countries grew from $1,500 to more than $12,000 (Pritchett 1995). Between 1960 and 1991, the ratio of income per person between individuals in the top one-fifth and the bottom one-fifth of the global income distribution rose from approximately 30-to-1 to more than 60-to-1 (United Nations Development Programme 1992, 34, 36). When the 1997 gross national product per person was adjusted for purchasing power parity, the low- and middle-income countries (with a combined population of 4.9 billion people) had $3,200 per person, while the high-income countries (with 0.9 billion people) had $22,800 per person (World Bank 1999, 191). Using purchasing power parity adjusted gross national product per person, the poorest 2 billion people on the planet have incomes of $1,400 per year, less than one-sixteenth of the average incomes of the richest billion. These comparisons of income between groups at different levels of economic development suffer from the same limitations as long-term comparisons of average GDP.

Related Changes in the Twentieth Century in the Environment

The economic and other collective activities of humans affect the planet far more than the sheer physical presence of humans. If the volume of all 6 billion humans were converted to soup and spread over the surface of the Earth, the result would be a film barely half a micrometer thick. Despite their small physical presence, humans have been a geological force on the face of the Earth since their mastery of fire hundreds of thousands of years ago. The intensity and diversity of human interventions in biotic and geological processes have grown enormously this century (Vitousek et al. 1997b).

The impact of human interventions on global biotic and geological systems is appropriately measured on an aggregate basis, although individual human well-being is appropriately measured per person. The reason is that the mass of the atmosphere, the area of the continents, the volume of the ocean, and other dimensions of the planet are independent of the size of the human population. For many planetary systems, human interventions are massive on a global scale. I shall mention as examples the global cycles of carbon, water, and nitrogen.

Atmospheric carbon emissions per person quadrupled from 300 to 1,200 kilograms of carbon per person per year between 1900 and 2000. Because population grew during the century, aggregate atmospheric carbon emissions rose from approximately 0.5 billion tons of carbon per year to 7.3 billion tons of carbon per year. (Tons are metric tonnes throughout.) In the steady-state, preindustrial global carbon cycle, the flux of carbon into the atmosphere from volcanic and tectonic sources was 0.2 billion tons of carbon per year, that from the entire land biota was 50 billion tons of carbon per year, and that from all sources was 191 billion tons of carbon per year (Watson and Liss 1998, 42, their figure 1). In this century human inputs of carbon into the atmosphere have changed from a negligible proportion to nearly 4 percent of all atmospheric carbon inputs. The partial pressure of carbon dioxide in the atmosphere rose in this century from 29 to 34–37 pascals. Atmospheric carbon dioxide concentrations are now higher than they have been in the last 150,000 years, a period that includes the emergence of modern humans and the multiple inventions of agriculture. The human and biological implications of this rise are hotly debated. Current models are the subject of controversy, some scientifically motivated and some politically motivated.

Between 1900 and 2000 (table 3.1), world water withdrawals grew from 500 cubic kilometers per year to levels variously estimated at 3,300 or 4,000 or 4,430 cubic kilometers per year, in addition to in-stream uses of 2,350 cubic kilometers per year (Postel, Daily, and Ehrlich 1996, 786, their figure 2). For comparison, the annual volume of available renewable freshwater probably lies in the range from 9,000 to 14,000 cubic kilometers per year. Postel et al. (1996) estimated "geographically and temporally accessible runoff" at 12,500 cubic kilometers per year. Thus, at the end of the twentieth century, humans withdrew annually from 24 percent (3,300/14,000) to 49 percent (4,430/9,000) of available renewable freshwater. The uncertainty in these estimates reflects current ignorance of humans' place in the world's water cycle. If in-stream uses are also considered, humans may exploit a majority of accessible renewable freshwater supplies and a substantial fraction of total global freshwater runoff (usually estimated at 41,000 cubic kilometers per year). This accounting does not consider other human uses of evapotranspiration.

In taking command of such a large fraction of freshwater runoff, humans have since 1950 constructed dams and reservoirs that impound more than 10,000 cubic kilometers of water, "as much water as there is total atmospheric moisture or equivalent to 10 times the Earth's biological water" (Chao 1995). The redistribution of this mass of water has measurably affected the rate of slowing of the earth's rotation and "has contributed a significant fraction in the total observed polar drift over the last 40 years" (Chao 1995, 3,529).

Human emissions of nitrogen in NO_x from the combustion of fossil fuels grew from 1.25 million tons per year to perhaps 25 million tons per year between 1900 and 2000 (table 3.1). The mass fraction of nitrates in ice grew from 45 parts per billion at the beginning of the century to 120 parts per billion at the end. Humans emit currently an estimated 40 percent of the nitrous oxide (N_2O), 70 percent of the ammonia (NH_3) and at least 80 percent of the nitric oxide (NO) emitted to the atmosphere from all sources (Vitousek et al. 1997a, 6, their figure 4).

Related Changes in Twentieth-Century Culture

Cultural changes in the last century have been no less dramatic than demographic, economic, and environmental changes. More people have had an opportunity to begin an education than ever before. Growing populations have generated increasing challenges to representative government. The gradual diffusion of the rights of citizenship has included unprecedented improvements in the status of women. These educational and civic improvements are correlated with, and may be causes of, declining fertility (Bledsoe et al. 1999).

One standard indicator of educational activity is the primary gross enrollment ratio (PGER). A gross enrollment ratio is calculated by dividing the number of children enrolled in school by the school-age population. Different countries define the ages of primary schooling differently. Because children who are over age or under age may also enroll in school, the PGER overrepresents the proportions of children of school age who are actually enrolled in school (Williams 1997, 122), and thus the PGER may exceed 100 percent.

In the wealthy regions of northwestern Europe, North America, and the Anglo Pacific, the PGER rose in the twentieth century from 72 percent to 103 percent. Latin America, the Caribbean, East Asia, and Southeast Asia saw much more dramatic increases, from as low as 4 percent in Southeast Asia to more than 100 percent in all these regions. Sub-Saharan Africa's PGER progressed from 16 percent to 85 percent. Late in the twentieth century, about three-quarters of the children eligible to attend primary schools in developing countries did so. The 130 million children who were out of school were disproportionately girls, and were mainly illiterate (Colclough 1993). These figures are probably no more reliable than are the demographic, economic, and environmental indicators quoted above.

Population growth poses increasing challenges to representative government. From 1900 to 2000, the number of people in the United States per U.S. senator grew from 0.84 million to 2.75 million, while the number per congressional representative grew from 0.19 million to 0.63 million. These increases probably understate considerably the relative increases in the number of voters per senator or representative. Women won the right to vote in the United States only in 1920. Moreover, the fraction of the American population in the age groups that are legally eligible to vote has probably increased from 1900 to 2000. Each senator and representative must try to listen to and speak to several times more people now than at the beginning of the century, even though a large fraction of the population does not vote. On the other hand, the means of communication to and from elected representatives, along with the cost and power of the mass media, have expanded enormously in the last century, so that purely demographic changes account for only part of the challenges to representative government.

In 1949 the British historian and sociologist T. H. Marshall identified three elements of citizenship: civil, political, and social. The civil element consists of individual freedoms: rights to personal liberty, freedom of speech, and religion; to property, contracts, and justice. The political element is the right to exercise political power as a voter and public official. The social element, for Marshall, meant "the whole range from the right to a modicum of economic welfare and security to the right to share to the full in the social heritage and to live the life of a civilized being according to the standards prevailing in the society." Marshall suggested that the formative period of civil rights occurred in the eighteenth century, of political rights in the nineteenth, and of social rights in the twentieth.

The improvement in the status of women in the twentieth century, and especially in its last third, may be the foremost example of the spread of the social element of citizenship. In 1946 the United Nations Commission on the Status of Women was formed to monitor and enhance the situation of women. The commission initiated a series of conventions: on the political rights of women in 1952, on the rights of women in marriage and divorce in 1957 and 1962, on the rights of women in employment in 1967, and by 1979 a Convention on the Elimination of All Forms of Discrimination against Women. These international conventions reflect aspirations more than achievements. By 1991 fewer than 5 percent of the world's heads of state, major corporations, and international organizations were women (United Nations 1991, 6–7).

For the mass of women, there were enormous changes. In the economically active population (consisting of those engaged in the cash economy, working for pay or looking for paying work), the number of women per 100 men rose from 37 in 1970 to 62 in 1990 globally (United Nations 1995). The increase in the economic activity of women was particularly dramatic in the developing regions of Asia and the Pacific, Latin America and the Caribbean, and Africa. Fertility fell sharply in these regions during the same years (although the decline was small in sub-Saharan Africa).

Half a century after Marshall spoke, the formative period of social rights is not yet over. The second half of the twentieth century saw the largest and fastest global increase of population ever to take place. Social rights might have spread further and faster had population increase been smaller and slower during these decades. The argument behind this speculation is that when the supply of workers is reduced, as it was in Europe after the Black Death in the fourteenth century, workers are valued more highly, other things being equal (North and Thomas 1973). Of course, a rise in the economic value of workers has no necessary translation into an increase in the value of people as citizens. The relations of power in a society influence whether the economic scarcity of workers augments their civil, political, and social rights.

How Is Population Predicted, and How Well?

The first requirement of predicting the future of population size and composition is knowing how many people there are at the beginning of the projection. The estimate of the world population in 1950 changed 17 times in U.N. *Demographic Yearbooks* from 1951 to 1996. Nico Keilman (personal communication, 18 August 1999, extending Keilman 1999, 20) reported that there were 11 changes upward and 6 changes downward, while Bongaarts and Bulatao (2000, 42) reported 13 changes upward and 4 changes downward. Evidently there is some uncertainty about the uncertainty. Perhaps 20 percent of the world's population (a number roughly equivalent to the population of China) was not censused in the 1990s, though obviously such an estimate depends on a guess about how many people have not been counted (Bongaarts and Bulatao 2000).

The major approaches to population projection and their results are reviewed, with varying levels of skepticism, by Hajnal (1957), Cohen (1995, 107–157), Lutz et al. (1999), and the U.S. National Research Council (edited by Bongaarts and Bulatao 2000).

Two approaches to predicting future population are common: demographic and exogenous. A demographic approach ignores the connections of population with the rest of the world and forecasts the trajectories of demographic variables. One variation on this approach, mathematical extrapolation, assumes that future population sizes are determined by present and past population sizes, and nothing more. A mathematical curve is fitted to the total sizes of a population at past times. The formula is used to continue the curve into the future. A second variation on this approach, now called "cohort-component projection," was invented in 1895 by the English economist Edward Cannan (1895). It is still used in most official and academic population forecasts, for example, by the United Nations Population Division (Zlotnik 1999). It requires knowledge of future birth rates and death rates by age group. A third variation of the demographic approach recognizes the variability in past birth rates and death rates and incorporates stochastic processes into the cohort-component method.

The forecasting errors of past demographic projections were analyzed quantitatively in several studies (reviewed in Cohen 1986). Three simple lessons may be drawn. First, the longer the gap between the time a population forecast is made and the target date of the forecast, the lower the accuracy of the forecast. When they are accurate at all, population forecasts are usefully accurate for less than a generation (up to 20 or 25 years). Second, for short-term forecasts (up to 5 or 10 years), simple projection methods, such as assuming constant geometric growth, are at least as good as complicated ones. Third, and perhaps most important, forecasters generally underestimate both the uncertainty of the forecasts they produce and the instability of the core assumptions from which those forecasts are derived.

The National Research Council report (Bongaarts and Bulatao 2000) compares cohort-component projections of the population size of individual countries, regions, and the whole earth against the United Nations' 1998 estimates of historical population sizes. The projections were prepared by the United Nations Population Division in 1973, 1980, 1984, and 1994 for all countries; by the World Bank in 1972, 1983, 1988, and 1990 for countries belonging to the World Bank; and by the United States Bureau of the Census in 1987 for developing countries. Projected and estimated population sizes were compared at 5-year intervals from the starting date of each projection to 2000.

When individual countries are used as the unit of analysis, deviations between the initial population estimate used in the projection and the currently estimated initial population account for 60 percent of the difference between the projected and estimated population for a 5-year projection. For a 10-year projection, the error in the initial population estimate accounts for about 40 percent of the discrepancy between projected and estimated population; for a 20-year projection, about 20 percent; and for a 30-year projection about 10 percent. Starting with the right country population size is an important component of forecasting future country population, especially in the near term.

As in previous retrospective analyses of population projections, longer projections are less accurate than shorter ones. The mean absolute percentage error (that is, the mean value of the magnitude of the difference between projected and estimated population size, expressed as a percent of estimated population size) is about 5 percent for projections of 5 years. The mean absolute percentage error increases by about 2.5 percentage points with each additional 5 years between the base year and the target year for the projection. The mean absolute percentage error for 30-year projections is 17 percent. Individual projection errors may be larger. For example, in 30-year projections, 1 country in 4 has a projection error of at least 20 percent and 1 in 10 of at least 40 percent. These high error rates are due partly to errors in the initially estimated rates of birth, death, and migration, partly to misspecified trends in these vital rates, and partly to unanticipated external shocks, sometimes called "demographic quakes."

Exogenous approaches to population projection relate demographic variables to external variables that are presumed to influence or control the course of demographic variables. The exogenous approach rests on the hope that external variables can be better predicted than demographic variables (Cohen 1999). One variant of the exogenous approach is the system model, most famously illustrated by *The Limits to Growth*. System models posit quantitative interactions of population growth and size with nondemographic factors such as industrialization, agriculture, pollution, and natural resources.

Exogenous forecasts are little favored by most demographers, though Sanderson (1999) is an important exception. Exogenous forecasts are built on shifting sands. For example, one might hope to forecast the future of life expectancy (or any other demographic variable) as a function of future economic development, perhaps measured by average income per person. The relationship between income per person and life expectancy has changed notably in the twentieth century (figure 3.1). Over the decades of this century, a given level of income was associated with a longer and longer life. Using the relation between income per person and life expectancy observed around 1900 would have grossly underestimated the life expectancy of the poor and middle-income

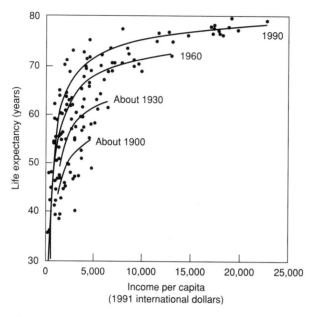

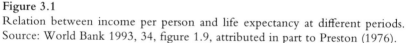

Figure 3.1
Relation between income per person and life expectancy at different periods.
Source: World Bank 1993, 34, figure 1.9, attributed in part to Preston (1976).

countries by the end of the century, even if it had been possible to predict correctly their economic progress.

Much of the resistance by demographers to developing population projections that incorporate economic, environmental, and cultural interactions with demographic variables is due, not to the failure of empirical attempts to do so, but to an a priori disciplinary narrowness that inhibits many demographers from even trying.

Could Population Change in the Twentieth Century Have Been Predicted from 1900?

If someone in 1900 had tried to predict the course of the human population in the twentieth century, it seems unlikely that he or she could have succeeded. The fall of fertility during the Great Depression was not foreseen at the beginning of the twentieth century, to the best of my knowledge. During the Great Depression, some demographers and many public figures were concerned by the apparently imminent demographic collapse of the West (Teitelbaum and Winter 1985). Apparently no one

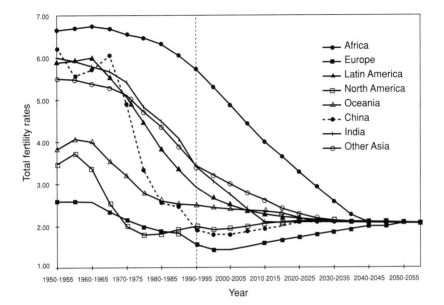

Figure 3.2
Total fertility rate (average number of children per woman's lifetime, at current age-specific birth rates) for major areas of the world, observed (to the left of the dotted vertical line) and anticipated in the medium-fertility scenario of the United Nations Population Division (1998b, their figure 1, 9). Reprinted by permission.

foresaw the baby boom in some Western countries after World War II. Some pre-war demographers anticipated a rising population in developing countries after World War II. However, all were surprised by the speed of decline in death rates and the magnitude of the subsequent rise in population. Apparently no one predicted that the global population growth rate would peak between 1965 and 1970. Nor was anyone able to forecast quantitatively the pace at which fertility would decline after 1970. The TFRs of different regions have varied widely across regions and over time (figure 3.2). The complexity of the observed pattern of TFRs (to the left of the dashed line in figure 3.2) contrasts starkly with the smooth simplicity assumed for the future (to the right of the dashed line).

In 1798, in an early example of an exogenous projection, Malthus assumed that population growth was limited by the area of arable land. For more than a century and a half after he wrote, the evidence appeared to confirm his assumption. As population grew, so did the area of arable

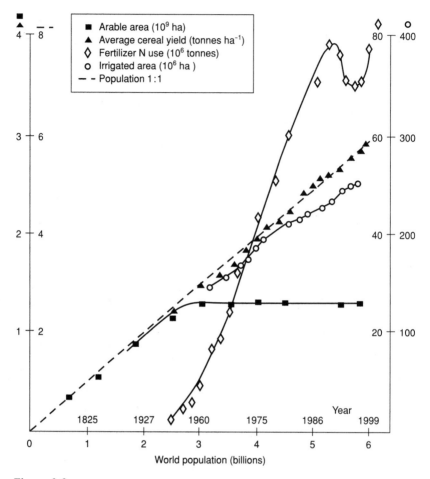

Figure 3.3
Relation between world population and arable area, average cereal yield, nitrogen fertilizer use, and irrigated area. Data from FAO Production Yearbooks. Source: Evans 1998, his figure 32, 205. Reproduced with the permission of Cambridge University Press.

land (figure 3.3). With a population of 3 billion or less, self-sufficient traditional agriculture could feed everyone, for example, with 2 billion hectares under cultivation, half of it yielding one ton per hectare of grain. Once world population passed 3 billion, self-sufficient traditional culture became impossible and intensification (extracting higher yields per hectare) became unavoidable (Evans 1998, 217). The area of arable land abruptly leveled off around 1.3 or 1.4 billion hectares. Although the total arable area has remained steady, the land cultivated now is not entirely the same land that was cultivated in 1960: some has been with-drawn from cultivation (as a result of urbanization and agricultural or industrial degradation) and new land of equal area has been recruited from natural ecosystems. Beyond 3 billion people, global average cereal yields have increased in close proportion to population size, at a steady ratio of one metric ton per hectare for each additional 2 billion people. After the invention of the Haber-Bosch process for nitrogen fixation, the production of artificial nitrogenous fertilizers increased much more rap-idly than population. After 1960, a variety of factors combined to raise cereal yields and to revolutionize the relationship between population and the land. These factors included chemical fertilizers, pesticides (invented in the years before, during, and after World War II), massive extensions of irrigation, and new cultivars of rice, wheat, and maize (Harrar 1970). The new cultivars had higher crop planting density made possible by changed plant architecture. Multiple cropping, better farm management, and new institutions for providing farmers with credit, in-formation, and other farm inputs also contributed to increased yields (Cohen and Fedoroff 1999).

A brief, incomplete list of some of the major inventions of the twentieth century that probably affected demographic variables (table 3.2) shows how difficult it would have been to predict these influences on the course of population. The miracle varieties of rice, wheat, and maize that feed billions today depend on the rediscoveries in 1900 of the work of Mendel and the subsequent development of cytogenetics and molecular genetics, as well as on the development of mathematical sta-tistics by Ronald A. Fisher and others at agricultural research stations in the first half of the century. Inventions of domestic appliances like the electric washer, the electric vacuum cleaner, and the automatic toaster reduced the time required for domestic labor, freeing homemakers for economic activity and increasing the opportunity cost of raising children. The invention of the radio, television, and other forms of telecommu-nication facilitated the diffusion of ideas concerning small families and social, economic, and political modernization. The synthesis of quinine, other antimalarials, vaccines, and antibiotics, and the invention of other cheap public health interventions made possible dramatic reductions in childhood mortality in developing countries after World War II. The consequences of sexual activity were changed by new ways to diagnose and treat syphilis and other sexually transmitted diseases, and by a variety

Table 3.2
Inventions and innovations during the twentieth century that affected demographic variables directly or indirectly.

Year	Innovation	Putative demographic effect	Source
1900	Correns, De Vries and von Tschermak discover 1866 paper of Mendel, leading to modern genetics	Foundation of scientific breeding of plants and animals	Evans 1998, p. 102
1901, 1907, 1918	Fisher invents electric washer, Spangler invents electric vacuum cleaner, Strite invents automatic toaster	Reduced domestic labor required, usually of women	Hoffman 1987, pp. 157–160
1901, 1916	Taylor, White invent high-speed steel alloy, Brearley invents stainless steel	Facilitated mechanization of agriculture, household appliances, scientific instruments	Hoffman 1987, pp. 157–160
1902, 1905, 1906	Marconi invents radio magnetic detector, Fleming invents radio tube diode, De Forest invents radio amplifier and radio tube triode	Facilitated diffusion of ideas of social, economic, and political modernization and of small families	Hoffman 1987, pp. 157–160
1903	Wright brothers invent heavier-than-air flight	Facilitated mobility of people and goods, promoted global economic integration, undermined manpower as basis of military power	Hoffman 1987, pp. 157–160
1906, 1910	August von Wassermann discovers test for syphilis; Ehrlich discovers Salvarsan (606) for syphilis treatment	Enhanced surveillance and clinical treatment of problems in reproductive health	Hoffman 1987, pp. 157–160
1907, 1917	Benjamin Holt invents first gasoline tractor with tracks; Henry Ford introduces Fordson tractor	Mechanized agriculture displaced horses and increased productivity of farm workers	Evans 1998, p. 119

1908, 1930	Haber-Bosch process discovered for catalytic combination of nitrogen and hydrogen to produce artificial ammonia; anhydrous ammonia first applied directly to soil	Basis of the modern nitrogenous fertilizer industry; made possible yield increases	Evans 1998, p. 120
1911	Kettering invents automobile self-starter	Step toward mechanization of transport and traction, increased mobility	Hoffman 1987, pp. 157–160
1912, 1913, 1916, 1922	Holst, Froelich discover vitamin C; McCollum, Davis discover vitamin A; McCollum discovers vitamin B, then vitamin D	Facilitated improvements in nutrition and survival	Hoffman 1987, pp. 157–160
1913, 1922, 1930	Burton invents cracked gasoline, Midgley invents lead ethyl gasoline, Ipatieff invents high octane gasoline	Increased productivity of farm workers, promoted urbanization and mobility, lowering fertility	Hoffman 1987, pp. 157–160
1913, 1918	Julien Tournois discovers that long nights initiate precocious flowering in hops and hemp; H. A. Allard and W. W. Garner, U.S. Department of Agriculture, discover that length of night controls flowering in tobacco and soybeans	Foundation for spread of plant varieties from tropics to higher latitudes and vice versa	Evans 1998, pp. 102–103
1917	Jones invents hybrid corn	Step toward increased crop yields, better nutrition and better survival	Hoffman 1987, pp. 157–160
1918	Dempster invents mass spectroscope	Crucial tool for analytical chemistry in industrial and biomedical research	Hoffman 1987, pp. 157–160

Table 3.2 (continued)

Year	Innovation	Putative demographic effect	Source
1918	Rabe synthesizes quinine	Eased control of malaria	Hoffman 1987, pp. 157–160
1927	Farnsworth invents electronic television	Facilitated diffusion of ideas of social, economic, and political modernization and of small families	Hoffman 1987, pp. 157–160
1927	Warner Brothers invent talking movies	Facilitated diffusion of ideas of social, economic, and political modernization and of small families	Hoffman 1987, pp. 157–160
1928	Morkrum, Kleinschmidt invent teletype	Facilitated diffusion of ideas	Hoffman 1987, pp. 157–160
1929, 1941	Fleming discovers penicillin, Florey and Chain discover practical use	Improved survival of children and adults	Hoffman 1987, pp. 157–160
1930	Midgley et al. invent low-boiling fluorine compound refrigerants	Improved preservation of foods and medicines, improving survival	Hoffman 1987, pp. 157–160
1931	Knoll, Ruska invent electron microscope	Crucial analytical tool for chemistry in industrial and biomedical research	Hoffman 1987, pp. 157–160
1934, 1945, 1948	Domagk discovers sulfanilamide; Waksman discovers streptomycin; Duggar discovers aureomycin	Massively reduced mortality from microbial infections	Hoffman 1987, pp. 157–160
1939	Paul Mueller synthesizes DDT (dichlorodiphenyltricholorethane, first discovered in 1874 by Zeidler) as insecticide for J. R. Geigy AG of Basel	Rapidly produced by Allies to control typhus in Italy and the Rhine, malaria in Southeast Asia; also used to reduce insect pests of crops	Hoffman 1987, pp. 157–160

1941	Simple synthesis invented for substituted phenoxyacetic acids, such as plant hormone 2,4-D (2,4-dichlorophenoxy-acetic acid), and groups in United States and United Kingdom independently suggest their use as selective weed killers for cereal crops	Increased yields of cereal crops, simplified crop rotations, reduced energy used to grow crops, opened possibility of reduced tillage	Evans 1998, p. 127
1944	Howard Aiken et al. invent automatic sequence computer	Changed ability to assemble and analyze demographic data, facilitated revolution in global communication	Hoffman 1987, pp. 157–160
1944	Bretton Woods agreement initiates post–World War II system of international trade	Led to unprecedented rise in global prosperity	Schild 1995
1945	Food and Agricultural Organization of the United Nations established	Drew international attention to present and prospective problems in national and world food supply, engaging attention of public and national governments to food-population balance	www.fao.org
1945–1953	25 synthetic organic pesticides introduced, including chlordane, toxaphene, aldrin, dieldrin, endrin, heptachlor, parathion	Improved food production and had significant environmental and health effects	Hoffman 1987, pp. 157–160
1947	Shockley, Brattain, Bardeen invent transistor	Basis of microelectronics revolution in telecommunications and computing	Hoffman 1987, pp. 157–160
1948	United Nations proclaims Universal Declaration of Human Rights	Promoted modernization, including rights of women	Evans 1998, p. 115

Table 3.2 (continued)

Year	Innovation	Putative demographic effect	Source
1951	Watson and Crick discover structure of DNA	Foundation of modern molecular genetics	Hoffman 1987, pp. 157–160
1951	Carl Djerassi directs synthesis of cortisone at Syntex laboratory, leading to synthesis of progesterone and orally active inhibitor of ovulation	Enlarged range of contraceptive choice	Djerassi 1981, pp. 240–244
1952	Population Council established	Supported research in social sciences and biomedicine to improve family planning effectiveness	www.popcouncil.org
1952	Hoffman-La-Roche and Domagk discover isoniazid for tuberculosis	Potential to reduce TB mortality	Hoffman 1987, pp. 157–160
1952	McGuire discovers erythromycin	Improved survival	Hoffman 1987, pp. 157–160
1953, 1954, 1955	Salk develops polio vaccine; Enders and Peebles develop measles vaccine; Sabin develops oral polio vaccine	Massively reduced mortality and morbidity from viral infections	Hoffman 1987, pp. 157–160
1957	Russians launch Sputnik, beginning use of Earth-orbiting satellites for human purposes	Led to global observations of human impact on Earth, facilitated diffusion of ideas	Hoffman 1987, pp. 497
1960	FDA approves birth control pill invented by Gregory Pincus and John Rock, marketed as Enovid	Enlarged range of contraceptive choice	Djerassi 1981, p. 253

1960, 1966	Rockefeller and Ford Foundations found International Rice Research Institute (IRRI), Philippines; and International Centre for Maize and Wheat Improvement (CIMMYT), Mexico	Started crucial institutions for development and propagation of the Green Revolution	Evans 1998, p. 148
1961, 1962	Jack Lippes develops plastic intrauterine contraceptive device, marketed in following year	Enlarged range of contraceptive choice	Diczfalusy 1997
1962, 1966	Norman Borlaug releases first Mexican dwarf wheat; International Rice Research Institute releases IR8 variety of dwarf rice, the first lodging-resistant, fertilizer-responsive rice for the tropics —both key players in the Green Revolution (term in use by 1968)	Improved yields, increasing aggregate production without expansion of cultivated land	Evans 1998, pp. 134, 138
1965	First regeneration of whole plants (tobacco) from single cells	Opened applications of plant cell culture to crop modification	Evans 1998, p. 130
1967, 1977, 1979	Smallpox eradication campaign is launched, last naturally occurring case of smallpox is reported, smallpox is eradicated	Controlled a major cause of human sickness and death in past centuries	http://Whqsabin.who.int:8082/smallpox.htm
1969, 1970, 1972	Photographs of Earth from Moon; Earth Day in United States; United Nations Conference on the Human Environment held in Stockholm and *Limits to Growth* published	Changed perceptions of human situation on Earth	Evans 1998, p. 133; Meadows et al. 1972

Table 3.2 (continued)

Year	Innovation	Putative demographic effect	Source
1971	Consultative Group on International Agricultural Research established to support international agricultural research centers in partnership with developing countries	Contributed to increased food production	Evans 1998, p. 134
Late 1970s, early 1980s	Epidemic of AIDS started in sub-Saharan Africa, Latin America, Caribbean, Western Europe, North America, Australia, New Zealand	Beginning of a global epidemic with massive consequences for mortality	United Nations Population Fund 1997, p. 7
1983	Ni is shown to be essential trace element for plant growth (part of a series of discoveries of essential trace elements over a century)	Made possible crop growth in deficient soils	Evans 1998, p. 105
1984	Functional antibiotic resistance gene is transferred from bacterium to tobacco	First reported transgenic plant began plant biotechnology revolution	Evans 1998, p. 162
1996	Genome sequence of budding yeast *Saccharomyces cerevisiae* published	First complete eukaryotic genome sequence	C. elegans Sequencing Consortium 1998
1998	Genome sequence (97 million bases) of nematode worm *Caenorhabditis elegans* reported	First genome sequence of a multicellular organism, of direct relevance to control of nematode parasites, and indirect relevance to control of all human diseases	C. elegans Sequencing Consortium 1998, p. 2012

References

C. Elegans Sequencing Consortium. 1998. "Genome Sequence of the Nematode *C. elegans*: A Platform for Investigating Biology," *Science* 282: 2012–2018, 11 December.

Diczfalusy, Egon. 1997. *The Contraceptive Revolution: An Era of Scientific and Social Development.* New York: Parthenon.

Djerassi, Carl. 1981. *The Politics of Contraception: Birth Control in the Year 2001.* San Francisco: W. H. Freeman.

Evans, Lloyd T. 1998. *Feeding the Ten Billion: Plants and Population Growth.* Cambridge and New York: Cambridge University Press.

Hoffman, Mark S. ed. 1987. *World Almanac and Book of Facts 1988.* New York: World Almanac, 157–160.

Meadows, Donella H., Dennis L. Meadows, Jirgen Randers, and William W. Behrens III. 1972. *The Limits to Growth: A Report for the Club of Rome's Project on the Predicament of Mankind.* New York: Signet, New American Library. 2d edition, 1974.

Schild, Georg. 1995. *Bretton Woods and Dumbarton Oaks: American Economic and Political Postwar Planning in the Summer of 1944.* New York: St. Martin's Press.

United Nations Population Fund. 1997. *AIDS Update 1997: A Report on UNFPA Support for HIV/AIDS Prevention.* New York: UNFPA.

of new contraceptives. Institutional innovation also played a major role in many fields with demographic impact, for example, in developing and promoting family planning (Population Council, founded in 1952), in agricultural innovation (Consultative Group on International Agricultural Research, founded in 1971), and in international trade (Bretton Woods agreement, concluded in 1944). To the extent that these inventions and innovations were unpredictable, one must expect similar surprises in the coming century. One must even allow for the possibility that the nature of the coming surprises will be unexpected.

In summary, population projections are uncertain because the initial data may be erroneous; the rates of birth, death, and migration in cohort-component models may be projected erroneously; external factors may change unexpectedly in exogenous projections; external factors may change as expected but the relationship between those factors and demographic rates may change; policies and programs may develop to influence the rates of birth, death, and migration; and feedbacks from anticipated population change may intervene to alter further population change in unanticipated ways. The social sciences have little ability to predict the aggregate course of the fundamental demographic processes of birth, death, and migration.

For a longer-term perspective, qualitative scenarios of the future are likely to be at least as interesting as detailed quantitative projections, provided the scenarios offer no false promises of reliability. Bellamy (1888, 1982) offered no explicit demographic projections, but his scenario of what life might be in the year 2000 remains full of interest.

A Speculative Scenario of the Twenty-First Century

Speculations about the future of population, environment, economics, and culture are not intended to divert attention from today's serious problems—the poverty, malnutrition, illiteracy, disease, and indignity of life for billions of people, plus unprecedented physical, chemical, and biological perturbations of the planet. These speculations aim to envision a positive future worth working toward. The future is at least partially an object of choice, and not entirely an inevitable outcome of an uncontrollable mechanical world.

I shall assume that the next century will not be afflicted by a lethal global pandemic of a novel infectious disease, by massively destructive warfare, or by a meteoric impact that darkens the skies for years. I assume no abrupt shift in ocean circulation and global climate that melts all polar ice, raises sea level by tens of meters, and ends conventional agriculture. All of these catastrophes are conceivable. None is especially unlikely. I exclude such possibilities because I have nothing useful to say about what would follow.

Population and Society

For the next quarter- to half-century, one can make four statements about the future of global population with fair confidence. First, the population will be bigger than it is now. Second, the population will increase less rapidly, absolutely and relatively, than it has recently. Third, the population will be more urban than it is now. Fourth, the population will be older than it is now.

Here are some details on each of these four points.

First, the twenty-first century is unlikely to see a reversal of world population growth for several decades at least. More young people are entering their childbearing years now than ever before in history. The 1998 long-term *low*-fertility projection of the United Nations estimated that global population will peak near 7.7 billion in the middle of the twenty-first century, and will fall to 5.6 billion by 2100. The world previously had 5.6 billion people around 1993. Unless future population growth is much lower than anticipated in the United Nations' low projection, the twenty-first century will have billions more people than the twentieth century.

Second, in the twentieth century, world population increased 3.8-fold. World population is very unlikely to increase 3.8-fold in the twenty-first century. At the end of the twentieth century, after 35 years of slowing population growth, a continued slowing of population growth in the twenty-first century seems very likely. Some demographers believe that another doubling of the earth's population is unlikely ever to occur (Lutz et al. 1997). If the rate of increase of population continues to fall, then the twentieth century was and will be the only century in the history of humanity to see a doubling of the earth's population within a single lifetime. Human numbers will probably never again nearly quadruple within a century. (But remember the baby boom! Surprises happen.)

Third, in Europe, the rush of people from the countryside to cities dates back to the eleventh century. Urbanization has occurred world-wide for at least two centuries. At the end of the twentieth century, there were perhaps 20 cities of 10 million people or more and 47 percent of all people lived in cities (I add the qualifier "perhaps" because of variations among countries' definitions of who is included in a major city and because of uncertainty in data on where people live). During 1990–1995, the world's urban population grew by 2.4 percent per year, 3 times as fast as rural populations grew (0.7 percent per year). The twenty-first century is unlikely to see a reversal in the relative growth of urban population. In its 1996 estimate of world urbanization prospects, the United Nations Population Division (1997b) estimated that almost all population growth in the next half-century will be located in cities, while the rural population of the world will remain nearly constant around 3 billion people. The U.N. Population Division (1997a) estimated that 61.1 percent of world population would live in urban areas by 2030 (83.7 percent in more developed regions, 57.3 percent in less developed regions). By 2030, the urban population would total 5.1 billion, 1.0 billion in the more developed regions and 4.1 billion in the less developed regions. If urbanization occurs as anticipated, then the twentieth century was and will be the last century in human history in which most people live in rural areas. In the next century, humanity will be predominantly urban. Of course, figures on urbanization disguise ambiguities and variations between countries in definitions of "cities" and "urban." While the numbers should not be taken too literally, the trend toward urbanization is clear.

Fourth, the twentieth century saw the world fraction of children aged 0–4 years gradually decline, and the world fraction of older people aged 60 years or more gradually increase. Both percentages met at 10 percent in the year 2000. This trend results from improved survival and reduced fertility. Improved survival raised the world's expectation of life from perhaps 30 years at the beginning of the twentieth century to more than 66 years at the beginning of the twenty-first century. Reduced fertility rates added smaller cohorts to the younger age groups. The twenty-first century is unlikely to see a reversal in the aging of world population. In its 1998 medium-variant projection, the United Nations estimated that by the middle of the twenty-first century, the fraction of the population aged 0–4 years will fall from 10 percent to less than 7 percent, while the fraction of the population aged 60 years or more will rise from 10 percent to more than 22 percent. In this projection, the ratio of older people to young children is expected to rise from 1-to-1 now to 3.3-to-1 in half a century. In all the variant projections developed by the United Nations, the ratio of elderly to young children is expected to grow. The lower future fertility, the higher the ratio of elderly people to young children. If the future resembles any of the U.N. projections, then the twentieth century was and will be the last century in human history to see younger people outnumber older people. The next century will be a world of predominantly older people. Among the elderly, women will outnumber men by as much as 2 to 1. New social arrangements among the elderly will arise.

For the very long-term future, one can make three statements about the future of global population with great confidence (Cohen 1995, 153–157). First, the future of human population growth is uncertain. Is the population of the world in the year 2200 likely to be closer to 2 billion or 15 billion people? No one knows. If different regions of the world have differing levels of fertility in 2200, where will the regions of high and low fertility be? No one knows. Second, in the long run, global population growth rates must necessarily be very close to 0 (though the same constraint need not apply to any sufficiently small region of the world). Global population has grown roughly 1,000-fold in the last 10,000 years, giving an average growth rate of 0.07 percent per year. It seems highly unlikely that Earth will shelter 6 trillion people 10,000 years in the future, hence the population must grow by much less than 0.07 percent per year on average over the next ten millennia. Third, in a stationary population, the average length of life equals 1 divided by the birth rate. Since global population must eventually become stationary on the average over time, people will eventually have to choose between having long lives on the average and having a high birth rate. At the global level, there is no way to have both.

The United Nations Population Division (1998) prepared official projections of future population sizes using the cohort-component method (figure 3.4). It is possible to obtain remarkably similar results by very rough calculations, at least for the year 2050. In 1999, the global population of 6 billion was increasing by almost 80 million people per year. Were growth to continue at this annual rate of 1.4 percent, the population size would double to 12 billion in roughly 50 years. Most demographers view this scenario as unlikely because the rate of increase in population size has been declining since 1965 and the absolute number of people added annually to the global population has been dropping since 1990.

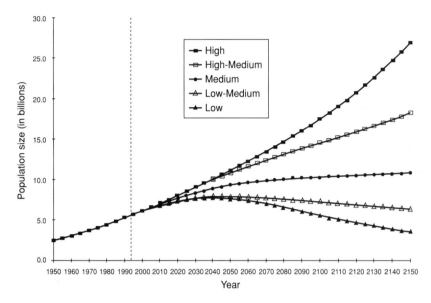

Figure 3.4
World population projections according to five main fertility scenarios of the
United Nations Population Division (1998b, their figure 4, 20). Values to the
right of the vertical dotted line are projected. Reprinted by permission.

If the annual increase in population were to drop linearly from
today's 80 million to zero over 50 years, then the average annual increase
would be 40 million per year for 50 years. Population would increase by
2 billion people to give a population size of 8 billion in the year 2050.
This scenario requires accelerating declines in fertility in presently poor
countries with high fertility rates.

Between the extremes of a constant relative growth rate and a rapid
decline to no population growth at all, it is plausible to imagine a population size in 2050 of 9 billion or 10 billion (United Nations Population
Division 1998a, b). There are few objective grounds for confidence
about the future trajectory of human fertility in the coming century.
Remembering that the human population numbered only 3 billion as
recently as 1960, population sizes of 8 billion or 12 billion can only be
viewed with awe.

In 1998, roughly 1.2 billion people—1 person in 5—lived in the developed countries, defined as North America north of the Rio Grande,
Europe, Japan, Australia, and New Zealand, and sometimes including

some smaller Asian countries. According to 1998 estimates (Population Reference Bureau 1998), the TFR of 1.2 billion people in the more developed regions was 1.6 children per woman, well below the replacement level of 2.1 children per woman. Little if any of the next half-century's population growth is expected to occur in these countries.

By contrast, the 3.5 billion people in the less developed regions outside China had a TFR of 3.8 children per woman and a doubling time of 35 years, at the end of the twentieth century. Unless the pace of economic and educational development accelerates markedly, the fraction of people living in developing countries will increase from 80 percent at the end of the twentieth century to 90 percent by 2050. The population density in the developed countries is currently about 22 people/km^2, while that in the developing countries is roughly 55 people/km^2. The latter number will roughly double to 100 people/km^2 if global population grows to 10 billion, largely as a result of increases in the developing countries. This is one person per hectare. Attaining acceptable qualities of life in developing countries at such population densities will be a challenge. The challenge has not been met even at today's population densities.

If the whole world had the level of fertility of the more developed regions today, world population would peak in the middle of the twenty-first century and then gradually decline. On the other hand, if fertility remained at its present high level in the less developed regions outside China, rapid population growth would continue, even without a resurgence of fertility elsewhere. In this case, another quadrupling of the Earth's total population in the coming century could result from three doublings (at 35 years each) of the population of the less developed regions outside China. While such growth cannot be precluded demographically, other factors might make such growth extremely difficult or impossible.

A century from now, humankind will live in a global garden, whether it be well or poorly tended (Cohen 1998, Janzen 1998). Most people will live in cities, surrounded by large, thinly populated zones for nature, agriculture, and silviculture. Worldwide, between 100 and 1,000 cities of 5 million to 25 million people each will serve their inhabitants' wants for food, water, energy, waste removal, political autonomy, and cultural and natural amenities. Some cities will serve people who want to live only with people ethnically and culturally like themselves. Other cities will serve people who are attracted by ethnic and cultural diversity. Different cities will gain shifting reputations as being favorable for young people, child-rearing, working, or retirement. The efficiency and quality of services that cities provide will depend on the quality of their management and on the behavioral skills and manners of their populations.

Just as feudal obligations were replaced by labor markets, other present rights and obligations will increasingly be replaced by markets. For example, there could be a worldwide market in permits for permanent residence in cities. The prices of these permits could be tacked on real estate or rental prices. City managements will compete to command market rewards for the public goods they are able to provide. Countries like the United States that insist on a person's right to leave his or her country of birth will have to decide if that implies a person's right to enter some other country.

Social and individual values will determine how far markets will be allowed to intrude into allocations previously determined by traditional means. Women around the world will demand and receive education and jobs comparable to men's education and jobs. Women will, therefore, have increased autonomy and power in the family, economy, and society. Partly as a consequence of women having attractive alternatives to childbearing and child-rearing, the number of children that women bear in a lifetime will most likely decline globally to the replacement level or below. As childbearing will occupy a falling fraction of most women's lengthening lives, women will intensify their demands for other meaningful roles. If the nuclear family of married adults and minor children comes to occupy a transient interval of a prolonged life cycle, the consequent reduction in average household size and composition could have substantial effects economically, environmentally, and culturally.

Though global human population growth could well end in the next century, some regions will be net exporters of people while others will be net importers. Rising pressures for migration from poorer to richer countries will strain traditionally xenophobic countries like Germany and Japan, as well as traditionally receptive countries like the United States, Australia, Sweden, and Argentina. Migrations will bring culturally diverse populations into increasing contact. The result will be many frictions as humans learn manners and tolerance. Intermarriages will make a kaleidoscope of skin colors.

Environment

A major challenge of the coming century will be coping with the environmental impacts of agricultural intensification. These impacts are partly physical (changes in the quality of soil after prolonged cultivation), partly chemical (effects of fertilizers and biocides beyond their intended targets, effects of methane and nitrogenous animal wastes), and partly biological (genetic, ecological, and epidemiological). If the 3 billion people in the rural areas of developing countries over the next half-century have to provide food and fiber to an enormously increased number of urban people in developing countries, it will be a challenge to do so without poisoning themselves and their environment, in the face of unpredictable climatic constraints (Evans 1998). Alternatives will be to acquire agricultural products from the developed world by trade or gift or to promote agricultural production within urban regions of developing countries.

Today's simplified agricultural ecosystems will be replaced by managed ecosystems of high complexity. Biological controls and farmer intelligence will aim to maximize yields while reducing biocidal inputs like today's pesticides and herbicides. Required agricultural inputs of nutrients and energy will be derived from human, animal, and industrial wastes rather than from today's fertilizers and fossil fuels. Unwanted effluents like eroded soil or agricultural runoff with pesticides and fertilizers will be eliminated or converted to productive inputs for industrial and urban use. Providing the farmer skills and supportive institutions required for such sophisticated agricultural management will be another major challenge.

Continental shelves, especially off Asia, will be further developed to provide food, energy, and perhaps living space. Oceanic food sources will be largely domesticated. The capture of any remaining wild marine animals will be managed like deer hunting now. The tropical forests that survive the onslaught of population growth and economic exploitation between 1950 and 2050 will be preserved as educational and touristic curiosities, like the immensely popular John Muir Woods north of San Francisco. Many forests will be meticulously managed for fiber, food, pharmaceuticals, and fun (that is, recreational exploration).

The atmosphere will also be managed. Rights to add carbon dioxide, methane, and other climatically significant trace gases and particles to the atmosphere will be traded in global markets for the services that natural ecosystems provide. Governments will recognize the potential of atmospheric and many other natural ecosystem services (Daily 1997) to generate taxes that can support other public goods. Gases will be manipulated as part of food production and wildlife management. For example, genetically engineered bacteria and farming practices will manipulate agricultural methane production.

People will revalue living nature as they realize that they do not know how to multiply old forests, coral reefs, and the diversity of living forms. People will increasingly value nature's genetic resources and aesthetic amenities. Conservation movements will gain renewed strength in collaborations with businesses.

The intensive management of continents, oceans, and the atmosphere will require massive improvements in data collection and analysis, and especially in concepts. A century hence, we will live on a wired Earth. Continents, air, and sea will be continuously sensed. Like the weather stations on land and the satellites that now monitor the atmosphere, the oceans and solid earth crust of the next century will have three-dimensional lattices of sensing stations at all depths. Mathematical · models of earth, air, and sea will aim to predict major events such as El Niños, hurricanes, earthquakes, volcanoes, major plumes of hot water from oceanic vents, and shifts in major ocean currents. These models will improve with at least million-fold improvements in computing power over the next century. Models will integrate not only the atmosphere, crust, and oceans, but also human and other biological populations including domestic animals, trees, cereal crops, and infectious diseases; economic stocks and flows, including all natural resources; informational stocks and flows, including scientific, literary, artistic, and folk traditions; and familial, social, institutional, and political resources and constraints. Comprehensive models will include factors beyond human control, such as solar flares, and will represent, though not predict, human decisions.

In spite of improvements in information, concepts, and management, the Earth will still bring surprises. Geophysical surprises will arise from an improved awareness of what the planet is doing, from inherent instabilities in geophysical systems described by the mathematics of chaos, and from rising human impacts. Surprising infectious diseases will continue to emerge from the infinite well of genetic variability. Historically, each factor-of-10 increase in the density of human settlements has made possible the survival of new human infections (Anderson and May

1991). Unless the sanitary infrastructure of the next century's megacities improves dramatically, large cities could become incubators for new infectious diseases. As more humans contact the viruses and other pathogens of previously remote forests and grasslands, dense urban populations and global travel will increase opportunities for infections to spread. However, people know far more now than in the past about how to prevent and contain the spread of infection. The ability to apply this knowledge depends on future political and social organization.

Economies

A slowing, cessation, or reversal of population growth need not entail a slowing or reduction in economic growth (Kosai, Saito, and Yashiro 1998). In the near-term, roughly a 4-fold increase in aggregate economic output will be required to bring the four-fifths of humanity living on a few thousand dollars a year up to the level of the one-fifth of humans living on roughly twenty thousand dollars a year. If poverty is eliminated from the Earth, the demand for positional goods (Hirsch 1976) should continue or be intensified, although environmental constraints may require those goods to take informational or symbolic form. As art dealers know, there is apparently no limit to the value that can be attached to rare beauty.

Economies will be increasingly integrated. Cities will concentrate the talent and resources required for international business. Hardly any complex product will be conceived, financed, engineered, manufactured, sold, used, and retired within the boundaries of a single political unit. Businesses will learn to profit from the eternity of atoms by designing products for use, return, and regeneration. Governments will find that a growing fraction of the power to control the economic well-being of their citizens lies outside their borders. Economic integration will give profit to those who can recognize the comparative advantage of other societies.

Information will become increasingly valuable. Those who can create it, analyze it, and manage effectively on the basis of it will be at a premium. Information technology and global economic integration will grow hand in hand. The definition of wealth may change toward one that is more information-rich and less material-intensive.

As the peoples of Asia, Latin America, and Africa grow wealthier (too slowly, and with too many major setbacks), their environmental fatalism and modest demands for food will be replaced by impatience with the accidents of nature, intolerance of environmental mismanagement, and refusal to eat less well than their neighbors. The need for careful global management, trusteeship, or stewardship will become irresistible—particularly stewardship of living resources, human and nonhuman.

Culture

Culture pervades everything that can be said about population, the environment, and economies. For example, culture conditions the productive and reproductive roles of men and women; defines which biological raw materials are seen as food and which are not; and shapes what consumers demand from the economy, including the balance of informational and material products.

An international common law—not a world government but rather international standards of behavior—will grow stronger and more comprehensive in a progression from technical, to commercial, to political law. International agreements on vaccination and on metric measures work because they benefit all who abide by them, and many who do not. Growing investments by multinational corporations will force the development of international contract law. Once the regional and global economic customs, institutions, and laws are firm, it will become too costly for nation-states or their successors to ignore them. Legal and economic resolutions of political conflicts will become more efficient than violent ones. Not all parts of the world will learn this lesson with equal ease.

A slowing or reversal in the growth of the human population in the twenty-first century could portend a more rapid spread of the three elements of citizenship identified by Marshall (1949). To understand why, it is useful to review the experience of Europe in the fourteenth and fifteenth centuries. This experience is one of the few documented examples of how societies responded to widespread—not merely local—population decline. Waves of the Black Death, probably related to today's bubonic plague, together with pervasive violence permitted or instigated by poor and sometimes malicious governments, killed from one-third (Cipolla 1993) to two-thirds (Herlihy 1997) of the European population. North and Thomas (1973) and Herlihy (1997) argued that this catastrophe shook Europe loose from a stable equilibrium of high population density, intensive grain production, and widespread poverty. Before the Black Death, admission to guilds had been hereditary or strictly limited. A scarcity of workers following the drop in population forced guilds to recruit more widely from among the poor. Parents shifted much of their bequests from pietistic charity to their children. Increased lands per person shifted diets toward more meat, the food of the rich previously. The scarcity of people raised the wages of both agricultural and urban laborers and stimulated the development of labor-saving technology. From an oversimplified economic perspective, when the supply of people dropped, the price of people rose. A dramatic fall in the abundance of people was followed by an increase in their value.

Cipolla (1993) argued that key factors in the development of Europe were the rise of urban society in the eleventh to thirteenth centuries, in which professionals had a prominent place, and the technological innovations in both agriculture and manufacturing that came with urbanization of the population. According to Cipolla, the Black Death saved these gains from being eaten up, as they were in Asia, by the rise of population.

However, numbers of people cannot be the whole story. If the decimation of the Amerindians following the European conquests raised the price of people in the New World, it led Europeans to tighten their control of the subjugated populations. This example shows that the effects on well-being of a major drop in population depend as much on the relations of power in a society as on numbers. To judge by the preventable ills of the human population today, people are collectively valued cheaply. Three-quarters of a billion people are chronically undernourished; at least another billion are malnourished; a billion adults are illiterate; perhaps 2 billion people are infected with the bacillus of tuberculosis (with hundreds of millions more under threat from other infectious diseases); and roughly four-fifths of the world's population lives on average annual incomes of at most a few thousand dollars.

The transition from a doubling of population in the last 40 years of the twentieth century to a possible absolute decline in the twenty-first century could be accompanied by a rise in the value of people, other things being equal. A perceived slowing in population growth could raise the incentives to nurture well those who are born. It could speed the worldwide diffusion of the civil, political, and social elements of good citizenship. When it can no longer be assumed that there will be plenty more people to come, then assuring that people have food, education, health, and a meaningful civic life may take on greater urgency. But as the example of the Amerindians shows, this positive outcome is by no means inevitable. If major changes for the better do occur, it will be to the lasting credit of humans that, this time, the demographic and social changes were in large part brought about or at least facilitated by the reproductive choices of individuals.

Geophysical and biological surprises, the revaluation of living nature, our greater dependence on people all over the world, our growing determination to act lawfully, and our own aging (individually and as a population) could increasingly inspire in many people a greater awe for the world, for others, and for ourselves.

Other Scenarios Are Possible

There is no shortage of scenarios for the future of population (Lutz 1994, 1996; United Nations 1997a, b; 1998a, b) or for the future of the entire world (McRae 1994, Coates et al. 1997, Ocko 1997, Bossel 1998, Hammond 1998). Bossel (1998) developed two scenarios, one called "competition" and the other called "partnership." For each scenario, he examined infrastructure, the economic system, the social system, individual development, government, environment, resources, and the future. The goals of his agenda for change included indicators for sustainable development, efficient technologies, education and information, the regionalization of economic activities, population control, the equitable distribution of work, the rights of affected systems, and participatory democracy. Hammond (1998) developed three scenarios called "market world: a new golden age of prosperity?"; "fortress world: instability and violence?"; and "transformed world: changing the human endeavor?" More than Bossel, Hammond emphasized the very different challenges faced by different regions of the world.

Bossel, Hammond, and I share the conviction that the future is at least partially a matter of choice. Many, perhaps most, things in the future are intrinsically hidden from us now. Nevertheless, we constantly make choices about investing, or not investing, in the next generation of humans individually and institutionally; about protecting the other species that support our life and make the planet habitable; and about conserving the physical setting of continents, oceans, and atmosphere.

We can foresee the consequences of our choices only dimly, but we can aspire to make choices that will improve our chances for a livable future.

Acknowledgments

I thank Sandra Waldman for helpful information, and Tim Besley, Chris Caswill, Richard Cooper, Paul David, Valerie Herr, Nathan Keyfitz, Jonathan Messerli, Richard O'Brien, Samuel Preston, Barney Rush, Peter Schwartz, and George Whitesides for helpful comments on earlier presentations and drafts of this material. I acknowledge with thanks the support of U.S. National Science Foundation grants BSR92–07293 and DEB 99–81552, and the hospitality of Mr. and Mrs. William T. Golden.

References

Ahlburg, Dennis A., and James W. Vaupel. 1990. "Alternative Projections of the U.S. Population." *Demography* 27(4): 639–652.

Anderson, R. M., and R. M. May. 1991. *Infectious Diseases of Humans: Dynamics and Control.* Oxford: Oxford University Press.

Ayres, Robert U., William H. Schlesinger, and Robert H. Socolow. 1994. "Human Impacts on the Carbon and Nitrogen Cycles." Pp. 121–155 in *Industrial Ecology and Global Change.* New York: Cambridge University Press.

Bellamy, Edward. 1888. *Looking Backward, 2000–1887.* Boston: Ticknor, 1888. Edited by Cecelia Tichi. Reprinted, 1982. Harmondsworth, Middlesex, England; New York: Penguin Books.

Berry, Brian J. L. 1990. "Urbanization." Pp. 103–119 in *The Earth as Transformed by Human Action,* ed. B. L. Turner et al. Cambridge: Cambridge University Press.

Bledsoe, Caroline H., John B. Casterline, Jennifer A. Johnson-Kuhn, John G. Haaga. eds. 1999. *Critical Perspectives on Schooling and Fertility in the Developing World.* Washington, D.C.: National Research Council, National Academy Press.

Bongaarts, John, and Rodolfo A. Bulatao, eds. 2000. *Beyond Six Billion: Forecasting the World's Population.* Panel on Population Projections, Committee on Population, Commission on Behavioral and Social Sciences and Education, National Research Council. Washington, D.C.: National Academy Press.

Bossel, Hartmut. 1998. *Earth at a Crossroads: Paths to a Sustainable Future.* Cambridge: Cambridge University Press.

Cannan, Edwin. 1895. "The Probability of a Cessation of the Growth of Population in England and Wales during the Next Century." *Economic Journal* 5, no. 20 (December): 505–515.

Chao, Benjamin Fong. 1995. "Anthropogenic Impact on Global Geodynamics due to Reservoir Water Impoundment." *Geophysical Research Letters* 22, no. 24 (15 December): 3529–3532.

Cipolla, Carlo M. 1993. *Before the Industrial Revolution: European Society and Economy, 1000–1700,* 3d ed. New York: W. W. Norton.

Coates, Joseph F., John B. Mahaffie, and Andy Hines. 1997. *2025: Scenarios of U.S. and Global Society Reshaped by Science and Technology.* Greensboro: Oakhill Press.

Cohen, Joel E. 1986. "Population Forecasts and Confidence Intervals for Sweden: a Comparison of Model-Based and Empirical Approaches." *Demography* 23, no. 1 (February): 105–126; 25, no. 2 (May 1988): 315.

———. 1995. *How Many People Can the Earth Support?* New York: W. W. Norton.

———. 1998. "A Global Garden in the Twenty-First Century?" *The Phi Beta Kappa Key Reporter* 63, no. 3 (Spring): 1–5.

———. 1999. "Should Population Projections Consider 'Limiting Factors'—and If So, How?" Pp. 118–138 in *Advances in Population Projections,* ed. W. Lutz, James W. Vaupel, and Dennis Ahlburg. Supplement to *Population and Development Review* 24.

Cohen, Joel E., and Nina V. Fedoroff, eds. 1999. *Colloquium on Plants and Population: Is There Time?* Washington, D.C.: National Academy Press.

Colclough, Christopher, and Keith Lewin. 1993. *Educating All the Children: Strategies for Primary Schooling in the South.* Oxford: Clarendon Press.

Crossette, Barbara. 1997. "How to Fix a Crowded World: Add People." *New York Times Week in Review,* 2 November, section 4, 1–3.

Daily, Gretchen C. 1997. *Nature's Services: Societal Dependence on Natural Ecosystems.* Washington, D.C.: Island Press.

Daly, Herman E., and J. B. Cobb. 1989. *For the Common Good: Redirecting the Economy toward Community, the Environment, and a Sustainable Future.* Boston: Beacon Press.

Eberstadt, Nicholas. 1997a. "The Population Implosion." *Wall Street Journal,* 16 October, section A, 22.

———. 1997b. "The Population Implosion." *The Public Interest,* Fall, 3–22.

Engelman, Robert, 1998. *Profiles in Carbon: An Update on Population, Consumption, and Carbon Dioxide Emissions.* Washington, D.C.: Population Action International.

Evans, Lloyd T. 1998. *Feeding the Ten Billion: Plants and Population Growth.* Cambridge: Cambridge University Press.

Gelbard, Alene, and Carl Haub. 1998. "Population 'Explosion' Not Over for Half the World." *Population Today* (Population Reference Bureau) 26(3): 1–2.

Hajnal, J. 1957. "Mathematical Models in Demography." *Cold Spring Harbor Symposia on Quantitative Biology* 22: 97–103.

Hammond, Allen. 1998. *Which World? Scenarios for the Twenty-First Century: Global Destinies, Regional Choices.* Washington, D.C.: Island Press.

Harrar, J. George. 1970. "Plant Pathology and World Food Problems." *Perspectives in Biology and Medicine* 13: 583–596.

Herlihy, David. 1997. *The Black Death and the Transformation of the West*, ed. Samuel K. Cohn, Jr. Cambridge: Harvard University Press.

Hirsch, Fred. 1976. *Social Limits to Growth*. Cambridge: Harvard University Press.

Holland, Elisabeth A., and Jean-Francois Lamarque. 1997. "Modeling Bioatmospheric Coupling of the Nitrogen Cycle through No_x Emissions and No_y Deposition." *Nutrient Cycling in Agroecosystems* 48: 7–24.

Janzen, Daniel H. 1998. "Gardenification of Wildland Nature and the Human Footprint." *Science* 279: 1312–1313.

Keilman, Nico. 1999. "How Accurate Are the United Nations World Population Projections?" Pp. 15–41 in *Frontiers of Population Forecasting*, ed. Wolfgang Lutz, James W. Vaupel, Dennis A. Ahlburg. Supplement to *Population and Development Review* 24. New York: Population Council.

Keyfitz, Nathan. 1993. "Increasing the Accuracy and Usefulness of the GDP." *Statistical Journal of United Nations Economic Commission for Europe* 10: 371–380.

Kosai, Y., J. Saito, and N. Yashiro. 1998. "Declining Population and Sustained Economic Growth: Can They Coexist?" *American Economic Review* 88(2): 412–416.

Laing, Jonathan R. 1997. "Baby Bust Ahead." *Barron's*, 8 December, 37–42.

Lutz, Wolfgang, ed. 1996. *The Future Population of the World: What Can We Assume Today?* London: Earthscan.

Lutz, Wolfgang, Warren C. Sanderson, and Sergei Scherbov. 1997. "Doubling of World Population Unlikely." *Nature* 387(6635): 803–805, 19 June.

Lutz, Wolfgang, James W. Vaupel, and Dennis A. Ahlburg, eds. 1999. *Frontiers of Population Forecasting*. Supplement to *Population and Development Review* 24. New York: Population Council.

Maddison, Angus. 1995. *Monitoring the World Economy 1820–1992*. Paris: Organisation for Economic Cooperation and Development.

Malthus, T. R. 1798, 1970. *An Essay on the Principle of Population*. Edited by A. Flew. London: Penguin.

Marshall, T. H. 1964. "Citizenship and Social Class." In *Class, Citizenship and Social Development*. New York: Doubleday and Co.

McRae, Hamish. 1994. *The World in 2020: Power, Culture, and Prosperity*. Boston: Harvard Business School Press.

North, Douglass C., and Robert Paul Thomas. 1973. *The Rise of the Western World: A New Economic History*. Cambridge: Cambridge University Press.

Ocko, Stephanie. 1997. *Doomsday Denied: A Survivor's Guide to the Twenty-First Century*. Golden: Fulcrum Publishing.

Office of Science and Technology Policy. Executive Office of the President. 1997. *Climate Change: State of Knowledge*. Washington, D.C.

Population Reference Bureau. 1998. *1998 World Population Data Sheet.* Washington, D.C.: Population Reference Bureau.

Postel, Sandra L., Gretchen C. Daily, and Paul R. Ehrlich. 1996. "Human Appropriation of Renewable Fresh Water." *Science* 271: 785–788.

Pritchett, Lant. 1995. "Divergence, Big Time." Policy Research Working Paper 1522. World Bank, Washington D.C.

Preston, S. H. 1976. *Mortality Patterns in National Populations: With Special Reference to Recorded Causes of Death.* New York: Academic Press.

Preston, S. H. 1995. "Human Mortality Throughout History and Prehistory." Pp. 30–35 in *The State of Humanity*, ed. Julian L. Simon. Cambridge, Mass.: Blackwell Publishers.

Raven, J. A. 1998. "Extrapolating Feedback Processes from the Present to the Past." *Philosophical Transactions of the Royal Society of London* B 353: 19–28.

Sanderson, Warren C. 1999. "Knowledge Can Improve Forecasts: A Review of Selected Socioeconomic Population Projections Models." Pp. 88–117 in *Frontiers of Population Forecasting*, ed. Wolfgang Lutz, James W. Vaupel, Dennis A. Ahlburg. Supplement to *Population and Development Review* 24. New York: Population Council.

Socolow, Robert, and Valerie Thomas. 1997. "The Industrial Ecology of Lead and Electric Vehicles." *Journal of Industrial Ecology* 1(1): 13–36.

Teitelbaum, Michael S., and Jay M. Winter. 1985. *The Fear of Population Decline.* Orlando: Academic Press.

United Nations. 1991. *The World's Women 1970–1990: Trends and Statistics.* Social Statistics and Indicators Series K, No. 8 ST/ESA/STAT/SER.K/8. New York: United Nations.

———. 1995. *Women in a Changing Global Economy: World Survey on the Role of Women in Development.* E.95.IV.1. New York: United Nations.

United Nations Development Programme. 1992. *Human Development Report 1992.* New York and Oxford: Oxford University Press.

United Nations Population Division. 1997a. *World Urbanization Prospects: The 1996 Revision, Estimates, and Projections of Urban and Rural Populations and of Urban Agglomerations.* ESA/P/WP.141, December 1997; Annex Tables 1, May 1997. New York: United Nations.

———. 1997b. *Urban and Rural Areas 1996.* Publication ST/ESA/SER.A/166. New York: United Nations.

———. 1998a. *World Population Estimates and Projections, 1998 Revision. Briefing Packet.* New York: United Nations.

———. 1998b. *World Population Projections to 2150.* ESA/P/WP.145, 30 March 1998. New York: United Nations.

———. 1999. *Comprehensive Tables.* Vol. 1 of *World Population Estimates and Projections, 1998 Revision.* New York: United Nations.

United States Bureau of the Census. 1975. *Historical Statistics of the U.S., Colonial Times to 1970.* Bicentennial edition. Washington, D.C.: U.S. Government Printing Office.

Vitousek, Peter, et al. 1997a. "Human Alteration of the Global Nitrogen Cycle: Causes and Consequences." *Issues in Ecology* (Ecological Society of America), no. 1, Spring.

Vitousek, Peter, Harold A. Mooney, Jane Lubchenco, and Jerry M. Melillo. 1997b. "Human Domination of Earth's Ecosystems." *Science* 277: 494–499.

Watson, Andrew J., and Peter S. Liss. 1998. "Marine Biological Controls on Climate via the Carbon and Sulfur Geochemical Cycles." *Philosophical Transactions of the Royal Society of London* B 353: 41–51.

Wattenberg, Ben J. 1997. "The Population Explosion Is Over." *The New York Times Magazine,* 23 November, pp. 60–63.

Williams, James H. 1997. "The Diffusion of the Modern School." Pp. 119–136 in *International Handbook of Education and Development: Preparing Schools, Students, and Nations for the Twenty-First Century,* ed. William K. Cummings and Noel F. McGinn. New York, Tokyo: Pergamon, Elsevier Science.

Woodward, F. I., M. R. Lomas, and R. A. Betts. 1998. "Vegetation-Climate Feedbacks in a Greenhouse World." *Philosophical Transactions of the Royal Society of London* B 353: 29–39.

World Bank. 1993. *World Development Report: Investing in Health.* New York: Oxford University Press.

World Bank. 1999. *World Development Report: Knowledge for Development.* New York: Oxford University Press.

World Resources Institute. 1998. *World Resources 1998–99.* New York: Oxford University Press.

Zlotnik, Hania. 1999. "World Population Prospects—the 1998 Revision." Working paper 19, Joint ECE-Eurostat Work Session on Demographic Projections. Statistical Commission and Economic Commission for Europe, Statistical Office of the European Communities (Eurostat), Conference of European Statisticians. Rome: ISTAT (Italian National Statistical Institute).

4

The Future of Energy from the Perspective of the Social Sciences

Clark C. Abt

Introduction

In governments and industries, great investment decisions must be made every year about what shall be done, what shall be invested, what shall be prepared for the ten-to-twenty year future. No sector of the world economy or industry feels this more profoundly than energy. No other issue than energy—where and how to get it, pay for it, supply it, produce it, defend and preserve it, consume it—affects every economy, society, and enterprise so pervasively.

Energy production, distribution, and consumption operate on a massive and pervasive scale, and take years—often over a decade—to design, organize, finance, build, and operate. Yet the energy supply required by industry and government and individual consumers changes all the time, with the growth and change of economic activity of energy consumers and producers. Planning energy production for a specific city or industry, for a decade hence, becomes complex when one must try to anticipate the main factors of supply and demand and cost. To plan energy production one needs to estimate energy demand. This is the essential problem of energy forecasting. Hundreds of billions of dollars are gambled annually on the accuracy of long-range energy forecasts. This is the world's biggest, longest money ball game, and forecasting it is much less certain and less well understood than forecasting the weather.

One reason that energy forecasting is more uncertain than weather forecasting is that energy demand and supply are mutually reactive. Weather does not care what the weather forecaster or weather consumers think or know or say about it—it has only to obey the laws of nature. Whatever we do about the weather, weather behaves as it will regardless of our response. True, humanity is collectively and cumulatively finally having an impact on weather's global warming with greenhouse gas emissions from energy production and consumption, but it is even less predictable how that affects local daily weather.

But with energy forecasting as with weather, failure to anticipate subtle cumulative long-term changes precipitate sudden short-term consequences—storm damage, electrical blackouts, rapid energy mode shifts by consumers faced with sudden price rises or supply disruptions, market failures following insufficiently prepared deregulation. In energy, the forecasted can react to the forecast. This is where social scientists, the scientists of human behavior, come in. They know something about human reactivity to events, about motivation, perception, and decision making under cross-pressures and uncertainty, which is exactly what energy forecasting is, because energy is pervasive in human biology, society, economy, technologies, and politics.

This is why it is essential and impossible to predict energy demand, supply, and prices. Yet energy and energy-intensive industries and governments must try, and repeatedly, because to produce and to consume is to plan, and to plan is to forecast. Forecasts, as distinct from predictions, are an envelope of alternative predictions conditional on alternative assumptions about current market structures and trends. The better energy demand and supply are forecasted, the better production can be planned to meet needs at acceptable cost and risk. The worse energy demand and supply are forecasted, the more dangerous to economy, society, and environment are the plans, and the less likely to meet needs in a timely, safe, and affordable manner. This is why it is important for independent, contrarian long-range forecasters to try to be more accurate; to *oppose with contrasting future scenarios from the extremes of the distribution of possibilities, the typical central tendency scenarios conventional econometric models produce.* The average almost never actually happens.

But what does it mean to be accurate as a forecaster? To be accurate the forecaster does not have to predict the future—that is not possible. *To be accurate the forecaster's forecast must include among the alternative possibilities the important ones that could occur, and the ones that actually do.* That is my own definition. *If important things happen that are not imagined as possible by forecasters, then who needs forecasters? If forecasters fail completely to anticipate the possibility of the actual, their forecasts are actually less than worthless—they are misleading.* To be inaccurate, the forecaster must *completely miss* the *possibility* of something that could happen, even with only modest probability, but that would be very important—perhaps fatal to goals achievement—if it did happen.

A long range forecast of the future, to be useful to government and industry planners who must make long lead-time commitments, should concern itself with forecasting a range of important and possible developments, not just a consensus view of current conventional wisdom's maximum likelihood point estimate expectation (as most government forecasts do).

We look at how well social scientists predicted the current state of world energy demand, predominant forms, technologies, sources, supplies, prices, and controlling powers in the past thirty years as they presented or assumed their pictures of the contemporary 1999 energy future in the 1970s and 1980s. We will see how accurate and comprehensive they were, where the forecasts were wrong, and something of how much this matters and for whom.

We also assess the performance of specific social sciences—mainly the economists, political scientists, and survey sociologists—and identify the capabilities and limitations of their energy and energy-relevant forecasting over the last twenty or thirty years. We then apply what we have learned from our many past forecasting mistakes and few successes to forecasting the next twenty-year energy future.

Social scientist forecasters, chiefly economists and political scientists, have a poor track record and a deservedly poor reputation for forecasting the future of energy demand, consumption, supply, prices, and technologies—and for understanding the interacting dynamics of energy economics, politics, and technologies. Even predicting the recent energy past is difficult, in the sense of convincingly identifying the causes and effects of the current situation. Who predicted the California electric energy supply crisis immediately following deregulation? What can we do to improve the forecasting of the future of energy? Here are a few suggestions.

First, *consider a wider range of outcomes than major current trends, and a broader set of dimensions (political, military, and social, in addition to economics and technology).* The U.S. Department of Energy (DOE) 2020 energy forecast neglects not only the future potential socio-political economic impact of rapid urbanization of billions of now rural poor people but even the growing technological change of currently small but rapidly growing worldwide activity and cost-competitiveness of abundantly distributed nonpolluting solar, wind, and biowaste energy supplies, and supporting technologies, tastes, and consumer preferences. The economic impact of major energy producer and consumer governments' interventions in energy markets, whether to massively develop, regulate, deregulate, or expropriate energy supply, is also not considered in the DOE forecasts.

Second, *sample survey more local informants in more diverse energy demand environments* to avoid the missing variables problem. One important example: DOE's energy demand and consumption estimates in their twenty-year projections for Asia, Africa, and Latin America wildly miss the rapidly swelling buildup of energy demand in poor rural areas of Less Developed Countries (LDCs), and rapidly growing urban areas. This demand growth is composed of both population and economic growth increases, and energy intensivity of use growth with increasing urbanization. Forecasts should warn us that such demand growth probably cannot be met within the twenty-year time frame by conventional sources alone. As demand growth outpaces conventional supply, the shorter construction lead times of cheaper mass-produced solar and wind systems could make up the gap.

Another example: Failing to survey important consumer groups in forecasting transportation energy demand. It is blithely assumed that poor people aspiring to a vehicle will insist on a 200-horsepower two-ton $20,000 sedan or nothing, and on this basis the demand for oil and oil-based transportation fuels is estimated for 2020—without consideration of affordability constraints, environmental constraints, even taste constraints, or the more energy-efficient substitution potential of cheaper hybrid electric vehicles.

Third, *pay attention to rapidly growing small absolute quantities of new technologies and energy sources to avoid measurement errors that will dramatically compound into gross oversights later* (things new and promising but small now). Since new energy sources, technologies, and innovations always start small, the initial measurement error of leaving them out altogether because they are "too small to count" (as for example the current under 1 percent world market penetration of solar and wind energy) can result, with rapid growth rates, in this initially small measurement error compounding over time to a gross oversight of what can become a major factor.

Aggregate global counts of energy innovations frequently mask significant developments in smaller countries or cities, and significant differences in local supply, demand, and costs—especially transportation costs. For example, wind energy supplies less than 1 percent of world energy, but in Denmark it supplies 11 percent, and the market value of one leading wind turbine manufacturer there, Vestas Wind Systems, grew tenfold in the last five years.

Another similar measurement error to be avoided is the failure to forecast a slowly gathering groundswell of public opinion and consumer preferences for new, environment-conserving energy products and services. These may initially represent only minority views and interests, as with the environmental movement. It was much underrated when still small in the early 1960s. If the current small but growing fraction of energy consumers interested in solar and wind energy and electric vehicles are dismissed as insignificant, it will lead to gross measurement errors later in the estimation of future energy demand.

The already enormous pent-up demand for energy-intensive consumer goods in the poorer three-fourths of the world is growing apace with the rapid diffusion of global TV communications. It can plausibly be argued that the range of twenty-year energy demand forecast envelopes, especially in LDCs, should be doubled to quadrupled by 3.5 percent to 7 percent average annual demand growth. Population growth alone accounts for half of that and per capita economic growth the other half, leaving nothing at all for growth of per capita energy consumption to the American ideal, which currently is two orders of magnitude greater than per capita use in the poor half of the world population.

The DOE forecast ignores the massive literature of market research on energy-related consumer behaviors, from purchases of automobiles to kitchen appliances, washing machines, refrigerators, air conditioning, home entertainment and office electronics. As electric lighting, telephones, TV, computers, and air conditioners inevitably penetrate third-world mass markets, electric energy demand will grow even faster than the growing urban population and urban electric power generating capacity, and much faster than beyond-grid rural populations. For most of the 2 billion people still without electricity who want these things, and are becoming aware of them through global village TV and radio coverage, extending the electric power grid or installing diesel motor-generators is too costly for them or their governments. But distributed solar home systems of the kind pioneered by Shell and Eskom in South African rural areas on a privately self-financed basis, are, as Nelson Mandela says, "safe, affordable, and friendly to the environment."

The main impact on Europe, North America, and Japan of this rising LDC consumer demand for electrification and electric products is to increase export trade. The rural poor consumers of Africa, Asia, and Latin America can best satisfy their demand for electricity-consuming products and better quality of life with some mix of domestically manufactured goods and imported ones from OECD nations. Electrification improves education, public health, and economic activity, and raises incomes. Both low- and high-income economies benefit from more trade. Long-range forecasting can avoid measurement errors and neglect of missing variables and the extremes of distributions by promptly recognizing productive social and technological innovations that are likely to become widely adopted on their merits.

An Evaluative Review of Past Energy Forecasting

A review of the performance of the social sciences in their long-range (ten to twenty years out) energy forecasting over the last thirty-five years found the following:

1. Mainly economic and technological forecasting, by economists and technologists. Almost no social, political, or military forecasting of events or trends affecting energy supply and demand.

2. Emphasis on demand and consumption forecasting, including the most energy-consuming technologies of manufacturing, housing, and transportation. Implicit assumption that market forces will always (and promptly!) generate enough supply to meet demand.

3. The spread of macroeconometric modeling methodology from university departments of economics to government and industry think tanks and independent research organizations, mostly in the United States but also in Europe and Japan.

4. The spread of mathematical process modeling from systems engineering through engineering project management (PERT—Program Evaluation and Review Technique) into Forrester's Industrial Dynamics. This was combined with mathematical optimization techniques of Linear Programming and Dynamic Programming, developed originally in military operations research, into "world modeling" for longer-range economic and natural resources forecasting (Meadows 1972). This approach has since been discredited as the resource depletion hypothesis proved untenable in the face of substitutes, but may be revived in more interdisciplinarily sophisticated forms by the growing awareness of global

environmental constraints. (I still remember a wise Japanese economist responding critically to my query of what he thought of Herman Kahn's book, *Japan As Number One*. He didn't think it would ever happen. Asked why not, he said simply, "Resource constraints.")

5. Thus far, attempts to extend short-term econometric modeling methods to long-term and multi-disciplinary forecasting (including social, political, cultural, and technological forecasting) have not been successful. Macroeconomic growth models, barely better than random in their two-year projections when there are no major disasters or structural changes, continue to be inappropriately extended to five- to twenty-year projections (as in DOE's 2020 energy forecast). These are usually too narrow and inaccurate to be of much use and are inferior to expert judgments.

Comparing the forecasts of energy ten, twenty, and thirty years ago with current reality, biases are found that distort the forecasts and result in systematic errors of commission. Important changes in energy supply and consumption technologies are overlooked or neglected repeatedly. Apparently few of these observed forecasting errors are fed back into subsequent long-range forecasting efforts to reduce biases and omissions, perhaps because they are forgotten by the time of subsequent forecasts. There does not seem to be any responsibility felt or the skill needed to improve comprehensiveness and accuracy in government forecasting. Industry long-range energy forecasting is not publicly available for assessment here.

Typically both errors of omission and commission are associated with specific disciplines or personality traits of forecasters. Technology forecasters tend to be positively biased toward what is technically feasible, and omit economic market forces motivating only the most profitable innovation of the scientifically possible. Economic forecasters tend to be positively biased toward what is economically most advantageous, maximizing market acceptance of competitive rewards for limited risk. They tend to omit new technologies penetrating under 1 percent of world markets (such as solar and wind), and question innovations that do not immediately meet market acceptance with doubts such as: "If it really worked better, why doesn't everybody buy it?" Only retrospective evaluation—hindsight—can identify these sources of forecasting error and transform them into corrections improving insight and foresight—*if* the sources of error do not also change.

How Well Did Social Scientists Predict the Present Energy Situation?

Back in the 1960s and 1970s, how well did energy economists predict the current (2000) state of world and regional energy demand? Smil (1993) reported that he had "collected two dozen American mid-to-short term energy forecasts of the country's total primary energy consumption in 1985. Expectedly, the closer they were made to the target year, the more realistic they tended to be, but even those looking ahead less than a decade were, on the average, about 25 per cent too high." The present writer compared U.S. total energy demand estimates from 1970 to 2000 from a Congressional National Fuels and Energy Policy Study (1972) with the actual total consumption from 1960 to 1997 (U.S. DOE Annual Energy Review 1997), and found a similar 23 percent too high forecast. It seems fairly clear that many of these forecasts were based on extrapolations of past trends with "business as usual" structures held constant, and assumed a continuing correlation of energy demand with population growth and per capita economic growth. This would make intuitive sense, were there not so many other countervailing factors such as new environmental laws and public concerns, increasing energy efficiency in production and consumption, an aggressive dictator constraining imports and pushing up prices, and reducing demand and consumption. And even the unexpectedly high rate of qualitative and quantitative economic growth in California in the last five years, and in telecomputing in the last ten, was not factored in *even as a less than trivial possibility*.

An example (mentioned by Smil) of a mix of accurate energy forecasting in the aggregate but erroneous in the components is the *Resources for Freedom Report of 1952* (President's Materials Policy Commission 1952). They came close to estimating actual total commercial energy use twenty-three years later, but got the proportions of individual fossil fuels wrong. Coal market share declined faster than was forecast, and oil and gas rose faster. They also incorrectly forecast that transportation energy use would grow more slowly than industrial energy use, while the reverse was the case (Landsberg 1988). It should not be surprising that large aggregates come out much as predicted—they have much inertia, and divergent elements tend to cancel each other out. However, from a policy and industry planning standpoint, component dynamics about which interventions can do something are much more important. And these they got mostly wrong.

In the Congressional National Fuels and Energy Policy Study (1972) cited above, there were other important forecasting errors and misunderstandings. The report states that "since most of the basic conflicts between environmental quality and energy production are due to the continuing high growth rate in energy demand, much discussion . . . centered on the effect of deliberate reductions in growth." This unfortunate misreading of the alleged (actually non-existent) conflict between growth and environment reflects resistance to both environmental concerns and excessive environmentalism.

In 1999 the U.S. Department of Energy (DOE) produced a report, *Performance of Past IEO (International Energy Outlook) Forecasts for 1990 and 1995*, to measure how well its IEO projections estimated future energy consumption trends. The report compares energy forecasts produced for 1990 and 1995, with the actual data published in DOE's *International Energy Annual 1996 (IEA96)*. The IEO projections extended from 1985 to 1995, and included total energy consumption forecasts for 1990 and 1995 for oil, natural gas, coal, and "other fuels." Forecasts included the United States, Canada, Japan, the United Kingdom, France, "West" Germany, Italy, the Netherlands, other OECD Europe, other OECD (Australia, New Zealand, U.S. Territories), OPEC, and other developing countries. Nuclear power forecasts were published separately after 1986. In 1990 the *IEO90* report expanded coverage to include energy forecasts for China, the Former Soviet Union, and the other centrally planned economies in the first edition to forecast the entire world's energy consumption.

How accurately did DOE's *IEO* forecast five- and ten-year energy consumption? Total regional energy consumption for the market economies in the 1985 to 1989 forecasts were between 2 percent and 5 percent lower than the actual consumption number published in *IEA96*. IEA forecasts of market economy energy consumption were also consistently lower than the actual 1995 data. There was a ten-year downward bias to consumption forecasts for market economies. Most of the error was for non-OECD countries, which perhaps reflects DOE's lower economic growth expectations for OPEC and other market economy countries outside OECD. Even the 1993 forecast for 1995 was over 10 percent lower than the actual. Is this good or bad? That large a variance in that short a forecast horizon of two years with no dramatic events intervening suggests very large energy demand forecasting errors over ten- and twenty-year periods, in which more dramatic events do intervene.

Energy consumption forecasts for the entire world were first released with *IEO90*, and have ever since been consistently higher than actual world energy consumed. DOE believes this to be the result of the "unanticipated" collapse of the Soviet economies. But some Sovietologists did forecast such a collapse, although it is uncertain when. It probably should have been considered as one of the alternative forecasts. *IEO90* estimated that the FSU would consume 66 quadrillion Btu, whereas only forty quads were actually consumed—a very large short-term underestimate.

More disturbing still is *IEO85*'s 40 percent underestimate of 1995 oil use in other developing market economies. Reflecting on past analyses affected by their historical context, the report points out that the *IEO85* published after the 1973–1974 OPEC oil price shock and the 1979–1980 Iranian revolution forecast, that oil would lose 5 percent share of total energy consumption to gas and coal in the market economies over the 1985–1995 period. Oil's share did not decline as forecast, but maintained a 45 percent share of energy consumption. Gas's share came in within a percent of the 22 percent share projected. But coal's share, which *IEO85* expected to increase to 22 percent in the market economies, presumably on pure price grounds, actually declined from 21 percent in 1985 to 18 percent in 1995. Some of the many political scientists studying "green" public opinion in Germany regarding pollution might have anticipated that, because the decline occurred mainly in Germany and the EU.

Forecasting the Cost of Energy 2020

Today oil still accounts for roughly 40 percent of world commercial energy supplies, down from 50 percent fifteen years ago. Thus the price of oil is still the most important raw material price in the world, and certainly the price that dominates the overall energy price. Oil still drives more of industrial civilization than coal, and still more than natural gas. Oil continues to be the single most internationally traded good, and until recently constituted 20 percent of world trade, peaking in the 1980s. This is why for the last forty years oil's major pervasive role in the world economy has made forecasting its price so important. (Still important, by 1995 oil was down to 7 percent of world trade.)

Because the price of oil is the dominant component of the world energy price, all energy-intensive industries—agriculture (25 percent of total cost inputs), aircraft, electric power generation, home heating, manufacturing, surface transportation (50 percent?)—must make long lead-time investments in plant, product, and energy supplies based on long-range forecasts of energy prices. So it is understandable that forecasting long-term oil prices has been so important to industry and government leaders. What is less obvious is why, despite the importance of doing so, and the obvious value of having at least roughly correct long-range oil price forecasts, they have been more often wrong than right. Inability to forecast oil prices has led to large costly overinvestment and underinvestment errors (as in California now), also creating much skepticism about economic forecasting itself.

It seems important to know whether the inability of oil analysts and macroeconomists to forecast demand, supply, and price of oil over the last twenty-five years is a problem intrinsic to only oil, or to the forecasting of all energy prices, or economic forecasting, or indeed all long-range (ten-to-twenty-year) forecasting itself. We want to know if we can, through study of past failures to forecast oil prices, better data, better analytical methods, incorporating contributions of other disciplines than economics, correct errors in forecasting energy demand, supply, and prices for different forms of energy, five to twenty years out.

If we cannot forecast prices of one kind of energy supply any better than another, then we have no rational basis for the long-range planning of the best mix of long lead-time investments in energy-producing power plants and energy-intensive industries and products. Should the World Bank and Chinese government invest in large coal-fired electric power plants on the coast (as the Asian Development Bank is doing), or in extending the massive Three Gorges hydroelectric dam project (as the Chinese government is doing), or in more nuclear power plants, solar electric and wind turbine systems (as the U.S. DOE, Denmark, Netherlands, Switzerland, and increasingly Germany and China are doing), oil exploration in the Spratly Islands, or some different mixes of these in different provinces? How can energy resources competing for markets and investment possibly be rationally planned and allocated to equalize risk-discounted marginal utilities if local prices cannot be forecasted?

A 1983 study by Daniel Yergin and Joseph Stanislaw of Cambridge Energy Research Associates and Arthur Andersen and Co., *The Future of Oil Prices: The Perils of Prophecy*, examined how forecasts of oil prices are developed, how they are perceived and used, and how they frequently fall into error. The study found that "in 1980–81 alone, on the order of

Table 4.1
Long-term forecast accuracy of the cost/price of different forms of energy.

Forecast **Accuracy** Actually Experienced	Long-term **Cost** Trends
Polluting and CO_2-Emitting Non-Renewable Fossil Fuels	
Coal: high accuracy for "dirty" coal, low for "clean" coal	for clean coal, going up
Oil: very low accuracy	Costs slowly going up
Gas: low accuracy	Costs going up
Non-CO_2-emitting nonrenewables	
Nuclear: low to medium Forecast Accuracy, depending on degree of safety demanded and regulated.	Costs: up
Nonpolluting renewables (generally high forecast accuracy)	
Solar: high forecast accuracy	Costs: going down
Wind: high forecast accuracy	Costs: going down
Hydroelectric: high forecast accuracy	Costs: staying about the same
Biowaste-fed fuel cells: moderate forecast accuracy	Costs: going down

half a trillion dollars was invested … on the assumption that oil prices would continue to rise throughout the century." They did not. That assumed forecast, they say, "will … add up to be one of the most expensive business errors ever." They conclude that future oil prices cannot be accurately predicted because of compounded and interacting uncertainties involving "new forces at work on energy and oil demand," changed industry structure, political upheavals and wars in oil-rich regions, unanticipated government decisions on taxes, tariffs, and subsidies, and changes in technology.

Three 1983 forecast statements illustrative of forecasting errors in the making are quoted: For the year 2000 the oil price "could be anywhere between $30 and $100 per barrel" (said a U.S. government forecaster, off by a factor of two to five); "Today's (1983) forecasting consensus: …. OPEC is able to maintain prices above $24 a barrel" (off by about 40 percent), and "The growth of non-oil supplies, principally coal and nuclear, is constrained by environmental concerns, their own economics, and the declining real price of oil." That may be true for coal and nuclear but neglects completely the rapid recent growth of non-oil energy supplies not at all constrained by environmental concerns or, in many locations, their own economics, namely solar and wind.

Yergin and Stanislaw correctly point out the failure of most fore-casters to anticipate the changes in demand, changes in government regulations and deregulation and its consequences, industry structure and the breakdown of the previously stable relationship between energy and economic activity, the risks of using single-line projections, unexpected political upheavals and wars, and so forth. Yet the DOE International Energy Outlook 1999 for World Oil Market forecasting to 2020 in 1999 makes most of these same errors.

Specific uncertainties not taken into account by DOE include major changes in demand: "The reference case projection anticipates rising demand, by about 1.8 percent per year, causing oil requirements to reach 110 million barrels a day by 2020." Why? This looks suspiciously like another single-line projection of oil and total energy demand, based on a regression line drawn on the last decade's time series of economic growth. It fails to consider how more stringent environmental regulations and availability of economically and environmentally competitive alternatives could displace oil, or how accelerated efficiencies in internal combustion engine efficiency could reduce transportation fuel demand even while economic activity rises.

"In all regions of the world, the largest increases in oil consumption are expected to result from oil's use as transportation fuel. By 2020 transportation is expected to account for 52 percent of world oil con-sumption, up from a 44-percent share in 1996." What spurious exacti-tude! This looks like another single-line trend extrapolation. But what if new cars get twice as fuel efficient as current stock, like the Toyota Prius hybrid electric that gets about fifty miles per gallon? And what about an increasing fraction being entirely electric vehicles, recharging their batteries from non-oil-powered generating stations (solar, wind, hydro, nuclear, gas, even coal, which would be much cheaper for China and India than oil)? Even if total car fleets expand greatly, losses of petroleum product demand to electrics and other fuel substitutes could greatly reduce that "52 percent" of oil consumption that transportation is expected to account for.

"The developing world, which accounted for less than one third of the world's oil consumption in 1996, is expected to account for 44 per-cent of the oil market by 2020. Almost 50 percent of the growth in oil consumption in developing economies occurs in developing Asia." That would be mostly China, India, Indonesia, and Pakistan; and most of this is transportation energy. Yet these countries already have some electric vehicles, a lot of coal and sunshine, and (except for Indonesia) little oil. Why wouldn't China and India reduce their costly oil import dependence and encourage automobile owners to buy EV's (electric vehicles) and HEV's to soak up some of their cheap coal-generated electricity with late night off-peak recharging, as Eskom has done in coal-rich, oil-poor South Africa, thereby saving the drivers money and air quality? That 44 percent transportation oil could easily be cut in half and half again by EV's being substituted for petrol-powered vehicles. Oil consumption in LDC's could drop if solar systems were installed en mass and used to recharge EV's. But the new power plants—cleaner gas and coal and solar photovoltaics—are not being built for the same reasons they were not built in California in the 1990s: too much investor uncertainty about price and environmental controls, too much NIMBY ("not in my backyard") reaction at potential building sites, too much apathy, and ignorance of viable technological options.

The Environmental Technologists' Hapless Forecasts of Renewable Energy

DOE and energy industry analysts up to the 1990s erred on the side of conservatism in forecasting the future of energy, but environmental enthusiasts also erred on the other side in prematurely predicting that wind power, solar power, and other nonpolluting renewable energy sources would soon make a significant contribution to European, U.S., and Japanese energy needs. While the strong market penetration wishfully predicted for renewables in industrialized countries where they were created has not yet happened except in a few northern European countries, they are being increasingly implemented in LDC's, and their performance and price reduction has often met or exceeded technical expectations and technological forecasts.

Concerns about the environment, economic growth, jobs, energy independence, national security, fairness, and monopoly power have all created controversy about the future of energy, and often about renewable energy technologies as either panacea or fraud. After thirty years of this debate the current reality is that the new renewable energy technologies of solar and wind, (excluding hydropower) have contributed less than one percent of the U.S., OECD, or world energy infrastructure. This has led some to question the viability of continued public and private investment in renewables, yet according to a recent Resources for the Future (RFF) study by Burtraw, Darmstadter, Palmer, and McVeigh (1999), evidence indicates that renewable energy technologies have lived up to their technical performance expectations and their public policy goals. How then explain their continued lack of commercial success to date? And should the same dismal result be forecast for the next two decades, as DOE does? We think not.

The RFF team evaluated five renewable energy technologies for their actual costs and performance, compared with the costs and performance forecast: biomass, geothermal, solar photovoltaic, solar thermal, and wind. They found that despite performance and cost containment goals achieved as forecasted, renewables failed to meet market penetration expectations. "They have succeeded ... in meeting expectations with respect to their cost."

In the 1970s, market forecasts for wind-generated electricity were optimistic, but by the 1980s and into the 1990s there was a shift downward, with wind energy consumption in the United States about flat and perhaps for that reason biasing its forecasts negatively.... Yet the optimistic projections about *costs* of wind-generated electricity were "realized or exceeded." "Wind has a current cost of about 52 mills (5 cents)/ kWh—," which is close to the average cost of conventional generation, and approaches and undercuts the marginal cost of new conventional fossil fuel plants in many favorable windy locations lacking local deposits of gas, oil, and coal.

Solar thermal and solar photovoltaic had similar disappointments in market penetration, despite better than promised cost performance. What was wrong with the theory of market penetration on the basis of comparable or superior price and performance? According to the RFF study: "To the extent that non-governmental organizations have historically championed renewable technologies, they might have been expected to have been the most optimistic about what renewables could do. We did not find this to be the case.... *NGO's were the most conservative* in their projections, as were studies by Edison Electric Power Institute." The RFF team's findings have, according to them, three implications: First, forecasts of costs for conventional generation are not more accurate, but *less* accurate than those for renewables, thus making financing of renewables less risky in reality, whatever the (mis)-perception. Second, the rate of technical change (and cost reduction) might be greater for a new technology than an older one; and Third, the declining price of conventional fuels in OECD was a moving baseline against which renewables had to compete, thus offsetting their growing cost reductions from scale economies.

Forecasting the Future of Energy to 2020

We now combine what has been learned from past forecasts and their errors with current knowledge, and apply it to forecasting the twenty-year energy future to estimate the magnitude and direction of the major differences between the worldwide energy future of 2020 and the present. Two approaches are presented: conventional macroeconomic projections, used by DOE; and interdisciplinary scenarios that include demographic, macroeconmic, and social and technological change projections, favored by the writer. Both examine aggregate regional and global trends of energy demand, uses, preferences, technologies, sources, supplies, prices, and trends in driving forces and deciding powers. From demographic, social, economic, political, technological, and environmental trends and their interactions with energy, qualitative twenty-year "macrotrends" were identified and are stated below:

In *Energy Politics*, power and control over energy supplies will become much dispersed, as the energy utilities shift from state monopolies to become deregulated, privatized, and more competitive. As energy industries restructure to cope with both more competition from utilities deregulation and increased environmental regulation, cost-competitive renewable energy sources become more interesting to investors, *but much more slowly than their advocates expect*. Widely distributed renewable energy technologies raise the importance of large sunny and/or windy land areas (including the sun-facing facades of urban high-rise buildings), relative to more geographically concentrated underground hydrocarbon resources. Ideally, increasing fractions of indigenous national energy supplies will be produced at lower cost than fossil fuel imports or transports from remote domestic sources. However, a winning political coalition that could make this happen has not yet been assembled in the United States, which is behind Europe in this respect.

However, as the case of California's deregulated energy market and attendant supply shortages and politically unacceptable price increases indicate, there is substantial risk of market failure in U.S. electricity supply deregulation—and not only in California.

Energy politics is an important aspect of world politics. In world politics, the United States is now the only fourfold military-economic- political-technological superpower. Europe is a threefold economic- political-technological superpower. Japan is a twofold economic-technological superpower. Russia remains a military-technological superpower, and China is a political superpower on the way to becoming an economic one. The significance of these facts of current world politics at the turn of the millennium is that the United States and Europe dominate but no longer unilaterally control world energy politics, which determines world energy trade, investment, and technological progress through trade investments. Almost all the leading energy companies are still American or European. American and European military forces are major consumers of energy but more important, the guarantors of freedom of the seas in energy trade and of free markets for energy exporters and importers.

Yet despite all their power, the increasing energy dependence of the' United States and its European allies, China, and Japan on imported oil creates increasing security risks and costs for them. (The United States imports about half its needs, Japan most of its needs.) Possibly as much as a third, or $100 billion, of the U.S. defense budget is needed to secure and protect essential access to foreign oil and the sea lanes of communication for trade and transport. The U.S. Navy expends nearly half of the U.S. defense budget, and defense of freedom of the seas and trade, including the oil trade, together with deterrence and defense against aggression toward friendly oil exporters such as Kuwait are its main missions.

These energy security costs are likely to increase over the next twenty years, with the relentless diffusion of nuclear and biological weapons technologies to countries controlling or threatening most of the major oil-producing countries, together with the persistence and probable increase in aggressive nationalist regimes in oil-producing developing areas, and the decline in the U.S. and NATO's *relative* conventional military power to deter or terminate regional and internal wars.

Energy Policy Options to Reduce Energy Import Dependence

The options open to the United States, Europe, China, and Japan to reduce energy import dependence include resorting to more domestic coal at heavy environmental cost (except in Japan), resorting to an unpopular (in the United States and Germany) buildup of nuclear power (which

France has accomplished but is rethinking), and investing in indigenous renewable resources such as solar, wind, and biowaste and the technologies to make them cost-competitive with domestic coal. All four great powers are pursuing these options which, if pursued effectively, reduce dependence on energy imports, limit the ability of foreign oil and gas producers to raise prices arbitrarily, provide examples for poor countries even more energy-import dependent (such as the Philippines), and improve relations with industrial allies and energy-importing LDCs.

In 1983 Harold Brown, former U.S. secretary of defense and a physicist who understood the technology and economics very well, predicted that "such renewable resources as solar heating and cooling, biomass conversion, wind power ... and solar electric power will be able to meet only a small percentage of U.S. energy needs for the rest of this century." He was right about that. He went on to say that "the bulk of the energy growth for U.S. central power stations during the next two decades will come from coal—perhaps some will come from natural gas." He overestimated coal and underestimated gas, but he well understood the choices and the lowest economic-military-political-environmental risk strategy then available: "It makes sense for the U.S. to undertake a major government-assisted program to diversify energy sources ... and encourage ... renewable energy resources." It makes even more sense now, not only for the United States but also for Europe, Japan, China, India, Pakistan, Brazil, and sub-Saharan Africa. But the DOE forecast for 2020 is not encouraging in this regard.

In *Energy Economics*, energy demand will increase enormously in the poorer half of the world population as global communications and TV show people everywhere the good material consumer life of the OECD that they have been missing. This pent-up energy demand in the LDCs will slowly but steadily be translated into *effective* demand—that is, demand with the ability to pay for what it wants—by the expected *reduction in local domestic renewable energy prices* made possible by favorable sunny and windy climates and economies of scale and specialization in renewable energy production machinery (PV and thermal solar, wind turbines, fuel cells). *Indigenous energy supply will increase greatly, particularly in poor, sunny LDCs* in Asia and Africa and Latin America, with the addition over the next two decades of many solar and wind turbine electric power plants coming on line, both in dispersed rural small units, and in grid-connected large urban PV-sheathed high-rise structures, and concentrated solar and wind energy "farms." *Average world energy prices may be driven down* by the rapid addition of new renewable energy supplies worldwide and in industrially advanced countries, and by widespread affluent environmentalist consumer preferences for them—unless demand grows even faster than supply, as it appears to be the case in the U.S.'s last decade. Prices may then go up or stay about the same, depending on the balance of the relative rates of expanding supply and expanding demand and technological progress in energy production and consumption efficiency.

It is up to some combination of government and industry massive investment in both renewable and the less environmentally damaging nonrenewable (gas) to redress the growing energy supply shortages. Where industry acts too slowly, and state and local governments erect regulatory barriers to new plants, as has happened in California, federal government acceleration of public investment seems essential. Where governments act too slowly, energy entrepreneurs may find opportunity for attractive private investment in renewables, as indeed Shell and British Petroleum are doing.

In *Energy Technologies*, continued progress in energy production, conversion efficiencies, and manufacturing will reduce the price of solar and wind-produced electricity, in sunny and windy areas, to less than the cost of fossil fuel energy except in those areas near coal mines and oil and gas fields. Electric vehicle technology will slowly develop safe, affordable, and economically and operationally competitive battery-powered and/or fuel-cell-powered cars, buses, and trucks that will reduce transport energy costs and environmental pollution, and gradually displace many internal-combustion engine-powered vehicles, particularly in oil-importing poor countries. Hydrogen turbines and motors may be developed after 2010 to power aircraft and intercity trucking, with hydrogen and electricity becoming the transportation fuel of choice after 2020–2030.

The rate at which renewables and hydrogen technologies are developed to first augment and then gradually replace carbon fuels economically will depend on the rate at which global warming, global unelectrified poverty, and electricity shortages cramping economic growth in highly developed areas such as California and coastal China are perceived as urgent threats by public opinion that is translated into effective political demand for joint action worldwide. This is probably one of the most uncertain areas of social sciences prediction. The present writer is fairly confident that political demand for expanded supply, both conventional and with the new clean technologies, will happen, but whether in ten, twenty, or fifty years remains most uncertain. What we *can* do is estimate the consequences of doing nothing differently, and contrast it with what we *could* do to ideally solve the sustainable energy-environment-growth problem, and argue for a self-fulfilling prophecy of energy policy success.

Ten Consequences of Energy Demand Outpacing Supply for the Twenty-year Future

Most simply, either major investments are made over the next five to ten years in greatly expanding electric power production from solar, wind, and water power clean renewable energy resources and gas production (as the least polluting and widely available fossil fuel), or, if these investments are not made in time to bring supply up to meet demand, world economic growth, and growth in all energy-importing countries (and even some exporting ones), will slow or stop.

1. Greatest growth in per capita and total national energy consumption and demand will come in the less developed countries (LDCs) of Africa, Asia, and Latin America. If massive investments in indigenous renewables are made in time, the LDCs may also enjoy the greatest growth in energy supply. There will also be unexpected growth spurts in energy demand in developed countries enjoying periods of unexpectedly rapid economic growth, such as the United States in the late 1990s, and these may or may not be accommodated by sufficiently prompt market-driven supply growth to avoid sacrifice of growth itself.

2. Worldwide, the compounding of increased per capita energy consumption associated with accelerated worldwide urbanization, motorization, mechanization, communication, democratization, marketization, militarization, and overall continued (though slightly falling) world population growth of 30–40 percent by 2020, could easily *triple or quadruple* total world energy demand by 2020, especially if latent, off-grid demand is included. We know of no government or industry environmentally sustainable plans to respond to this worldwide impending energy shortage, the lowest estimate of which we can already forecast with some confidence.

How could world energy demand consumption possibly increase as much as fourfold in the next twenty years, versus DOE's 65% forecast!

if world population growth is only 32 percent at current rates and might even drop to 30 percent (unless President Bush's order canceling U.S. sponsorship of worldwide birth control education is widely ignored)? The basis for the fourfold energy demand consumption growth projection for 2020 is the compounding of an assumed 33 percent to 40 percent population growth, multiplied by a doubling of the urbanized and motorized world population over the next twenty years, from 50 percent in 2001 to 75 percent in 2020 (and its attendant tripling to quadrupling of urban per-capita energy consumption), further doubled by an average 3.5 percent economic growth that by itself doubles energy consumption even if all other factors remain unchanged. (1.33 to 1.4 × 6 billion = 8 to 8.4 billion 2020 population, 75 percent of whom or 6 to 6.3 billion will be urban for an additional 3–3.3 billion urban added to the current 3 billion, each consuming thrice to tenfold the energy of their rural counterparts thus increasing average year 2000 per capita energy intensivity by 1.66 to 2.00, all multiplied by 2 for world economic growth, yields averaging 3.5%/year for 20 years, 1.33 to 1.4, ×1.66 to 2.00, ×2.0 = 3.3 to 4 times current 2000 energy consumption or demand.) Most of the fourfold increase in 2020 energy consumption demand is attributable to the unprecedented urbanization and consequent order of magnitude greater per capita energy consumption of the newly doubled urban and previously unelectrified and unmotorized rural population of LDCs. This immense demographic shift and its socio-economic impacts are totally neglected in the DOE 20-year forecast.

3. All currently produced forms of energy from all currently available sources will be needed and wanted by at least some countries and large populations, to meet world energy demand growing more rapidly than any single current source of supply. The world is not remotely running out of total energy, but it *is* (slowly) running out of major nonrenewable sources such as coal, oil, gas, and (more quickly) the arable land environment and healthy air quality urban environment.

4. The most rapidly growing sources of renewable and nonpolluting energy will be wind and solar, of three types: solar heating, solar photovoltaic (PV)-electric, and solar-thermal electric. Solar energy may develop into the major market share of energy supply in most poor countries and areas, not because it is nonpolluting and not globally warming, but because for most oil-poor sunny countries it is most eco-

nomical, most politically independent, most secure (from interrupted or overpriced imports), and most reliable. In rural small distributed units, it is also cheaper than wind turbines, which must be large to be efficient. In cities not near seaside wind farms (such as Copenhagen and Amsterdam), building-integrated photovoltaics (BIPV) will increasingly clad the vertical sun-facing surfaces of high-rise structures at construction costs comparable to conventional curtain walls, and supply most of their peak daytime electrical loads.

Operating examples of this new distributed energy-*producing* building technology of BIPV curtain walls exist now in Europe and Japan, and are designed and may be operating in the United States in the decade. European examples include a twelve-story office building in Bern, Switzerland, and a six-story electric company office building in Bremen, Germany. In Japan, the best example of BIPV is the Kyocera Corporation's twenty-story headquarters building in Kyoto. In the United States, one of the first major examples being planned is the new Abt Associates headquarters building in Cambridge, Massachusetts.

5. Nuclear power will continue to grow, even in LDCs with plentiful sources of fossil fuels and solar energy, because it is prized for its dual use for military and scientific power.

6. Solar, wind, and other locally more cost-competitive renewable energy sources will become self-financing through private, rural micro-finance—already successfully demonstrated in several LDCs (such as Rockefeller Brothers'-financed Soluz in Latin America, and Shell/Escom's joint venture in South Africa), and more slowly in industrialized countries seeking environmental and energy security and independence with building-integrated photovoltaics in cities.

7. Large-scale private industry will lead government, not the reverse, in implementing widespread economically successful solar home and office heating, air conditioning and lighting, and rural electrification—because it is profitable, reliable, and safe.

8. Urban building-integrated photovoltaics of solar electricity-generating screening walls on high-rise buildings, together with urban electric vehicles, may rescue the economy, environment, and esthetics of the world's poorest, most crowded cities from increasing brownouts, higher prices, and pollution, first in subtropical and then in temperate zones.

9. There will not be any significant acceleration of the rate of technological change in the next twenty years, nor has there been in the

last fifty, nor is one needed to achieve the above increases in sustainable energy supply. Solar and wind power are mature technologies now.

10. There will be an acceleration of the rate of social and political and material change in the 2–3 billion of the world's currently poor, uneducated, unelectrified, underrepresented, and disenfranchised people, as the global diffusion of (solar-powered) satellite TV, radio, and telephone communications give ideas and show images of affluent and relatively equitable market democracies. Further diffusion of military technologies as means of achieving justice will also motivate and facilitate change, or punish the unwilling.

On the basis of the economics of scarcity differentially affecting fossil fuel and solar energy, and on the basis of increasing economies of scale in PV production and application, there are clear fifty-year trends in the gradual and continuing real price increases of fossil fuels, when environmental, extraction, transportation, and defense cost externalities are finally internalized. At the same time, there have been steady decreases in the price of solar-generated heat and electricity, currently dropping at the rate of about 20 percent per year as a result of technical advances and economies of scale in ever-expanding production. In most sunny, poor developing countries and regions without large, easily extractable domestic supplies of oil and gas—and that is most of them—the cost curves for solar distributed point-of-use-generated power, versus centralized fossil-fuel-generated power have already crossed in the last five years. This fact has been obscured by macroeconomic models treating countries like points in space and thus neglecting the greater transportation costs of fossil fuel energy from centralized sources dispersed to users, the subsidized artificially low price of gasoline in the United States, and by the technological ignorance and risk aversion of most conventional energy production financings, including those by the World Bank. (Two major oil companies, British Petroleum and Shell, have invested more in solar energy than the World Bank and the U.S. government combined, or any private investment fund. Why? They must think they know something about the future of energy!)

The major means by which the large external costs of fossil fuels have been masked by government subsidies in the United States are: (1) tax subsidies, (2) government program subsidies, (3) protection costs for the defense of oil sources and shipments, and (4) environmental, health, and social costs. A large fraction of this is believed due to defense, specifically the U.S. Navy that spends about half of the U.S. $300 billion defense budget. We had a large navy while we were still an oil-exporting nation, but for other reasons—first the Nazi and Imperial Japan threats, then the Soviet naval threat. With these threats gone or greatly diminished, one of the chief reasons for maintaining a large navy is to protect the sea lanes of communication and our oil-exporting allies in the Middle East. (My own rough estimate is that as much as one-third and a minimum of one-fifth of the $150 billion U.S. Navy's annual cost, or $30 billion to $50 billion, is spent for defense of American, European, and Japanese access to Mideast oil.)

In the United States alone, just for gasoline for automobiles, these fossil fuels "external" costs total $558 billion to $1.69 trillion per year, which, when added to the retail price of gasoline, results in a per gallon real price of $5.60 to $15.14" (International Center for Technology Assessment 1999).

Four Technological Changes Drive Energy Transformations

Over the last five centuries, four technological changes have driven the major energy transformations in supply sources, demand, prices, and uses of energy: changes in communications technology, transportation technology, building technology, and military technology. They continue apace.

Communications technology diffuses awareness and desire for the most attractive and useful technological advances in all fields of human endeavor. Now that many of even the poorest villages worldwide enjoy at least communal television sets receiving satellite TV broadcasts, images of the highest standards of living are known and desired universally. The poorest millions of peasants now aspire to electrically lit homes, stoves and refrigerators, automobiles, and perhaps guns. They've seen it on TV!

Transportation technology is driven by the universal needs and desires of human commerce for mobility, freedom of movement, and independence. Military technology fully mobilizes available communications and transportation technology (and indeed all other technologies).

Building technology changes will be most significant in the next twenty years, as the LDCs undergo unprecedented urbanization and build hundreds of new one-million-inhabitants cities. Early in the last century came the advent of the skyscraper, which is now a common sight in newly grown cities of even the poorest countries. The previous major housing technology change was from outdoor to indoor plumbing. With most of the world population massively shifting from rural to urban living, high-rise, energy-intensive construction of energy-intensive structures will accelerate, even in the face of energy and capital shortages. As energy shortages develop in these new cities (as they already have in most of them), energy-efficient buildings will be in demand, and photovoltaic curtain wall construction technology and fuel cell energy storage technology will advance to make energy-*producing* buildings and energy-self-sufficient buildings increasingly cost-effective, common, and possibly even required in new construction.

The U.S. Department of Energy's Forecast of the 2020 Energy Future, and What Is Wrong with It

The most comprehensive publicly available long range energy forecast in the United States is the U.S. Department of Energy's *International Energy Outlook 1999*, Report #:DOE/EIA–0484(99). The contents are critically reviewed below. Many misjudgments, in this writer's opinion, are omissions, excessive caution, and reliance on discredited assumed relationships of energy to growth.

U.S. DOE World Energy Consumption: "Energy consumption in 2020 will increase by 236 quadrillion Btu—or about 65 percent—relative to the 1996 level." "World energy consumption reaches 612 quadrillion Btu by 2020." "Energy consumption in the developing world is expected to more than double. . . ."
Comment: This appears to be a massive underestimation of energy demand. The 2 billion population of the developing world alone, growing at an average annual rate of 2 percent for twenty years, will grow 40 percent to 3 billion. If total energy consumption in these areas only doubles, it would mean that per capita energy consumption remains about half again as much as in 1996. Given that a large part of the average per capita energy consumption of this population includes roughly 1.5 billion people in Asia and Latin America of the 2 billion worldwide without electricity, this forecast effectively dooms most of them to remain unelectrified for the next twenty years! And growing in number from 1.5 to 2 billion, unelectrified! That is unrealistic.

While these 1–2 billion poor people might want to consume electricity, they may not be able to afford it for twenty years using currently common technologies. Social research in Africa and Asia among poor rural people indicates that many spend about \$5–8 per month on home lighting with kerosene or paraffin or batteries. At the same time Shell and Eskom in South Africa, and Brazil, Soluz/Winrock in Latin America, and others in Asia (including a U.S. DOE solar homes program in Western China), already provide off-grid solar electric home systems at \$8 a month or less.

In 2020 the world population will be about 8 billion, or 2 billion more than in 2000. Assuming at least equal average per capita energy consumption of those with electricity now (4 billion of the world's 6 billion 2000 population that grows to 5.3 billion), and no other sources of increased energy consumption, world energy consumption would grow by 5.3/4 or 33 percent. However, if a probable average annual Gross World Product increase of 3.5 percent is factored in, and GWP doubles between 2000 and 2020, total energy consumption is likely to double for these 5.3 billion electricity consumers. Doubling incomes tends to roughly double energy consumption among this poor and low-income majority, as they get TV and electric appliances and motor vehicles. Thus the energy consumption of the 4 billion electrified in 2000 and now grown to 5.3 billion in 2020 is likely to at least double on a per capita basis, bringing the total to at least 10.6/4.0 of the slightly smaller 1996 figure, or 2.65 times the 1996 figure of $612 - 236 = 376$ quads, or $2.65 \times 376 = 996$ quads—or a minimum of about 60 percent more energy consumption than the DOE 2000 forecast of 612 quadrillion Btu.

Now add the additional energy consumption of the 1–2 billion previously without electricity, and assume that 1 billion of them consume energy in 2020 at the (low) average rate of the other 7 billion—a reasonable assumption consistent with contemporary energy industry plans for massive worldwide rural electrification with a variety of means, including fossil-fueled grid power, wind and solar home systems. This increases 2020 world energy consumption by another 8/7 or 14 percent to 996×1.14 or 1135 quadrillion Btu—nearly double DOE's forecast of 612 quads. For an alternate estimate of fourfold increase in 2020 world consumption assuming 400 quads 2000 consumption, see above.

When there are plausible reasons why an important forecast by a powerful and influential government may miss a major change by a factor of two or more, while engaged in tunnel vision in extrapolating the contemporary with spurious exactitude, social scientists have an obligation to raise the issue and debate alternatives. Typical American or northern European behavior (already quite different from U.S. behavior) is not necessarily a useful guide to how poor Chinese, Indian, African, Latin American, or Indonesian farmers (totaling about half the world's population) might regard the opportunity to consume more energy, even of a limited and unfamiliar sort, given the lack of attractive alternatives. Given the diffusion of TV, it is possible that poor rural people will soon be satisfied with nothing less than a 3 kW grid-connected home electrical system capable of simultaneously powering electric stoves, air conditioning and washers and dryers, and a five-passenger sedan, that they will not long accept a 300-watt solar home system giving them only lighting and TV and radio and perhaps a small refrigerator or sewing machine, that they will not long accept a cheap short-range, battery-powered utility vehicle of the sort built and sold for $5,000 in Katmandu.

U.S. DOE The World Oil Market: "A moderate view of future oil market. . . . Sustained high levels of oil prices are not expected, whereas continued expansion of the oil resource base is anticipated."

". . . prices fell by one third on average from 1997 levels." "The world oil price in 1998 was the lowest since 1973." "Oil consumption in 1998 was lower than anticipated largely because of the recession in Southeast Asia." "Oil demand is expected to reach 110 million barrels per day by 2020, requiring an increment to world production of 30 to 40 million barrels per day." "Over the past 25 years oil prices have been highly volatile. In the future one can expect volatile behavior to recur principally because of unforeseen political and economic circumstances." "Oil currently accounts for 40 percent of world commercial energy supplies. . . . In 2020, oil is expected to represent 37 percent of total energy supply."

Comment: The DOE forecast for the 2020 real price of oil ranges from $15 to $30 a barrel, a factor of only two and a much narrower range than the factor of six which extended from $11 to $66 from 1970 to 1999. Obviously no one has a clue. What can we learn from this apparent uncertainty in the future of energy? That oil in the long term is the most uncertain form of energy, in terms of price and supply and demand. The important thing about oil and gas, besides their dominance of current energy markets, is their uncertainty and unreliability of sufficient and predictably economical supply at any point in time. This makes economic and technological forecasting simultaneously more difficult and more urgent for rational matching of supply growth with demand growth. Oil and gas are not commodities to be relied on as the pre-dominant sources of energy over the long term. A government or an industry would want to know with what it could replace them, if they suddenly became unobtainable or unaffordable.

Beyond natural gas, the DOE forecast suggests no likely substitutes for oil, and none for gas. Yet substitutes may be forced on oil-poor and gas-poor populous countries like China, India, Japan, and the EC, by agricultural-environmental concerns growing much worse, by inter-ruptions of oil supply by war or politics, by a major shift in demand away from oil, or by a pervasive technological change that puts oil at a relative disadvantage to other widely available fuels, or finally by that old and excessively used and misused correlate, the rate of economic growth.

A major shift in demand away from oil could come from its re-placement as the preeminent transportation fuel, by electric fuel for recharging electric vehicle batteries, generated by some other energy source than oil—it might be renewables, nuclear, gas, or coal. Urban traffic congestion, air pollution, and the threat of global warming put steady pressures on vehicle manufacturers to develop and produce elec-tric vehicles and hybrids, as well as much more efficient fossil-fuel vehi-cles. Dozens of models are in development worldwide and a few electric vehicle (EV) and hydroelectric vehicle (HEV) models are in serial pro-duction in Japan, the United States, and France.

Another shift of demand away from oil could be the replacement of jet fuel by hydrogen, generated by electrolysis of water with electricity generated from renewables. This is unlikely to become economically competitive in the next twenty years, but might within the next fifty. With hydrogen and renewables there is the possibility of an almost complete elimination of CO_2 products of combustion. If global warming threats accelerate, the shift to the solar-hydrogen energy economy may be accelerated.

U.S. DOE Natural Gas: "Natural gas is the fastest growing primary energy source. Because it is a cleaner fuel than oil or coal and not as controversial as nuclear power, gas is expected to become the fuel of choice...."

Comment: This is correct for now. By 2010, half way through the forecast period, the fastest growth natural gas now enjoys might begin to be displaced by solar PV and wind, particularly in those countries (like China and South Africa) that would have to use scarce foreign exchange to import gas and have plentiful and cheaper indigenous supplies of sun and wind. An interesting aspect of natural gas is its development of international pipeline infrastructure that could someday serve to distribute hydrogen, the ideal transportation fuel of the future.

U.S. DOE Coal: "In the IEO99 forecast, coal's share of total world energy consumption falls only slightly from 25 percent in 1996 to 23 percent in 2020. Its historical share is nearly maintained, because large increases in energy use are projected for the developing countries of Asia, where coal continues to dominate many national fuel markets.... China and India are projected to account for 33 percent of the world's total increase in energy consumption over the forecast period and 90 percent of the world's total increase in coal use (on a Btu basis)."

Comment: Coal need not dominate China and India electricity generation in 2020 if locally cheaper renewables far from the coal mines, such as solar and wind, are fully exploited. If energy transport costs are included, locally plentiful renewables in nongrid areas are already cheaper than remotely located coal. The World Bank recently committed nearly $100 million to wind turbine procurement for western China, where wind power is cheaper than coal if coal transportation costs are included. This may signal a shift from years of World Bank investing of hundreds of millions of dollars in China coal-fired power plants.

U.S. DOE: "In China ... coal continues to be the primary fuel in a rapidly growing industrial sector, in view of the nation's abundant coal reserves and limited access to alternative sources of energy."

Comment: On the contrary, in China (and India, South Africa, and the United States) there *is* plenty of access to alternative energy sources— solar, wind, and hydro—which in a ten-year national effort could replace much of the coal with superior economic/environmental performance. PV and wind turbine manufacturing jobs could replace coal miners' jobs.

U.S. DOE: "Because the Kyoto Protocol is not currently a legally binding agreement, the projections do not reflect the commitments made by the signatory countries to reduce or moderate their emissions of greenhouse gases. If their commitments do become legally binding, however, it is likely that the coal outlook for the industrialized countries will differ substantially from the *IEO99* projections . . . coal consumption in the industrialized countries is projected to increase by 12 percent . . . from 35.8 quadrillion Btu in 1996 to 40.0 quad Btus in 2020."

Comment: Since the Kyoto Protocol, legally binding or not, is a clear statement of intention and desire on the part of the industrialized countries to cut their carbon emissions from primarily coal, why does DOE not even consider in their 2020 forecast how these nations might economically shift from coal to locally plentiful renewables of solar, wind, and hydro energy that, when externalities are internalized, are cheaper?

U.S. DOE: ". . . coal . . . is projected to lose market share to natural gas" in Europe and North America. "Despite declines in some regions, world coal consumption has increased from 84 quadrillion Btu in 1985 to 93 quads in 1996 . . . increases in coal consumption include the U.S., Japan, and Asia. Declines have occurred in Western and Eastern Europe and the FSU. In Western Europe coal consumption declined by 30 percent between 1985 and 1996, displaced . . . by growing use of natural gas and, in France, by nuclear power. . . . Although coal has lost market share to oil, natural gas, and nuclear power, it continues to be a key source of energy, especially for electric power generation—in 1996 . . . 38 percent of the energy consumed worldwide for electricity generation." "World coal consumption is projected to increase by 2.4 billion tons, from 5.2 billion tons in 1996 to 7.6 billion tons in 2020. World coal consumption in 2020 could be as high as 9.2 billion tons or as low as 5.7 billion tons, based on alternative economic growth rate assumptions."

Comment: This set of alternative assumptions perpetuates the fallacy that environmental remediation must compromise economic growth. Why could not world coal consumption in 2020 equally well be as low as 1 billion or 2 billion tons, "based on alternative assumptions" not just about growth rates but also about renewable non-CO_2-emitting energy sources being substituted for coal? It is not fanciful to believe that the necessary combination solar/wind/hydroelectric/nuclear energy infrastructure to replace coal expansion could be built within the next five to fifteen years.

U.S. DOE: "China is projected to add more than 220 gigawatts of new coal-fired generating capacity by 2020 and India approximately 60 gigawatts."

Comment: Unless DOE can read China's State Planning Commission's mind concerning long lead-time, energy-planning decisions, why not at least consider that Chinese engineers and economic planners may find it feasible and preferable to replace half or more of this DOE-forecasted new coal-fired generating capacity with a combination of additional hydro, solar, and wind energy? We know they are experimenting with it. In parts of western and southwest China remote from the northeast coal fields, hydro, solar, and wind are already cheaper than coal when coal transportation costs are included.

U.S. DOE: "Coal's share of the world's total primary energy consumption is expected to decline from 25 percent in 1996 to 23 percent in 2020.... The coal share ... consumed ... for electricity generation also declines from 38 percent in 1996 to 34 percent in 2020."

Comment: Why not decline even more to 20 percent or 10 percent, if we were really serious about global climate change and global warming risk and respiratory disease reduction in China? It is quite possible over twenty years to replace much of coal's primary energy production in the main coal-burning countries (China, India, South Africa) with combinations of much cleaner natural gas and entirely nonemitting solar and wind energy sources.

U.S. DOE: "... most coal-fired capacity in Southeast Asian countries is not fitted with FGD equipment, primarily because of cost ... public concern over pollution in Southeast Asia is likely to increase as living standards rise, but at present the emphasis is on increasing electricity generation to ensure economic growth.... In late 1998 ... 5,000 villagers in southern Thailand staged a protest against plans for three new coal-fired power plants in the region ... people living in close proximity to the ... lignite-fired plant in N. Thailand have suffered serious respiratory problems ... the potential magnitudes and costs of additional environmental restrictions for coal are uncertain, ... costs for coal-fired generation will increase."

Comment: The sum of increasing environmental costs, air pollution reduction costs (for stack gas scrubbers, etc.), and labor and public health costs will keep increasing for coal, the more it is expanded (as DOE says it will be in China and India). The ever-increasing total cost of coal, together with the ever-decreasing cost of solar and wind renewables through economies of scale in PV and wind turbine manufacturing, keeps increasing in the areas where renewables are the least cost source of energy. A comprehensive twenty-year forecast should include these trends of potentially crossing cost curves and provide maps showing successively smaller areas of coal use.

U.S. DOE: "... the most significant emerging issue for coal is the potential ... international agreement to reduce emissions of carbon dioxide and other greenhouse gases. ..."

Comment: It is unlikely for an international agreement to reduce greenhouse gases emissions, for example, with emissions trading and carbon taxes, according to energy economists studying and promoting it. (Richard Schmalensee, MIT, personal communication). While having theoretical attractiveness and creating an industry for economists, the difficulties of negotiating such a complex international agreement among many sovereign states with many opposing interests seem insurmountable. Thus the most significant issue for coal is not the slim potential for such an agreement being effectively implemented, but rather how to avoid the need for such an agreement, by substituting renewable energy for coal, and negotiating economic offsets and alternative employment for coal miners in PV and wind turbine production.

U.S. DOE: "Total recoverable reserves of coal around the world are estimated at 1,088 billion tons—enough to last another 210 years at current production levels. 60 percent ... are located in three regions: the U.S. (25 percent), FSU (23 percent), and China (12 percent). Australia, India, Germany, and South Africa ... account for an additional 29 percent."

Comment: Two hundred and ten years is not so long to look ahead to exhaustion of the world's coal. ... Fortunately most countries rich in coal are plentifully endowed with solar and wind renewable nonemitting energy reserves that can gradually replace coal economically.

U.S. DOE: "In Western Europe, environmental concerns play an important role in the competition among coal, gas, and nuclear power. Recently, other fuels—particularly natural gas—have been gaining an increasing economic advantage over coal. Coal consumption in Western Europe has declined by 35 percent over the past 7 years. ... The decline ... is expected to continue over the forecast period but at a slower rate."

Comment: Why only a slower rate? Why not equally possibly at a faster rate, as wind and solar play an ever-increasing role in Denmark, the

Netherlands, Britain, and Germany along the North Sea coastlines, Norway and Sweden, the Iberian peninsula, and the Adriatic; as solar energy becomes fully exploited in southern Spain, France, Italy, and Greece, and the large underutilized hydroelectric potential of the Balkans is developed? Since Europe has already taken the lead in environmentally sustainable energy development, why not keep it, and be a role model for the rest of the world? Europe has shown that it can substitute nongreenhouse gases-emitting renewable energy for coal and oil, first with hydroelectric power in Switzerland and Norway, then with nuclear power in France, in the last decade with wind turbines in Denmark, energy-independent solar-powered buildings in Netherlands, Germany, and England, and energy-conserving nonpolluting electric vehicles in France, Italy, and Germany.

U.S. DOE: "For Africa as a whole, coal consumption is projected to increase by 48 million tons between 1996 and 2020, primarily to meet increased demand for electricity. Contributing to the increase in electricity demand is South Africa's commitment to an aggressive electrification program, which aims to increase the percentage of households connected to the electricity grid from 44 percent at the end of 1995 to 75 percent by 2000."

Comment: This is quite misleading. There is plenty of pent-up demand for electricity in South Africa and southern Africa, but it is not a demand for more coal or coal-generated electricity. Eskom—South Africa's predominant electric utility—has the mandate for rural electrification of roughly 25 million of the 40 million South Africans without electricity in 2000. The financial resources do not exist to extend the grid to 75 percent of the population—from 15 million in 2000 to a doubled 30—by 2010, or even by 2020. There is a better alternative available that has realistic hope of electrifying 75 percent of the country by 2020, but it does not involve expanding coal consumption. Coal-fired power plants and coal reserves already have excess production capacity, and a continuing shortage of economically affordable rural distribution capacity. (During apartheid coal energy had been built up to achieve transport fuel independence by producing coal-based synthetic oil, a very expensive product.) For the next decade at least, the best hope for rapid and economical self-financed rural electrification is the Shell-Eskom joint venture, or others like it, to provide 50,000 photovoltaic solar home systems on an affordable $8/month fee for service basis. Initiated in 1998, it will add significantly to electric energy consumption in South Africa, but not to coal consumption.

U.S. DOE Nuclear Power: "Nuclear power remains flat."

Comment: Much depends on how militarized the world is in the first quarter of the twenty-first century. The chief incentives to countries to develop nuclear power are to acquire nuclear weapons capabilities (for deterrent defense, intimidation, or aggression) or for scientific prestige, rarely simply to mobilize a nongreenhouse gases-emitting energy source. If nuclear weapons states increase in number from the current ten, as seems likely with the impending ballistic missile defense-stimulated new nuclear arms race, or if a very limited nuclear war breaks out (e.g., India-Pakistan, Iraq-Israel) and is terminated before much escalation, a new worldwide demand for nuclear reactors for dual use may well result. A U.S. national ballistic missile defense risks provoking a new nuclear arms race with China, and then India and Pakistan, because first China will feel the need to expand their "minimum deterrent" ICBM force to avoid its being rendered ineffectual. Then, of course, countries threatened by China, such as India and possibly Taiwan and Japan, may be tempted to expand their own arsenals, as will India's potential nuclear adversary, Pakistan, and so on and on.

Anticipation of any of these disasters could stimulate the regrowth of nuclear power again, particularly in ambitious LDCs not closely aligned with one of the nuclear superpowers. Also, if China feels threatened or ambitious to challenge U.S. military power, China may push for a greatly expanded nuclear power capability, again for dual use.

In the United States, half of the current 22 percent nuclear power capacity will be lost by 2020. This has serious long-term implications for U.S. energy independence and security, unless the decline is compensated by increases in other large, plentifully available, and cost-competitive domestic energy sources such as solar, wind, hydro, and gas. If the decline in domestic nuclear energy is uncompensated by indigenous renewable resources and gas, the United States will become 75 percent dependent on foreign oil and gas imports (compared to 50 percent now), or on resorting to the environmentally costly domestic coal supply. Both alternatives put the United States into potential conflict with countries seeking to control oil and gas exports, or who wish to equalize environmental burdens, and this may add further to defense costs. Fusion power is not an option soon and is unlikely to become commercially available before 2050.

How Feasible Is the Ideal Solar Energy Age of 2020+?

There is nothing in an ideal solar-electric-powered civilization of 2020–2050 that does not already exist today in small quantities, except perhaps solar-electric farm machinery. The solar photovoltaic manufacturing industry had roughly a billion dollar revenue in 1998, and is growing at 20–30 percent per year. Energy-independent buildings producing more electricity from PV than they consume over the course of a year have been built in the Netherlands and England. Large-scale rural solar electrification projects producing thousands of solar electric home systems were under way in the late 1990s in western China, Southern Africa, and Central America—some of them, Shell's in South Africa and Soluz's in the Dominican Republic, on an economically self-sustaining, profitable, privately financed basis.

Practical electric vehicles meeting the needs of urban and suburban commuters have been produced in quantity in France, Japan, the United States, and other countries, and in prototype form by most major automobile manufacturers worldwide. A cheap electric jitney bus (cost under $5,000) has been successfully manufactured by the dozens and used in Katmandu, Nepal, since 1997. Although no one has yet mass-produced a cheap EV competing on both performance and cost with internal-combustion petrol-powered cars, several automobile manufacturers have built prototypes. For interurban extended range travel beyond today's typical EV's eighty-mile range at highway speeds, rapid (eight-minute) recharging stations for standard lead-acid batteries have been developed by Southern California Edison and other utilities. Electric utilities worldwide—Tokyo Electric, Southern California Edison, Boston Edison, Electricite de France, German utilities, and Eskom in South Africa—have been promoting and sponsoring small fleets of electric vehicles since the early 1990s, motivated by the desire to sell more off-peak electric power profitably for EV overnight recharging, bringing average generating capacity closer to peak capacity and thus through load balancing saving the capital costs of adding capacity.

There is really no outstanding scientific or technological question concerning the practical worldwide application of these now fifty-year-old technologies of photovoltaic solar cells. EVs (electric vehicles) and lead-acid batteries are over 100 years old. The main issues and obstacles are economic and political. The cost issue is basically a chicken-and-egg one of which comes first, mass production to permit price reductions through economies of scale, to make EVs affordable to the hundreds of millions of low-income first time car buyers who would gladly buy an EV if it were cheaper to buy (as it could be) and refuel (as it already is) than an IC car or minibus—or mass marketing to promote sales of the first expensive generation of EV's. The political issues are much more complicated, because the price of gasoline is so highly tax subsidized in the United States that even environmental regulation has not overcome the apparent but ultimately false economic advantage of cheap mass-produced, gasoline-powered vehicles.

Forecasting Energy Demand/Consumption to 2020 and Beyond

The ideal solar-electric age assumes that, given that the supply of solar energy is practically unlimited, energy demand is constrained only by other costs associated with collecting, processing, and using solar energy, and the satisfaction of the civilization's other needs. Thus energy demand, in an ideal solar energy age, might be expected to grow much faster than in the contemporary world where higher energy costs, including environmental costs and rural distribution and hook-up costs constrain consumption.

One need only consider how even the rudimentary solar electrification of most of the 2 billion people currently without electricity, even at much lower intensity of per capita use, would add to 2020 energy consumption and effective demand. Assuming, as an extreme example, that the presently unelectrified poorest 2 billion of a 2000 world population of 6 billion grows to an electrified 3 billion in a 2020 world population of 9 billion, and that there is uniform per capita energy consumption at the 2000 average (which will be exceeded by the highest income quartile and not reached by the poorest), 2020 total world energy demand would be about double that of 2000—and that without any per capita economic growth. Factoring in an average 3.5 percent world economic growth rate over the twenty years, we get another doubling in energy consumption, for a total twenty-year economically and culturally "ideal" and environmentally benign increase in energy consumption to four times that of 2000, or 400 percent. It could be more, under this ideal solar-electric scenario, because it is almost unconstrained by environmental costs, and only slightly by common materials supply costs and technology, capital, and labor. It could also be much less, as consumer habits, governments, industries, institutions, and sunk investments in conventional fuels continue to be slow to change.

It is clear from the U.S. Department of Energy's *International Energy Outlook 1999* that this possible and (from renewable sources) desirable increase in energy consumption is not taken into account, when the report's "reference case projects that energy consumption in 2020 will increase by 236 quadrillion Btu—or about 65 percent—relative to the 1996 level. More than half the increment is expected in the developing countries, where strong economic growth in the long term is expected to increase the demand for energy over the projection period." The difference between the 400 percent growth in "ideal" mostly solar-electric energy consumption (both grid and off-grid), and the DOE Report's 65 percent growth in mostly conventional fossil fuel-powered grid energy consumption, is the difference between a forecast of a theoretical ideal that may not be reached by 2020 or 2050 or ever unless deliberate government policies, industry actions, and consumer preferences change, and change the linear extrapolation of long-term "business as usual" trends in energy consumption, government regulation, consumer habits, and their economic growth correlates.

The DOE projections do correctly recognize that "more than half" of the even modest 65 percent growth in world energy consumption will come in the developing countries in the next twenty years. However, given that 2 billion people in the LDCs are currently without electricity, the distribution of 33 percent of the energy growth over 3 to 4 billion people or half the world's population in LDCs, by conventional (and costly) fossil fuels, indicates the perhaps unconscious but nevertheless appalling expectation that most of the 2 billion now unelectrified will stay that way beyond 2020. Will the unelectrified 2 billion poor accept that? We do not know but we doubt it. The LDCs half a billion middle-income urban population could soak up those extra 78 quads ($0.33 \times 236 = 78$) just in their own urban living standards improvement.

Conclusion

We have asked how well social scientists predicted the current state of world and regional energy demand, predominant forms, technologies, sources, supplies, prices, and controlling powers, and the answer was, with few exceptions, not very well.

Energy demand was both overestimated and underestimated. Economists assumed it would continue to have a close relationship with economic growth in the industrialized world, and underestimated it badly in the developing world. Economists overestimated gasoline's elasticity of demand in the OPEC oil shock, and underestimated the price elasticity of energy independence substitution efforts. The persistence of the predominant form of energy at the beginning of the period, coal, was overestimated, as was the predominant form of energy in the second half of the fifty-year period, oil, which became displaced by gas more rapidly than anticipated.

Political scientists and economists studying technological change overestimated energy technologies for recovering economically competitive quantities of shale oil, and underestimated the productivity of exploratory logging and well recovery technologies. Political scientists consistently underestimated the safety of nuclear technology, and overestimated the speed of the spread of nuclear weapons from the diffusion of civilian nuclear power technology (Albert Wohlstetter et al. 1977). American and French political scientists and economists who wanted nuclear power for their countries for other reasons consistently overestimated its economic competitiveness. (Remember how nuclear power would be "too cheap to meter"?)

Supplies, and reserves of oil and gas were consistently underestimated, much as *future supplies of economically utilized wind and solar energy remain underestimated.* Economists mostly underestimated the future price of oil until the OPEC shock of 1973, then overestimated it until the years before the Shah's overthrow and the Iran oil crisis of 1979, after which they first overestimated it again, then underestimated it, and then again overestimated it into the 1990s. Most of the time the economists either over- or underestimated the all-important oil price. Furthermore, no one has yet estimated the *real* price of oil with all externalities incorporated.

American political scientists did little better in forecasting who would and would not control or affect the price of oil, and what political instabilities would impact the control of the oil and its price. They failed to anticipate the fall of the Shah and OPEC and the Gulf War, incorrectly (at least in the United States) forecasted that OPEC would not hold, then again incorrectly overestimated OPEC's control with respect to non-OPEC sources, and were generally behind rather than ahead of what was happening in the political control of oil and its price.

Transportation energy consumption constraints imposed by environmental regulations and their attendant costs have not really been studied much by survey sociologists working as market researchers for government regulatory agencies or energy and transportation companies, so we cannot claim that they correctly or incorrectly forecasted any significant consumer energy demand or voter political demand reactions. For the next ten years the great California electricity deficit will be a rich lode for political pollsters and opinion researchers.

When survey sociologists and political scientists working as market researchers for automobile manufacturers attempted to forecast consumer preferences for bigger more powerful cars versus smaller lighter more energy-efficient cars, they did not come up with anything conclusive and, in at least one case, when coming to conclusions differing with the car company's prevailing beliefs about its customers' preferences, were fired. Political scientists studying public opinion on environmental regulation of energy industries have also not been prominent in forecasting major changes.

Where the forecasts were wrong, how much did this matter and to whom? They were wrong most of the time in the most important energy subsectors of oil, nuclear, and very wrong, particularly in forecasting the price of oil from 1973 until 1999. It mattered enormously to many oil companies and many thousands—possibly millions—of investors in oil worldwide, and to the governments of the oil-exporting countries dependent on oil revenues and the governments of oil-importing countries dependent on affordable and predictable energy prices. Hundreds of billions of dollars of investment were lost most years by investors, energy companies, and governments both directly and indirectly as a result of false expectations about oil prices raised by misleading and insufficiently contingency-covering forecasts. It mattered a lot to many and still does.

We have asked how well the social scientists predicted the future of energy in the past thirty years, and we have gotten our answer: not very well. On supplies they were inaccurate, on forms incomplete, on demand inconsistent and mostly wrong, on uses more or less correct because uses did not change much, and on prices mostly wrong in either over- or underestimating the timing, speed, direction, and magnitude of significant price changes, particularly in the main traded energy commodity of oil.

By what social sciences methods were these more often wrong than right energy forecasts made? Predominantly by the methods of macroeconometric modeling, and related economic analyses. Lacking almost completely were political science, historical and social survey analyses of multiyear interacting political, military, economic, and technological factors in decision making by national and industrial leaderships that determine what governments and industries actually do to find, produce, distribute, price, sell, buy, use, and consume energy. These are notably and regrettably absent from the energy forecasting literature.

Which methods of long-range energy forecasting provided the most insights and accuracy? One hesitates to say those that were not used, because then where would be the proof? All we have is negative evidence that the methods most commonly used—those of economics and macroeconomic modeling—were too narrowly cast in time and function, and failed to produce even roughly accurate results most of the time. These methods did badly with their mid-1970s energy forecasts for the 1990s, even when using retrospectively corrected improved methods and knowledge gained from their previous ten years' experience and errors. Some energy historians, such as political scientist Daniel Yergin in *The Prize*, are more likely to have better judgment and more valuable insights using the methods of historical analysis.

The picture of the twenty- and forty-year energy future envisioned then for the present was, however, roughly right in its qualitative aspects, but that did not require econometric modeling to forecast. It did not require economic analysis so much as a long look at cultural and economic history to see that the energy requirements of the slowly changing world economy and political culture would not change radically; nor would consumer preferences and tastes change quickly for comfortably heated homes, energy-inefficient cities, tall buildings making the most of high land values, affordable energy-intensive consumer products, fast, heavy gas-guzzling cars and big and fast passenger aircraft, and more energy-intensive weaponry fed into the world's nonnuclear wars continue indefinitely until global warming, global war, or global winter end our negligent energy joy ride.

How did existing knowledge enable us to foresee key changes in the energy future to 2020 from the present, in the present analysis? The key changes we were most interested in were changes in the mix of energy supply sources, changes in the mix of energy demand and use, and changes in energy prices for diverse types, diverse uses, in diverse locations. These questions have very different answers for the wealthy industrial countries of Europe, North America, and Japan, than for the larger poor countries worldwide where 2 billion people today are without electricity. The difference in the energy demand and supply forecasts for the rich and poor countries is not reflected in the DOE 2020 forecast, which assumes that the poor LDC parts of the world want to and will go the wasteful energy ways of the wealthy industrialized countries, whether they can afford to or not. We believe this to be a massive parochial error.

Existing technology and economic knowledge enables us to foresee these changes in the energy future of 2020 as different for the LDCs and for the present fossil-fuel path of the wealthy industrialized countries. Existing knowledge of economic geography, agricultural economics, and renewable energy technologies enables us to forecast with some confidence at least the strong possibility of:

• a substantially changed world energy *demand* forecast (much increased)
• a substantially changed world energy *supply* forecast (even more increased)
• a substantially changed world energy supply *composition* forecast (much diversified)
• a changed world energy *price* forecast (mainly reduced, after five to ten years)
• a changed world energy *environmental impact* forecast (much improved)
• a changed world energy *distributional equity and efficiency* forecast (improved)

These are not trivial differences between the U.S. DOE and the ideal 2020 energy future forecast. There is reason to believe that significant portions of the international energy industries' 2020 energy forecasts lie somewhere between these two extremes of *DOE's* "business as usual" forecast of major recent trends (to the neglect of the fastest-growing minor ones), and the present writer's openly advocated solar-powered economic growth forecast. Documented evidence and demonstrations of this belief are being sought.

References

Abt, Clark C. 1997. "China's Sustainable Growth Maximized by Avoiding Agricultural and Energy Shortages with Renewable Energy Resources for Farming, Irrigation, Transport and Communications." Paper presented at the International Conference, "China's Economy with Moderately Rapid and Stable Growth" Beihai City, Guanxi Province, China, 2–4 September.

———. 1998. "The Role of the State in Renewable Energy Efficiency Contributions to Economic Growth, with an Example: Energy Self-Sufficient Solar PV-Clad Buildings for Low-Cost Rural Housing and Electric Transport." University of Pretoria Conference on "Challenges of the Next Millennium for Public Administration" and National Policy Institute of South Africa (NAPISA), 5 and 10 November.

———. 1999. "Chapter XII A: Solar Energy-Driven World Economic Development." SolarGuide.Com., http://www.solarguide.com/articles/clarkabt-c12.html. Accessed Jan. 4, 1999.

———. 1999. "Fast, Safe, and Fair Economic Growth through Renewable Energy Technology." Eastern Economic Association Annual Meeting, Boston, 14 March.

———. 1999. "Solar Energy-Driven Growth in Africa, Brazil, and China." Unpublished paper.

Abt, Clark C., and Hsiang-Ling Han, 1998. "Brazil's Environmentally Sustainable Economic Growth Accelerated by Renewable Energy Technologies, with Forecasts (An Example of Environmentally Sustainable Growth in Sunny Countries)." A paper presented at the Project LINK Fall Meeting, hosted by Instituto de pequisa Economia Aplicada (IPEA), Rio de Janeiro, Brazil, September 18, 1998.

———. 1998. "Energy Efficiency and Sustainable Economic Growth of Oil-Importing Countries." Project LINK Annual Meeting, United Nations, New York, 19 March.

———. 1998. "Renewable Energy Efficiency and Economic Development of South Africa: A Geocoded Macro-Mezzo-Micro Socio-Economic Forecasting Model of How Improved Energy Efficiency Creates Jobs, Exports, Improved Capital and Labor Productivity, Investment, Per Capita Economic Growth, Social Integration, and Quality of Life." Third Conference on Econometrics, University of Pretoria, South Africa, 18 June.

———. 1999. "Solar Energy-Driven Economic Growth in Africa, Brazil, and China." Paper at Eastern Economics Association Annual Meeting, Boston, 13 March.

———. 1999. "Solar-Powered Economic Growth." Unpublished book manuscript.

Atkinson, Giles, Richard Doubourg, Kirk Hamilton, Mohan Monasinghe, David Pearce, and Carlos Young. 1997. *Measuring Sustainable Development: Macroeconomics and the Environment.* Cheltenham, England: Edward Elgar.

Kulsum Ahmed, with Dennis Anderson. 1994. *Renewable Energy Technologies: A Review of the Status and Costs of Selected Technologies.* Washington, D.C.: The World Bank.

Bell, Daniel. 1999. *The Coming of Post-Industrial Society: A Venture in Social Forecasting.* New York: Basic Books.

———. 1986. "The Limits of the Social Sciences." Chapter 15 in *Advances in the Social Sciences, 1900–1980: What, Who, Where, How?* Edited by Karl W. Deutsch, Andrei Markovits, John Platt. Cambridge: Abt Books.

Bernstein, Mark, et al. 1999. *Developing Countries and Global Climate Change: Electric Power Options for Growth.* Arlington, Virginia: RAND, Pew Center on Global Climate Change.

Brown, Harold. 1983. *Thinking about National Security.* Boulder: Westview Press.

Brown, Lester R., Christopher Flavin, and Hilary French. 1998, 1999, 2000. *STATE OF THE WORLD 1998, 1999, 2000—A Worldwatch Institute Report on Progress Toward a Sustainable Society.* New York: W.W. Norton.

———. 1995. *Who Will Feed China: Wake-Up Call for a Small Planet.* New York: W.W. Norton.

Brown, Lester R., Michael Renner, and Christopher Flavin. 1997. *Vital Signs 1997: The Environmental Trends That Are Shaping Our Future.* Worldwatch Institute. New York: W.W. Norton.

Cline, William R. 1992. *The Economics of Global Warming.* Washington, D.C.: The Institute for International Economics.

Claussen, Eileen, and Lisa McNeilly. 1998. *Equity and Global Climate Change.* Arlington, Virginia: Pew Center on Global Climate Change.

Cooper, Richard. 1998. "Toward a Real Global Warming Treaty." *Foreign Affairs,* March–April 1998.

Dasgupta, Partha. 1997. *Environmental and Resource Economics in the World of the Poor.* Washington, D.C.: Resources for the Future.

Deck, Leland, Ellen Post, Matthew Wiener, and Cathy Cunningham. 1996. *A Particulate Matter Risk Assessment for Philadelphia and Los Angeles.* Cambridge: Abt Associates Inc.

Deutsch, Karl W., Andrei Markovits, John Platt, eds. 1986. *Advances in the Social Sciences. 1900–1980: What, Who, Where, How?* Cambridge: Abt Books.

Dornbusch, Rudiger, and James M. Poterba, eds. 1991. *Global Warming: Economic Policy Responses.* Cambridge: MIT Press.

Fay, Chris. 1995. Chairman and CEO, Shell UK Ltd., Speech in Scotland, "Analysis of Future Trends in Energy Supply and Demand, Royal Dutch/Shell Group."

Geller, Howard, Regiane M. de Bare, Carlos E. Lima, Marcos Lima, Geraldo Pimentel. 1997. Evaluation of the Energy Savings Due to Brazil's National Electricity Conservation Program. Speech presented to American Council for an Energy-Efficient Economy, Washington, D.C.

Goldemberg, Jose. 1996. *Energy, Environment, and Development.* London: Earthscan Publications.

Grubb, Michael. 1995. *Renewable Energy Strategies for Europe. Volume I: Foundations and Context.* The Royal Institute of International Affairs, Energy and Environmental Programme. London: Earthscan Publications.

Grubb, Michael, and Roberto Vigotti. 1997. *Renewable Energy Strategies for Europe. Volume II: Electricity Systems and Primary Electricity Sources.* The Royal Institute of International Affairs, Energy and Environmental Programme. London: Earthscan Publications.

Han, Hsiang-Ling. 1998. "The Macro-Mezzo-Micro Model for Energy Efficiency and Sustainable Economic Growth of Oil-Importing Countries (An Economic Forecasting Model of Energy Efficiency Improvements)." Appendix to the paper "An Economic Forecasting Model of Energy Efficiency Improvements" presented at the Project LINK Spring meeting, United Nations, New York.

————. 1999. "Is Renewable Energy Technology Economically Competitive in the Market Place?" Unpublished paper.

Hankins, Mark. 1995. *Solar Electric Systems for Africa.* Commonwealth Science Council, London, and AGROTEC UNDP/OPS Programme for Agricultural Operations Technology, Harare, Zimbabwe.

Hill, Robert, Phil O'Keefe, and Colin Snape. 1995. *The Future of Energy Use.* London: Earthscan Publications.

Holm, Dieter. 1996. *Manual for Energy Conscious Design.* Directorate of Energy for Development, Department of Minerals and Energy, Pretoria, South Africa.

Holm, Dieter, and Reinhold Viljoen. 1996. *Primer for Energy Conscious Design.* Directorate of Energy for Development, Department of Minerals and Energy, Pretoria, South Africa.

Kahn, Herman. 1961. *On Thermonuclear War.* Princeton: Princeton University Press. See especially the military technology and comparative Soviet and U.S. economic growth forecasts made in 1960 for 1973 (506–507). Most were mistaken. Even the five-year (1965) and ten-year military technology forecasts (476, 489) were more than half wrong. Yet in its profound formulation of the nuclear strategy of the United States and the U.S.S.R. for the next thirty years, it was fundamentally prophetically accurate and comprehensive. The main issue *mis*estimated by Kahn was how *slowly* military technology would change from 1960 to 1990, particularly the H-bomb-delivering deterrent triad.

Khalema-Redeby, Lucy, H. Mariam, A. Mbewe, and B. Ramasedi. 1998. *Planning and Management in the African Power Sector.* London and New York: Zed Books.

Kiss, Gregory. 1999. *Abt Associates Office Building Integrated Photovoltaic Analysis.* New York: Kiss & Cathcart, Architects, and Personal Communications.

Leggett, Jeremy. 1999. Chief executive and managing director, The Solar Century Ltd. Personal communication regarding the first solar-powered house in the United Kingdom, costing $8,000 per kilowatt—producing 145 percent of daily energy needs from photovoltaic roof tiles.

Arthur D. Little, Inc. 1995. *Building-Integrated Photovoltaics (BIPV): Analysis and U.S. Market Potential.* Lisa Frantziz, Program Manager. Cambridge: Arthur D. Little, Inc.

McNelis, Bernard, Anthony Derrick, and Michael Starr. 1992. *Solar-Powered Electricity: A Survey of Photovoltaic Power in Developing Countries.* London: Intermediate Technology Publications.

Osborn, D. E. 1998. Supervisor SMUD Solar. "Friends of SMUD Solar (FOSS) Update, July 18, 1997." Sacramento Municipal Utility District (dosborn@smud.org), Personal communication, 26 August.

Post, Ellen, Leland Deck, and Mathew Wiener. 1996. *An Analysis of the Monetized Benefits Associated with Alternate Particulate Matter Standards in the Year 2007.* Cambridge: Abt Associates Inc.

Runci, Paul, and Jack Riggs. 1998. *2020 Vision: The Energy World in the Next Quarter Century.* Aspen: The Aspen Institute.

Sinton, J., ed. 1996. *China Energy Databook.* Berkeley, California: Lawrence Berkeley National Laboratory, LBL-32822 Rev. 4, UC-900.

Smil, Vaclav. 1993. *China's Environmental Crisis.* Armonk, New York: M.E. Sharpe.

———. 1993. *Global Ecology.* London and New York: Routledge. See especially figure 1.3, "How Not to Forecast," and figure 1.4, "Futility of Forecasting."

———. 1994. *Energy in World History.* Boulder: Westview Press.

Solow, Robert M. 1970. *Growth Theory.* New York: Oxford University Press.

Statistical Abstract of the United States, 1995–1996. Austin, Texas: Reference Press.

Stiglitz, J. E. 1974. "Growth with Exhaustible Natural Resources: Efficient and Optimal Growth Path." *Review of Economic Studies,* Symposium, 123–137.

United Nations. 1992. *Prospects for Photovoltaics: Commercialization, Mass Production, and Application for Development.* Advanced Technology Assessment System, Department of Economic and Social Development. New York: United Nations.

U.S. Congress. Office of Technology Assessment. 1995. *Report on Energy Technology for Surface Transport.* Washington, D.C.

U.S. Department of Energy. 1998. *Support to the U.S. Government's Initiatives on Climate Change: Statement of Work.* Washington, D.C.

U.S. Department of Energy. 1999. *International Energy Outlook 1999.* DOE/EIA-0484(99). Washington, D.C.

U.S. Department of Energy. Energy Information Administration, Office of Integrated Analysis and Forecasting. 1996. *The National Energy Modeling System.* DOE/EIA-0581(96). Washington, D.C.

U.S. Environmental Protection Agency. Office of Air and Radiation. 1997. *The Benefits and Costs of the Clean Air Act, 1970 to 1990.* Washington, D.C.

von Weizsacker, Ernst, Amory B. Lovins, and L. Hunter Lovins. 1998. *Factor Four: Doubling Wealth—Halving Resource Use*. London: Earthscan Publications.

Wang, Anhua, and Yu Wang. 1999. "The Benefits of 100,000 Solar Home Systems in Western China. Unpublished paper. Ganzu PV Company, Lanzhou, China.

Wohlstetter, Albert, et al. 1977. *Swords from Ploughshares*. Chicago: University of Chicago Press.

World Bank 1997, 1998, 1999. *World Development Report 1997–99*, New York: Oxford University Press.

U.S. Congress. 1972. Committee on Interior and Insular Affairs, U.S. Senate, pursuant to S. Res. 45. A National Fuels and Energy Policy Study, serial No. 92-29, GPO.

U.S. Department of Energy. 1997. *Annual Energy Review, 1997*. Washington, D.C.

U.S. Department of Energy, 1999. *International Energy Outlook 1999*. Washington, D.C.

Yergin, Daniel, Joseph A. Stanislaw et al., 1984. *The Future of Oil Prices: The Perils of Prophecy*. Cambridge: Cambridge Energy Research Associates and Arthur Andersen & Co.

5

Modeling Climate Change Impacts and Their Related Uncertainties

Stephen H. Schneider

Throughout human history, climate has both promoted and constrained human activity. In fact, humans only very recently have been able to reduce their dependence on climate through advances in technology and organization. On the other hand, human actions affect climate. Are our actions causing the climate to change in ways or at rates that will threaten natural systems or make human adaptations difficult? What actions can we or should we take to alleviate the effects of human action on climate change? To approach these questions, we often use mathematical modeling and computer simulations to aid our understanding of the relationship between human action and global climate change. The most comprehensive models of atmospheric conditions are three-dimensional, time-dependent simulators known as general circulation models (GCM). Integrated assessment models (IAM) are important tools to study the impacts of climate change on the environment and society as well as the costs and benefits of various policy options and decisions.

I present a brief overview of the climate debate, modeling, and the current understanding of the climate processes. I discuss how IAMs evaluate the effects of human-induced climate change and the implications of policy options. The critical role of uncertainty is highlighted. Finally, I suggest areas for further consideration.

Can a Forecast Climate Signal Be Detected in the Climate Record?

Twenty thousand years ago, a mere blink in geologic time, a visitor to the now-productive U.S. corn belt would not be sitting in the heart of one of the world's foremost granaries, but rather in open spruce parkland forest, where many of the tree species seen are the same kinds that are found today 500 to 1,000 kilometers north in the boreal forests of Canada (e.g., Wright et al. 1993). Similarly, if we could somehow have been flying over the Great Basin in the U.S. West we would have seen the massive fossil lakes, some stretching hundreds of miles like former Lake Bonneville in Utah, and the now-fossil beaches (currently visible flying into Salt Lake City, Utah Airport, or over Mono Lake, California) from those high water stands that date back 10,000 to 15,000 years ago. The Ice Age, which at its maximum some 20,000 years ago was about 5° to 7 °C colder than our current global climate, disappeared in, what is to nature, a relatively rapid period of about 5,000 to 10,000 years. The average rate of temperature change from the Ice Age to the current 10,000-year period of relative climate stability, our so-called Holocene Interglacial, is about 1 °C change for every thousand years. There were more rapid periods embedded within this time frame (e.g., Broecker 1997), but for the moment, let's only consider the sustained average rates.

Not only did such changes correspond with radical alterations to the ecosystems of the earth, but they have been implicated in the extinction of what is known as the charismatic megafauna (woolly mammoths, saber tooth tigers, etc.). Fossil pollen evidence tells us that the vegetation habitats during the more "rapid" parts of the transition from ice age to interglacial around 10,000 to 12,000 years ago saw what paleoclimatologists call "no analog habitats," that is, combinations of pollen abundances that do not exist on Earth today (Overpeck et al. 1992). All of this change was natural, of course, and there are two reasons for mentioning it in our context of a human perspective. First, to remind us that the climate and ecosystems change by themselves, without influence of humans (the latter is what we call anthropogenic causation), and, two, that climate change of several degrees on a global average basis is a very significant change from the point of view of natural systems.

Explanations of the Ice Age vary, the most popular one being a change in the amount of sunlight coming in between (a) winter and summer and (b) the poles and the equator. These changes in the distribution of seasonal or latitudinal sunshine are due to slow variations in the tilt of the earth's axis and other orbital elements, but these astronomical variations alone cannot totally explain the climatic cycles (e.g., Crowley and North 1991). If these orbital variations and other factors (such as the increased reflectivity of the earth associated with more ice) are combined, our best climate theories (embodied through mathematical models that are composed of the physical laws of conservation of mass, energy, and momentum) suggest that the Ice Age should have been several degrees warmer than it actually was—especially in the Southern Hemisphere. What could account for this extra cold? Perhaps the models are not sensitive enough, that is, they do not respond sufficiently to a change in so-called "radiative climate forcing," which is the change in the amount of radiant energy coming to the earth from external factors like orbital variations or extra ice. Another (more likely, I think) possibility is that something else also changed at the same time.

These theories can be better reconciled with what happened between ice ages (i.e., during interglacials) if one assumes that several watts of energy over every square meter of the earth were taken away in the ice age by some other mechanism at a global scale. But what could be such a mechanism? The obvious candidate would be a change in the composition of the earth's atmosphere, which affects both its reflectivity and its heat-trapping capacity (e.g., decreases in the well-known greenhouse effect or increases in atmospheric dust). But what evidence is there that greenhouse gases, for example carbon dioxide, methane, nitrous oxide, or water vapor, had lower concentrations 20,000 years ago than in the interglacial? In the 1980s that evidence came through loud and clear from the ice caps of the world. Air trapped in these glaciers provides a library of the history of the earth's atmosphere back over 200,000 years. It shows that during the past two ice ages carbon dioxide concentration was about 40 percent less and methane half of the average value during the current and penultimate interglacials (e.g., Eddy and Oeschger 1993). It also shows that since the Industrial Revolution carbon dioxide has increased beyond any levels experienced in the past 250,000 years (at least) by about 30 percent and methane by 150 percent—two figures that virtually no knowledgeable scientist disputes (e.g., IPCC 1996a and 2001a). Moreover, nearly all climate scientists agree that these documented increases in greenhouse gas concentrations are a result of so-called anthropogenic emissions, which are driven by increasing numbers of people pursuing higher standards of living and achieving those growth-oriented goals, through activities such as clearing land, or burning fossil fuels.

If the carbon dioxide and methane decreases in the last ice age help to explain the ice-age coldness, can they tell us something about how the anthropogenic increase of these gases due to human activities might cause climate change in the future? The answer is "not directly," for it is possible that there are other factors we have not accounted for in the ice-age story that could well have been involved, and there are still many unanswered questions associated with the ice-age cycles. It is simply a circumstantial bit of evidence that suggests that the estimated levels of carbon dioxide and methane gases during the ice ages are consistent with the predictions of the greenhouse effect (e.g., Hoffert and Covey 1992). During the ice ages, when surface temperatures were lower by about 5 °C to 7 °C, the estimated levels of greenhouse gases were about half of current levels. From this and other information about ice caps and the distribution of sunlight, we infer that a doubling of CO_2 would raise surface temperatures by about 3 °C plus or minus 1.5 °C. This is known as the "climate sensitivity range." The magnitude of climate sensitivity that best helps to explain the Ice-Age coldness is 2–3 °C. If the best estimate of the temperature change associated with a doubling of CO_2 were ten degrees warming, which is twice the value at the high end of the climate sensitivity range thought by the mainstream climate scientist today (e.g., IPCC 1996a and 2001a), then the ice ages should have been even colder than they were. On the other hand, if the earth would only warm up by half a degree or less if CO_2 doubled, then it would be tougher to explain the magnitude of the ice ages without finding some other mechanism not yet identified. Of course, the latter is possible. So, what other lines of circumstantial evidence or direct evidence do we have for estimating the sensitivity of the climate to greenhouse gas increases?

We know from quite literally thousands of laboratory experiments and direct measurements, millions of balloon observations, and trillions of satellites data bits, that the basic structure of the energy flows in and out of the earth's atmosphere is relatively well understood. We know that water vapor, carbon dioxide, and methane trap enough energy on the earth to warm the surface up about 33 °C relative to that which would occur in their absence.

This well-known natural greenhouse effect is not under dispute and has been known for a century and a half. Nor do most climatologists dispute that there has been about an 0.6 °C (plus or minus 0.2 °C) globally averaged warming trend at the earth's surface over the past century, nor that 1998 was by several tenths of a degree the warmest year globally in the instrumental record (IPCC 2001a). In much greater dispute is whether a small increment in this envelope of greenhouse gases since the Industrial Revolution would produce a noticeable response (i.e., a "climate signal"). It is difficult to detect a small climate signal (less than 0.5 °C) because the natural variability of global surface temperature is several tenths of a degree Celsius from year to year. Also, century-long 0.5 °C global warming trends are not unknown historically, and may have occurred about every thousand years or so. However, as Mann, Bradley, and Hughes (1999) show, the latter half of the twentieth century stands out remarkably as above the climatic noise of the millennium as the warmest period.

The debate over whether that signal has been detected and can be attributed to human activities has been intense. This intensity has been based upon significant recent pieces of evidence (e.g., Santer et al. 1996, Wigley et al. 1998)—albeit each piece is circumstantial—and a few loud, well-publicized denials (e.g., Robinson and Robinson 1997, Singer 1997) that the totality of evidence has any meaning (e.g., see the reviews by Edwards and Schneider 1997, 2001). In the absence of clear, direct empirical evidence, one often has to use either circumstantial evidence or incomplete bits of direct evidence with uncertainties attached—and the nature of those uncertainties explained. When the preponderance of such evidence gets strong enough, then most scientists begin to accept, tentatively of course, the likelihood of causal connections (e.g., chapter 8 of IPCC 1996a). Some people shed their skepticism at different levels than others, so naturally there will be a cacophonous debate over whether a climate signal has been "detected," let alone whether it can be attributed to human activities. One can always find some scientist who will want 999 out of a 1,000 probability of certainty, and others who will accept the proposition at 8 or 9 chances out of 10. And if one adheres to the "precautionary principle," he or she might accept 2 chances out of 10 for a concerning outcome to be concerned. This is not "exact science," but a value judgment about the acceptability and meaning of a significant, but not conclusive, body of evidence. The scientific job is to assess (a) what can happen and (b) what the odds are of its happening (see, for example, this discussion in chapter 6 of Schneider 1997a). Let me discuss this process further.

I have mentioned the ice ages since this is a "natural experiment" that we use, not to forecast a climate map of the future, but to build understanding of climate processes and to validate the tools that we do use to forecast the future (e.g., Schneider 1993)—that is, our climate theories embodied in mathematical models. Are there any other such natural experiments? The answer is "yes, there are several," the two most prominent being (1) episodic volcanic eruptions which throw dust in the stratosphere that reflects for a few years a few watts per square meter of solar energy that otherwise would have reached the lower atmosphere and (2) the seasonal cycle. Let's consider volcanic eruptions first.

Volcanic dust veils should cool the planet. In fact, the effects of the last major eruption, Mt. Pinatubo in 1991, had been independently forecasted by a number of climate modeling groups to cool the earth's lower atmosphere for a few years on the order of several tenths of a degree. Indeed, that is roughly what happened. However, it can be argued that a few tenths of a degree cooling, or warming for that matter, might be a natural internal fluctuation in the earth's climate system, and indeed, as noted earlier, fluctuations of that magnitude are a part of the natural background "climatic noise." How then can we distinguish the climatic signal of the volcanic eruption from the noise of the natural internal variability? In any one eruption it is difficult to do so since the signal to noise ratio is about one, that is, the magnitude of the cooling expected is about equal to the magnitude of the natural internal fluctuations in nonvolcanic years, and therefore for any one volcanic dust event we cannot have very much confidence that a signal has been observed. The fact that the Pinatubo results support the prediction doesn't, by itself, give a lot of confidence, although as a circumstantial bit of evidence it is quite useful. However, another volcanic eruption in 1983, El Chichón, also was followed by several tenths of a degree cooling, as was the effect after the eruptions of Mt. Agung in 1963 or Mt. Krakatoa in 1883.

A number of scientists (e.g., Mass and Schneider 1977) looked at the results from several volcanic eruptions and discovered a clear and obvious correlation between climate and volcanic eruptions. The evidence suggests that a volcanic dust veil in the stratosphere removes a few watts of energy over every square meter of the earth for a few years, and thus, cools the lower atmosphere by a few tenths of degrees—the very magnitude predicted by the same computer models that we use to forecast the effects of a few watts per square meter of sustained (i.e., over a century or more) heating from global greenhouse gas increases.

What other natural experiments might we have to test climate sensitivity? Another one that happens every year is the change in seasons. Winter predictably follows summer, being some fifteen degrees colder in the Northern Hemisphere and five degrees colder than summer in the Southern Hemisphere. The reason the Southern Hemisphere has a smaller seasonal cycle is because it has much more ocean than land, and water has a higher heat-retaining capacity than land or air. Since a season is not long enough for the planet to reach an equilibrium temperature change, therefore, the more land-dominated Northern Hemisphere has lower heat storage capacity and thus a larger seasonal cycle of surface temperature. How well do the climate models do in reproducing this change? The answer is "extraordinarily well." Although the absolute temperatures that models may simulate can be off by as much as five or six degrees in some regions of the world for some seasons, the models' capacity to reproduce the amplitude of the seasonal cycle of surface air temperatures, by and large, is quite good. (It is less good for some other variables, however, particularly for the hydrological systems—see chapter 5 of IPCC 1996a, and the technical summary of IPCC 2001a.) If we were making a factor of ten error in our estimate of the climate sensitivity, either positive or negative, it would be difficult for the models to reproduce the different seasonal cycle surface temperature amplitudes over land and oceans as well as they do. This is thus another piece of circumstantial evidence suggesting that the current estimate of climate sensitivity is not off by a factor of ten, as some "contrarians" assert. Indeed, indirect evidence like ice ages, volcanic eruptions, and the seasonal cycle simulation skills of models are prime reasons why many of us in the scientific community have for more than twenty-five years expected that clear signs of anthropogenic climate change were not unlikely by the twenty-first century (e.g., see p. 11 of Schneider and Mesirow 1976—in which I projected that "demonstrable climatic changes could occur by the end of this century").

In summary, then, in my opinion it is unlikely that natural variability is the explanation of all recent climate change, especially that which has been documented in the last half of the twentieth century—a point emphasized recently by IPCC (2001a). However, since much of the debate over detection and attribution of human-caused climate change hinges on the projections of climatic models, it is necessary to have at least a cursory understanding of how they work. Although it is impossible to treat more than the highlights of the nature and use of climatic models in only a few pages or so, I nonetheless offer the following section in the hopes of reducing somewhat the confusion that may exist in many peoples' minds after listening to the often acrimonious and technically complex debate over climatic models and their credibility.

Overview of Climate Modeling Fundamentals

Engineers and scientists build models—either mathematical or physical ones—primarily to perform tests that are either too dangerous, too expensive, or perhaps impossible to perform with the real thing. To simulate the climate, a modeler needs to decide which components of the climatic system to consider and which variables to include. For example, if we choose to simulate the long-term sequence of glacials and interglacials (the period between successive ice ages), our model needs to include explicitly the effects of all the important interacting components of the climate system operating over the past million years or so. These include the atmosphere, oceans, sea ice/glaciers (cryosphere), land surface (including biota), land subsurface, and chemical processes (including terrestrial and marine biogeochemical cycles), as well as the external or "boundary forcing" conditions such as input of solar radiant energy (e.g., IPCC 1996a).

The problem for climate scientists is separating out quantitatively cause and effect linkages from among the many factors that interact within the climate system. It is a controversial effort because there are so many subsystems, so many forcings, and so many interacting complex sets of processes operating at the same time that debates about the adequacy of models often erupt. These difficulties are compounded because it is sometimes difficult to determine a trend when there is a large variation around the trend, let alone the possibility that there can be trends in that variability as well.

Modeling the Climate System

So how are climate models constructed? First, scientists look at observations of changes in climate variables, such as temperature, ozone level, and so forth. This allows us to identify correlations among variables. Correlation is not necessarily cause and effect—just because one event tracks another doesn't mean it was caused by it. To assess high confidence to a conclusion, one has to actually prove the relationship is causal and explain how it happened. Especially for cases where unprecedented events are being considered, a first principles or deductive, rather than a purely empirical-statistical, approach is desirable. However, observations can lead to a hypothesis about cause and effect that can be tested. The testing is often based on simulations with mathematical models run on a computer. The models, in turn, need to be tested against a variety of observations, both present and paleoclimatic. That is how the scientific method is typically applied. When a model, or set of linked models, appears plausible, they can be fed unprecedented changes such as projected human "global change forcings" (or pressures placed on the climate system from outside the system, in this case, pressures from human activities) and then be asked to make projections of future climate, ozone levels, forests, species extinction rates, and so forth.

The most comprehensive weather simulation models produce three dimensional details of temperature, winds, humidity, and rainfall all over the globe. A weather map generated by such a computer model—known as a general circulation model or GCM—often looks quite realistic, but it is never faithful in every detail. To make a weather map generated by computer we need to solve six partial differential equations that describe the fluid motions in the atmosphere. It sounds in principle like there's no problem: we know that those equations work in the laboratory; we know that they describe fluid motions and energy and mass relationships (e.g., Washington and Parkinson 1986). So why then aren't the models perfect simulations of the atmospheric behavior?

One answer is that the evolution of weather from some starting weather map (known as the initial condition) cannot be uniquely determined beyond about ten days—even in principle—due to the chaotic internal dynamics of the atmosphere. A weather event on one day cannot be said to determine an event thirty days in the future, all those commercial "long-range" weather forecasts notwithstanding. But the inherent unpredictability of weather details much beyond ten days doesn't preclude in principle accurate forecasts of long-term averages (climate rather than weather). The seasonal cycle is absolute proof of such deterministic predictability, as winter reliably follows summer and the cause and effect is known with certainty. Unfortunately, this distinction between the "in-principle" unpredictability of long-term weather and the possibility of long-term climatic projections is often missed in the public debate, especially by nonclimate scientist authors with political agendas (e.g., Robinson and Robinson 1997).

Grids and Parameterization

The other answer to the imperfection of general circulation model simulations, even for long-term averages, is that nobody knows how to solve those six complex mathematical equations exactly. It's not like an algebraic equation where one can get the exact solution by a series of simple operations. There isn't any known mathematical technique to solve such coupled, nonlinear partial differential equations exactly. We approximate the solutions by taking the equations, which are continuous, and breaking them down into discrete chunks, which we call grid boxes. A typical GCM grid size for a "low resolution" model is about the size of Germany horizontally and that of a "high resolution" GCM is about the size of Belgium. In the vertical dimension there are two (low-resolution) up to about twenty (high-resolution) vertical layers that typically span the lowest 10–40 kilometers of the atmosphere. Some refer to the grid box as the smallest "grain size" in the model, like the size of the dots in a newspaper photo.

In addition, we have a problem of scale: how can we treat processes that occur in nature at a smaller scale than we can resolve by our approximation technique of using large grid boxes? For example, clouds are very important to the energy balance of the Earth-atmosphere system, since they reflect sunlight away and trap infrared heat. Unfortunately, none of us have ever seen a single cloud the size of Belgium, let alone Germany; thus, we encounter the scale problem. We cannot calculate clouds explicitly because individual clouds are typically the size of a dot in this grid box—that is, they are much smaller than the grain size of our model. We can put forward a few reasonable propositions on cloud physics: if it's a humid day, for example, it's more likely to be cloudy; if the air is rising, it's also more likely to be cloudy.

GCMs can explicitly predict the average humidity in the grid box, and also whether the air is rising or sinking on average. Using this, we can write what we call a parametric representation or "parameterization" to connect large-scale variables that are resolved by the grid box (such as humidity) to unresolved small-scale processes (individual clouds). Through this parameterization, we can predict grid box-averaged cloudiness. So-called "cumulus parameterization" is one of the important—and controversial—elements of GCMs that occupies a great deal of effort in the climate modeling community. Although the models are not ignoring cloudiness, neither are they explicitly resolving individual clouds. Instead, modelers try to get the average effect of processes that can't be resolved explicitly at smaller scales than the smallest resolved scale (the grid box) in the GCM (e.g., Trenberth 1992). Developing, testing, and validating many such parameterizations is the most important task of the modelers (e.g., Root and Schneider 1995), since these parameterizations determine critically important issues like climate sensitivity. Recognizing both the strengths and shortcomings of climate model is crucial to appreciating the value and limitations of GCMs in increasing our understanding of climate change and its impacts.

The Greenhouse Effect

If the earth only absorbed radiation from the sun without giving an equal amount of heat back to space by some means, the planet would continue to warm up until the oceans boiled. We know the oceans are not boiling, and surface thermometers plus satellites have shown that the earth's temperature remains roughly constant from year to year (the interannual globally averaged variability of about 0.2 °C or the 0.5 °C warming trend in the twentieth century, notwithstanding). This near constancy, within a few watts per square meter, requires that, in some form, about as much radiant energy leaves the planet each year in some form as comes in. In other words, a near-equilibrium or energy balance has been established. The components of this energy balance are crucial to the climate.

All bodies with temperature give off radiant energy. The earth gives off a total amount of radiant energy equivalent to that of a black body— a fictional structure that represents an ideal radiator—with a temperature of roughly $-18\,°C$ (255 °K). The mean global surface air temperature is about 15 °C (288 °K), some 33 °C warmer than the earth's black body temperature. The difference is due to the well-established natural greenhouse effect.

The term greenhouse effect arises from the classic analogy to a greenhouse, in which the glass allows the solar radiation in and traps much of the heat inside. However, the moniker is a bit of a misnomer because the mechanisms are different. In a greenhouse the glass primarily prevents convection currents of air from taking heat away from the interior. Greenhouse glass is not primarily keeping the enclosure warm by its blocking or reradiating infrared radiation; rather, it is constraining the physical transport of heat by air motion.

Although most of the earth's surface and all clouds (except thin, wispy clouds) are reasonably close approximations to a black body, the atmospheric gases are not. When the nearly black-body radiation emitted by the earth's surface travels upward into the atmosphere, it encounters air molecules and aerosol particles. Water vapor, carbon dioxide, methane, nitrous oxide, ozone, and many other trace gases in the earth's gaseous envelope tend to be highly selective—but often highly effective—absorbers of terrestrial infrared radiation. Furthermore, clouds (except for thin cirrus) absorb nearly all the infrared radiation that hits them, and then they reradiate energy almost like a black body at the temperature of the cloud surface, which is colder than the earth's surface most of the time.

The atmosphere is more opaque to terrestrial infrared radiation than it is to incoming solar radiation, simply because the physical properties of atmospheric molecules, clouds, and dust particles, tend on average to be more transparent to solar radiation wavelengths than to terrestrial radiation. These properties create the large surface heating, or greenhouse effect, that occurs when the atmosphere allows a considerable fraction of solar radiation to penetrate to the earth's surface and then traps (more precisely, intercepts and reradiates) most of the upward terrestrial infrared radiation from the surface and lower atmosphere. The downward reradiation further enhances surface warming and is the prime process causing the greenhouse effect.

This is not a speculative theory, but a well-understood and validated phenomenon of nature (e.g., Raval and Ramanathan 1989). The most important greenhouse gas is water vapor, since it absorbs terrestrial radiation over most of the infrared spectrum. Even though humans are not significantly altering directly the average amount of water vapor in the atmosphere, increases in other greenhouse gases, which warm the surface, cause an increase in evaporation, which increases atmospheric water vapor concentrations, leading to an amplifying or "positive" feedback process known as the "water vapor-surface temperature-greenhouse feedback." The latter is believed responsible for the bulk of the climate sensitivity (Ramanathan 1981). Carbon dioxide (CO_2) is another major greenhouse gas. Although it absorbs and re-emits considerably less infrared radiation than water vapor, CO_2 is of intense interest because its concentration is increasing due to human activities—creating what is known as "anthropogenic radiative forcing." Ozone, nitrogen oxides, some hydrocarbons, and even some artificial compounds like chloro-fluorocarbons are greenhouse gases that are also increasing due to human activities. The extent to which these gases are important to the climate depends upon their atmospheric concentrations, the rates of change of those concentrations and their effects on depletion of stratospheric ozone. In turn, lower levels of stratospheric ozone can indirectly modify the radiative forcing of the atmosphere below the ozone layer thus off-setting a small fraction of the otherwise expected greenhouse warming signal.

The earth's temperature, then, is primarily determined by the planetary radiation balance, through which the absorbed portion of the incoming solar radiation is nearly exactly balanced over a year's time by the outgoing terrestrial infrared radiation emitted by the climatic system to the earth. As both of these quantities are determined by the properties of the atmosphere and the earth's surface, major climate theories that address changes in those properties have been constructed. Many of these remain plausible hypotheses of climatic change. Certainly, *the natural greenhouse effect is established beyond a reasonable scientific doubt*, and accounts for natural warming that has allowed the coevolution of climate and life to proceed to this point (e.g., see Schneider and Londer 1984). The extent to which human augmentation of the natural greenhouse effect (i.e., global warming) will prove serious is, of course, the current debate—along with discussions over the potentially offsetting cooling effects of "anthropogenic aerosols" (particles created in the atmosphere primarily from emissions of sulfur dioxide, primarily from burning of high sulfur coal and oil—Schneider 1994; IPCC 1996a and 2001a). (More recently there is some concern that soot particles from unfiltered coal burning, biomass fires, or diesel engines might absorb extra sunlight and further warm the climate, but this debate is still marked by great uncertainties (Jacobson, 2001.))

Model Validation

There are many types of parameterizations of processes that occur at a smaller scale than our models can resolve, and scientists debate which type is best. In effect, as discussed earlier, are these parameterizations an accurate representation of the large-scale consequences of processes that occur on smaller scales than we can explicitly treat? These include cloudiness, radiative energy transport, turbulent convection, evapotranspiration, oceanic mixing processes, chemical processes, ecosystem processes, sea ice dynamics, precipitation, mountain effects, and surface winds. In forecasting climatic change, then, validation of the model becomes important. In fact, we cannot easily know in principle whether these parameterizations are "good enough." We have to test them in a laboratory. That's where the study of paleoclimates has proved so valuable (e.g., Hoffert and Covey 1992). We also can test parameterizations by undertaking detailed small-scale field or modeling studies aimed at understanding the high-resolution details of some parameterized process the large-scale model has told us is important. The Second Assessment Report of IPCC (IPCC 1996a) Working Group I, devoting more than one chapter to the issue of validation of climatic models, concluded that:

> the most powerful tools available with which to assess future climate are coupled climate models, which include three-dimensional representations of the atmosphere, ocean, cryosphere and land surface. Coupled climate modeling has developed rapidly since 1990, and current models are now able to simulate many aspects of the observed climate with a useful level of skill. [For example, as noted earlier, good skill is found in simulating the very large annual cycle of surface temperatures in Northern and Southern Hemispheres or the cooling of the lower atmosphere following the injection of massive amounts of dust into the stratosphere after explosive volcanic eruptions.] Coupled model simulations are most accurate at large spatial scales (e.g., hemispheric or continental); at regional scales skill is lower.

One difficulty with coupled models is known as "flux adjustment" —a technique for accounting for local oceanic heat transport processes that are not well simulated in some models. Adding this element of empirical-statistical "tuning" to models that strive to be based as much as possible on first principles has been controversial (see Shackley et al. 1999). However, not all models use flux adjustments, and those that do seem to get very similar global climate sensitivities to those that don't (e.g., see the discussion and references in IPCC 2001a; see also Rahmstorf and Ganopolski 1999). Nearly all models, with or without this technique, produce climate sensitivities within or near to the standard IPCC range of 1.5 to 4.5 °C. Even though they do not seem to have a major impact on globally averaged climate sensitivity, flux adjustments do, however, have a large influence on regional climatic projections.

Improving coupled models is thus a high priority for climate researchers since it is precisely such regional projections that are so critical to the assessment of climatic impacts on environment and society (e.g., IPCC 1996b; 1997, 1998, and 2001b).

Transient versus Equilibrium Simulations

One final issue needs to be addressed in the context of coupled climate simulations. Until the past few years, climate modeling groups did not have access to sufficient computing power to routinely calculate time-evolving runs of climatic change given several alternative future histories of greenhouse gases and aerosol concentrations. That is, they did not perform so-called transient climate change scenarios. (Of course, the real earth is undergoing a transient experiment—e.g., Schneider 1994.) Rather, the models typically were asked to estimate how the earth's climate would eventually be altered (i.e., in equilibrium) after CO_2 was artificially doubled and held fixed indefinitely rather than increased incrementally over time as it has in reality or in more realistic transient model scenarios. The equilibrium climate sensitivity range has remained fairly constant for over twenty years; assessments by various national and international groups indicate that, were CO_2 to double, climate would eventually warm at the surface somewhere between 1.5 and 4.5°. (Later on we will address the issue of the probability that warming above or below this range might occur, and how probabilities can even be assigned to this sensitivity.)

Transient model simulations exhibit less immediate warming than equilibrium simulations because of the high heat-holding capacity of the thermally massive oceans. However, that unrealized warming eventually expresses itself decades to centuries later. This thermal delay, which retards the climate signal and can lull us into underestimating the long-term amount of climate change, is now being accounted for by coupling models of the atmosphere to models of the oceans, ice, soils, and an interactive biosphere (so-called earth system models—ESMs). Early generations of such transient calculations with ESMs give much better agreement with observed climate changes on Earth than previous calculations in which equilibrium responses to CO_2 doubling were the prime simulations available. When the transient models at the Hadley Center in the United Kingdom and the Max Planck Institute in Hamburg, Germany, were also driven by both greenhouse gases (which heat) and sulfate aerosols (which cool), these time-evolving simulations yielded much more realistic "fingerprints" of human effects on climate (e.g., chapter 8 of IPCC, 1996a and also IPCC 2001a). More such computer simulations are needed to provide greater confidence levels in the models. Nevertheless, scientists using coupled, transient simulations are now beginning to express growing confidence that current projections of climate changes are plausible (a number of papers have been published very recently at a number of centers showing that the best explanation of the twentieth-century climate trend is a combination of natural factors like solar variations and human forcings such as greenhouse gases, aerosols, and ozone changes, e.g., Wigley et al. 1998 or IPCC, 2001a). In my opinion, the "discernible" human impact on climate trends is becoming clearer and should be considered as likely.

One current problem for regional impact assessment efforts is the great complexity of transient coupled ESMs; each submodel creates a significant burden for data requirements, computational resources, and validation possibilities. Practical considerations typically prohibit the coupling of a large number of very highly spatially resolved models of atmosphere, oceans, ice, or biota to be run in transient mode over centuries of simulated time. Therefore, modelers often use highly parameterized (or reduced-form) models to allow practical computations given limited resources (e.g., Root and Schneider 1995). Downscaling (e.g., Mearns 1997) or hybridization across vastly different spatial scales of highly resolved and highly parameterized models for special purposes will be a fundamental feature of climatic impact assessment for the foreseeable future (e.g., Mendelsohn et al., 2000). Therefore, there will be a continuous need for protocols to evaluate the credibility of such hybridized modeling systems that cycle between detailed and highly aggregated models—see, for example, the discussions in Root and Schneider 1995.

Some of the validation protocols could, as noted earlier, include: (1) intercomparisons of highly aggregated models with a limited set of highly resolved test runs or special field experiments, (2) intercomparisons of such hybrid models with different designs against each other, (3) tests of the ability of such models' simulations to capture known and salient features of the actual natural/social systems, and, for example, the ability of all models to demonstrate reasonable sensitivity responses to known forcing events (e.g., physical submodels should respond reasonably to volcanic dust veils or changes in the earth's orbital elements and the impact of price shocks, or trade policy changes on societal models should bear resemblance to actual societal impacts).

Transients and Surprises

However, a very complicated coupled system like an ESM is likely to have unanticipated results when forced to change very rapidly by external disturbances like CO_2 and aerosols. Indeed, some of the transient models run out for hundreds of years exhibit dramatic change to the basic climate state (e.g., radical change in global ocean currents—e.g., Rahmstorf 1997; Schneider and Thompson, 2000; and Mastrandrea and Schneider 2001). Thompson and Schneider (1982) first investigated the question of whether the time-evolving patterns of climate change might depend on the *rate* at which CO_2 concentrations increased. They used very simplified transient energy balance models to illustrate the importance of rates of forcing on regional climate responses. For slowly increasing CO_2 buildup scenarios, their model predicted the standard outcome: the temperature at the poles warmed more than the tropics.

Any changes in equator-to-pole temperature difference help to create altered regional climates, since temperature differences over space influence large-scale atmospheric wind patterns. However, for very rapid increases in CO_2 concentrations a reversal of the equator-to-pole difference occurred in the Southern Hemisphere. If sustained over time, this would imply difficult-to-forecast transient climatic conditions during the century or so the climate adjusts toward its new equilibrium state. In other words, the harder and faster the enormously complex climate system is forced to change, the higher the likelihood for unanticipated responses. Or, in a phrase, *the faster and harder we push on nature, the greater the chance for surprises*—some of which are likely to be nasty.

Noting this possibility, the Summary for Policy Makers of IPCC Working Group I concluded with the following paragraph (IPCC 1996a, 7):

Future unexpected, large and rapid climate system changes (as have occurred in the past) are, by their nature, difficult to predict. This implies that future climate changes may also involve "surprises." In particular these arise from the nonlinear nature of the climate system. When rapidly forced, nonlinear systems are especially subject to unexpected behavior. Progress can be made by investigating nonlinear processes and subcomponents of the climatic system. Examples of such nonlinear behavior include rapid circulation changes in the North Atlantic and feedbacks associated with terrestrial ecosystem changes.

Of course, if the climate system were somehow less "rapidly forced" by virtue of policies designed to slow down the rate at which human activities modify the land surfaces and atmospheric composition, this would lower the likelihood of nonlinear surprises. Whether the risks of such surprises justify investments in abatement activities is the question that integrated assessment (IA) activities (see next section) are designed to inform (IPCC 1996c and 2001c). The likelihood of various climatic changes, along with estimates of the probabilities of such potential changes, are the kinds of information IA modelers need from climate scientists in order to perform IA simulations (Schneider 1997b and 2001). I turn next, therefore, to a discussion of methods to evaluate the subjective probability distributions of scientists on one important climate change issue, the climate sensitivity.

Subjective Probability Estimation

What does define a scientific consensus? Morgan and Keith (1995) and Nordhaus (1994a) are two attempts by nonclimate scientists, who are interested in the policy implications of climate science, to tap the knowledgeable opinions of what they believe to be representative groups of scientists from physical, biological, and social sciences on two separate questions: first, the climate science itself, and, second, policy-relevant impact assessment. The Morgan and Keith surveys show that although there is a wide divergence of opinion, nearly all scientists (e.g., table 5.1) assign some probability of negligible outcomes and some probability of very highly serious outcomes, with few exceptions, like Richard Lindzen at MIT (who is scientist number 5 on figure 1 taken from Morgan and Keith).

In the Morgan and Keith study, each of the sixteen scientists listed in table 5.1 participated in two separate several-hour, formal decision-analytic elicitations of their subjective probability estimates for a number of factors. Figure 5.1 shows the elicitation results for the important climate sensitivity factor. Note that fifteen out of sixteen scientists surveyed (including several 1995 [and 2000] IPCC Working Group I Lead Authors—I am scientist 9) assigned something like a 10 percent subjective likelihood of small (less than 1 °C) surface warming from doubling of CO_2. These scientists also typically assigned a 10 percent or so probability for extremely large climatic changes—greater than 5 °C, roughly equivalent to the temperature difference experienced between a glacial

Table 5.1
Experts interviewed in the study. Expert numbers used in reporting results are randomized. They do not correspond with either alphabetical order or the order in which the interviews were performed. From Morgan and Keith (1995).

James Anderson, Harvard University	Michael MacCracken, U.S. Global Change Research Program
Robert Cess, State University of New York at Stony Brook	Ronald Prinn, Massachusetts Institute of Technology
Robert Dickinson, University of Arizona	Stephen Schneider, Stanford University
Lawrence Gates, Lawrence Livermore National Laboratories	Peter Stone, Massachusetts Institute of Technology
William Holland, National Center for Atmospheric Research	Starley Thompson, National Center for Atmospheric Research
Thomas Karl, National Climatic Data Center	Warren Washington, National Center for Atmospheric Research
Richard Lindzen, Massachusetts Institute of Technology	Tom Wigley, University Center for Atmospheric Research/National Center for Atmospheric Research
Syukuro Manabe, Geophysical Fluid Dynamics Laboratory	Carl Wunsch, Massachusetts Institute of Technology

and interglacial age, but occurring a hundred times more rapidly. In addition to the lower probabilities assigned to the mild and catastrophic outcomes, the bulk of the scientists interviewed (with the noted exception) assigned the bulk of their subjective cumulative probability distributions in the center of the IPCC range for climate sensitivity. What is most striking about the exception, scientist 5, is the lack of variance in his estimates—suggesting a very high confidence level in this scientist's mind that he understands how all the complex interactions within the earth-system described above will work. None of the other scientists displayed that confidence, nor did the Lead Authors of IPCC SAR (or the TAR five years later). In fact, several scientists interviewed by Morgan and Keith expressed concern for "surprise" scenarios. For example, scientists 2 and 4 explicitly display this possibility on figure 5.1, whereas several other scientists—myself among them—implicitly allow for both positive and negative surprises, since they assigned a considerable amount of their cumulative subjective probabilities for climate sensitivity outside of the standard 1.5 to 4.5 range. This concern for surprises is consistent with the concluding paragraph of the IPCC Working Group I Summary

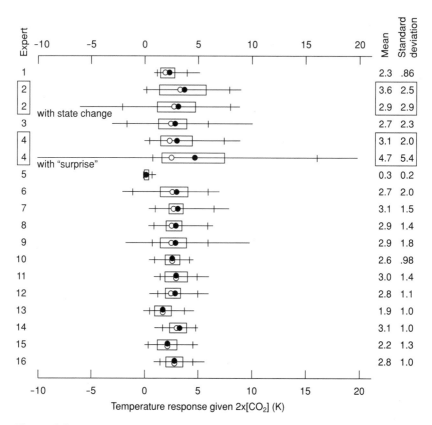

Figure 5.1
Box plots of elicited probability distributions of climate sensitivity, the change in globally averaged surface temperature for a doubling of CO_2 ($2x[CO_2]$ forcing). Horizontal line denotes range from minimum (1 percent) to maximum (99 percent) assessed possible values. Vertical tick marks indicate locations of lower (5) and upper (95) percentiles. Box indicates interval spanned by 50 percent confidence interval. Solid dot is the mean and open dot is the median. The two columns of numbers on right-hand side of the figure report values of mean and standard deviation of the distributions. From Morgan and Keith (1995).

for Policy Makers quoted above and the studies of Rahmstorf (1997), Broecker (1997), and Stocker and Schmittner (1997).

IPCC Lead Authors, who wrote the Working Group I Second Assessment Report, were fully aware of both the wide range of possible outcomes and the broad distributions of attendant subjective probabilities. After several caveats and a number of sentences highlighting such uncertainties, the Report concluded: "Nevertheless, the balance of evidence suggests that there is a discernible human influence on the climate." The reasons for this now-famous subjective judgment were many, such as the kinds of factors listed above. These include a well-validated theoretical case for the natural greenhouse effect, validation tests of both model parameterizations and performance against present and paleoclimatic data, and the growing "fingerprint" evidence that suggests horizontal and vertical patterns of climate change predicted to occur in coupled atmosphere-ocean models have been increasingly evident in observations over that past several decades. Clearly, more research is needed to produce higher confidence, but enough is already known to warrant assessments of the possible impacts of such projected climatic changes and the relative merits of alternative actions to both mitigate emissions and/or make adaptations less costly. That is the on-going task of integrated assessment analysts, a task that will become increasingly critical in the twenty-first century. To accomplish this task, it is important to recognize what is well established in climate data and modeling and to separate this from aspects that are more speculative. That is precisely what IPCC (1996a) had attempted to accomplish, and IPCC (2001a) carried out to a greater degree. The latter was aided by a lengthy discussion of consistent methods to treat uncertainties, and to use common terms in defining high or low subjective confidence levels. This was facilitated by an IPCC uncertainties "guidance paper," several drafts of which were circulated to IPCC lead authors and revisions made by an iterative process among the lead authors and the guidance paper authors (see Moss and Schneider 2000).

Assessing the Environmental and Societal Impacts of Climatic Change Projections

One of the principal tools used in the assessment of climate change impacts is integrated assessment models (IAMs). These models are often comprised of many submodels adopted and adapted from a wide range of disciplines. In IAMs, modelers "combine scientific and economic aspects of climate change in order to assess policy options for climate change" control (Kelly and Kolstad 1999).

One of the most dramatic of the standard impacts of climatic warming projections is the increase in sea level typically associated with warmer climatic conditions. A U.S. Environmental Protection Agency study (Titus and Narayanan 1996) used an unusual approach: combining climatic models with the subjective opinions of many scientists on the values of uncertain elements in the models to help bracket the uncertainties inherent in this issue. Titus and Narayanan (1996) used formal elicitations on uncertain parameters from teams of experts of all persuasions on the issue and calculated the final product of their impact assessment as a statistical distribution of future sea-level rise, ranging from negligible change as a low-probability outcome, to a meter or more rise, also with a low probability (see figure 5.2). The midpoint of the probability distribution is something like half-meter sea-level rise by the end of the next century.

Since the EPA analysis stopped there, this is by no means a complete assessment. In order to take integrated assessment to its logical conclusion, we need to ask what the economic costs of various control strategies might be and how the costs of abatement compare to the economic or environmental losses (i.e., impacts or damages as they are called) from sea-level rises. That means putting a value—a dollar value typically—on climate change, coastal wetlands, fisheries, environmental refugees, and so forth. Hadi Dowlatabadi, then at Carnegie Mellon University, led a team of integrated assessors who, like Titus, combined a wide range of scenarios of climatic changes and impacts, but, unlike the EPA studies, added a wide range of abatement cost estimates into the mix. Their integrated assessment was presented in statistical form as a probability that investments in CO_2 emissions controls would either cost more than the losses from averted climate change or the reverse (Morgan and Dowlatabadi 1996). Since their results do not include estimates for all conceivable costs (e.g., the human or political consequences of persons displaced from coastal flooding), the Carnegie Mellon group offered its results only as illustrative of the capability of integrated assessment techniques. Its numerical results have meaning only after the range of physical, biological, and social outcomes and their costs and benefits have

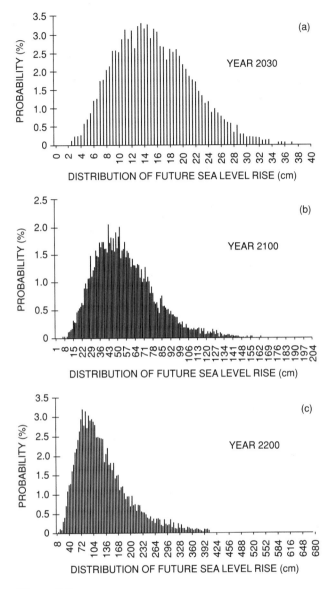

Figure 5.2
Plots showing the probability of various rises of sea level in the years 2030, 2100, and 2200, calculated on the basis of the "Monte Carlo" estimation technique, combining experts' probability distributions for model parameters. From Titus and Narayanan (1994).

been quantified—a Herculean task. Similar studies have been made in Holland by a Dutch effort to produce integrated assessments for policy makers. Jan Rotmans, who heads one of their efforts, likes to point out that such modeling of complex physical, biological, and social factors cannot produce credible "answers" to current policy dilemmas, but can provide "insights" to policy makers that will put decision making on a stronger analytical basis (Rotmans and van Asselt 1996). Understanding the strengths and weaknesses of any complex analytic tool is essential to rational policy making, even if quantifying the costs and benefits of specific activities is controversial (e.g., Schneider 1997b).

William Nordhaus has made heroic steps to put the climatic change policy debate into an optimizing framework. He is an economist at Yale University who has long acknowledged that an efficient economy must internalize externalities (in other words, find the full social costs of our activities, not just the direct cost reflected in conventional "free market" prices to private firms or individuals). He has tried to quantify the external damage from climate change and balance it against the costs to the global economy of policies designed to reduce CO_2 emissions. His "optimized" solution produces a carbon tax, designed to internalize the externality of damage to the climate by increasing the price of fuels in proportion to how much carbon they emit, thereby providing an incentive for society to use less of these fuels—in essence a "polluter pays" principle.

Nordhaus (1992, 1994b) imposed carbon tax scenarios ranging from a few dollars per ton to hundreds of dollars per ton of carbon emitted— the latter would effectively limit coal use in the world economy. He showed that, in the context of his model and its assumptions, these carbon emission fees would cost the world economy anywhere from less than 1 percent annual loss in Gross National Product to a several percent loss by the year 2100. The efficient, optimized solution from classical economic cost-benefit analysis is that carbon taxes should be levied sufficient to reduce the GNP as much as it is worth to avert climate change (e.g., the damage to GNP from climate change). He *assumed* that the impacts of climate change were equivalent to a loss of about 1 percent of GNP. This led to an "optimized" initial carbon tax of about five dollars or so per ton of carbon dioxide emitted rising by several fold to 2100. In the context of his modeling exercise, this would avert only a few tenths of a degree of global warming to the year 2100, a very small fraction of the 4 °C warming his model projected.

How did Nordhaus arrive at climate damage being about 1 percent of GNP? He assumed that agriculture was the most vulnerable economic market sector to climate change. For decades agronomists had calculated potential changes to crop yields from various climate change scenarios, suggesting some regions now too hot would sustain heavy losses from warming whereas others, now too cold, could gain. Noting that the United States lost about one-third of its agricultural economy in the heat waves of 1988, and that agriculture then represented about 3 percent of the U.S. GNP, Nordhaus felt the typically projected climatic changes might thus cost the U.S. economy something like 1 percent annually in the twenty-first century. This figure was severely criticized because it neglected damages from health impacts (e.g., expanded areas of tropical diseases, heat-stress deaths, etc.), losses from coastal flooding or severe storms, security risks from boat people created from coastal disruptions in South Asia or any damages to wildlife (e.g., Sorenson et al. 1998), fisheries, or ecosystems (e.g., IPCC 1996b and 2001b) that would almost surely accompany temperature rises at rates of degrees per century as are typically projected. It also was criticized because his estimate neglected potential increases in crop or forestry yields from the direct effects of increased CO_2 in the air on the photosynthetic response of these marketable plants. Nordhaus responded to his critics by conducting a survey, similar to that undertaken by Morgan and Keith, but this time focused on the impacts of several scenarios of climatic change on world economic product—including both standard market sector categories (e.g., forestry, agriculture, heating and cooling demands) and so-called nonmarket sectors like biological conservation, international equity, and national security. Respondents gave aggregate losses, but also were asked what fraction of those losses were specified in markets (i.e., in Standard National Accounts) and what fraction would be nonmarket. Respondents were not asked to specify which numeraires they used in each case, an issue I'll return to below.

When Nordhaus surveyed the opinions of mainstream economists, environmental economists, and natural scientists (I am respondent number 10 in Nordhaus 1994), he found that the former expressed less anxiety, by a factor of twenty, about the economic or environmental consequences of climate change than the latter (see figure 5.3, in which the bulk of the economists estimates lay toward the left-hand side of the distribution and the natural scientists toward the right). However, even

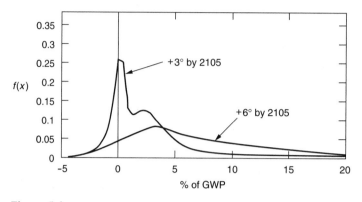

Figure 5.3
Probability distributions ($f(x)$) of climate damages (market and nonmarket components combined) from an expert survey in which respondents were asked to estimate tenth, fiftieth, and ninetieth percentiles for the two climate change scenarios shown. From Roughgarden and Schneider (1999). Data from Nordhaus (1994a).

the conservative estimates of economists Nordhaus surveyed considered there to be at least a 10 percent probability that typically projected climate changes could still cause economic damages worth several percent of gross world product (the U.S. GNP is soon to be around 10 trillion dollars, accounting for about 20 percent of the global total), even when these economists didn't include estimates for possible costs of "non-market" damages (e.g., harm to nature or loss of ecosystem services). One ecologist who did explicitly factor in nonmarket values for natural systems went so far as to assign (for 6 °C warming in a century) a 10 percent chance of 100 percent loss of GNP—the virtual end of civilization! While Nordhaus observed that those who know the most about the economy are "comparatively unconcerned," I countered with the obvious observation that those who know the most about nature are comparatively very concerned (e.g., Roughgarden and Schneider 1999, from which figure 5.3 is adapted).

Five Numeraires
One reason for the differences between economists' and natural scientists' relative degrees of concern was the fraction of damages assigned to nonmarket categories. Roughgarden and Schneider (1999) analyzed the Nordhaus (1994a) elicitation data set and found that most respondents who had estimated large damages placed the bulk of them in the non-

market basket, and the converse for those with low damage estimates. This raises a major issue about the dimensions of damages, which need even finer subdivision than the market and nonmarket binary characterization. Schneider et al. (2000) summarize this issue of the dimensions of climate damage as the "Five Numeraires": monetary loss, loss of life, quality of life (including coercion to migrate, conflict over resources, cultural diversity, loss of cultural heritage sites, etc.), species or biodiversity loss, and changes in distribution/equity.

Any comprehensive attempt to evaluate the societal value of climate change should include, for example, such things as loss of species diversity, loss of coastline from increasing sea level, environmental displacement of persons, change in income distributions, and agricultural losses or gains. The environment also possesses intrinsic worth without a clear market value, such as its aesthetic appeal, which suggests that the environment should be treated as an independent variable in utility. In a sense, this is what is meant by "existence value"—a priority is placed on preserving the environment, even if we don't intend to personally experience it. This is in addition to the "option value" of the environment, which we may want to preserve for our possible personal use in the future. There is little agreement on how to place a dollar value on the nonmarket impacts of climate change, such as the loss of human life, biodiversity, or ecosystem services.

The point of this discussion is that it is essential for analysis of costs of climate change impacts or mitigation strategies to consider explicitly alternative numeraires and to be as clear as possible which is being used and what is omitted. Moreover, before any aggregation is attempted—e.g., cost-benefit optimization strategies—authors should first disaggregate costs and benefits into several numeraires and then provide a "traceable account" (Moss and Schneider 2000) of how they were reaggregated. Such transparency is essential given the normative nature of the valuation of various consequences characterized by the five numeraires.

We will not easily resolve the paradigm gulf between the relatively optimistic and pessimistic views of these specialists with different training, traditions, and world views. But the one thing that is clear from both the Morgan and Keith and Nordhaus studies is that the vast majority of knowledgeable experts from a variety of fields admits to a wide range of plausible outcomes in the area of climate change—including both mild and catastrophic eventualities—under their broad umbrella of possibilities. This is a condition ripe for misinterpretation by those who are unfamiliar with the wide range of probabilities most scientists attach to climate change issues (e.g., Ravetz 1986). The wide range of probabilities follows from recognition of the many uncertainties in data and assumptions still inherent in climate models, climatic impact models, economic models, or their synthesis via integrated assessment models (see Schneider 1997a, b).

Moreover, these uncertainties "cascade" as wide ranges are given for projections of very different "storylines" for how future societies will be structured (Nakicenovic and Swart, 2000); these storylines condition the range of emissions scenarios, which in turn are expanded by uncertainties in biogeochemical modeling of the dispersion of emissions, compounded further by uncertainties in climatic modeling, climatic impact assessments, and eventually uncertainties in the costs of adaptation and mitigative activities—themselves a function of the very assumptions of how future societies will be structured, since these precondition both adaptive and mitigative capacities (see chapters 2 in both IPCC 2001b and c). This complex interaction where projections of future social conditions govern emissions, which in turn control climatic effects, but in which impacts are not a straightforward response to climatic effects, since adaptations modulate impacts and adaptive capacity, is a function of how future societies are structured—which determined the emissions in the first place. In other words, integrated assessment models need to deal simultaneously with the interconnections among emissions scenarios and adaptive and mitigative capacities of societies over time. This will render single-scenario cost-benefit methods, regardless of how many numeraires are considered, highly tentative, and will be a major challenge to the application of any fixed analytic method to estimating the full range of implications of a variety of social structural assumptions or climate policy proposals (e.g., see chapter 1 of IPCC 2001b). This challenge certainly will keep integrated assessors busy for decades to come.

It is necessary in a highly interdisciplinary enterprise like the integrated assessment of climate change problems that a wide range of possible outcomes be included, along with a representative sample of the subjective probabilities (e.g., Schneider 2001 or Wigley and Raper 2001) that knowledgeable assessment groups like the IPCC believe accompany each of those possible outcomes. In essence, the "bottom line" of estimating climatic impacts at a planetary scale is that both "the end of the

world" and "it is good for business" scenarios are the two lowest probability outcomes, and that most knowledgeable scientists and economists
consider there to be a significant chance of climatic damage to both
natural and social systems. Under these conditions—and the unlikeli-
hood (for reasons given in the above paragraph) that research will soon
eliminate the large uncertainties that still persist—it is not surprising that
most formal climatic impact assessments have called for cautious, but
cost-effective positive steps both to slow down the rate at which humans
modify the climatic system and to make natural and social systems more
resilient to whatever changes do eventually materialize (e.g., National
Academy of Sciences 1991). No such assessments recommend a "wait-
and-see" attitude simply because uncertainty is a structural feature of this
complex socio-natural system (e.g., Lempert and Schlesinger 2000). It
remains to be seen how long it will take for this cautions but positive
message to penetrate international climate policy negotiations currently
under way.

References

Broecker, W. S. 1997. "Thermohaline Circulation, the Achilles Heel of Our Climate System: Will Man-Made CO_2 Upset the Current Balance?" *Science* 278: 1582–1588.

Crowley, T. J., and G. R. North. 1991. *Paleoclimatology*. New York: Oxford University Press.

Eddy, J. A., and H. Oeschger, eds. 1993. *Global Changes in the Perspective of the Past*. New York: John Wiley and Sons.

Edwards, P. N., and S. H. Schneider. 1997. "The 1995 IPCC Report: Broad Consensus or 'Scientific Cleansing'?" *Ecofables/Ecoscience* 1(1): 3–9.

———. 2001. "Self-Governance and Peer Review in Science-for-Policy: The Case of the IPCC Second Assessment Report." Pp. 219–246 in *Changing the Atmosphere: Expert Knowledge and Global Environmental Governance*, ed. C. Miller and P. N. Edwards. Cambridge: MIT Press.

Hoffert, M. I., and C. Covey. 1992. "Deriving Global Climate Sensitivity from Paleoclimate Reconstructions." *Nature* 360: 573–576.

Intergovernmental Panel on Climatic Change (IPCC). 1996a. Climate Change 1995. *The Science of Climate Change*. Contribution of Working Group I to the Second Assessment Report of the Intergovernmental Panel on Climate Change. Edited by J. T. Houghton, L. G. Meira Filho, B. A. Callander, N. Harris, A. Kattenberg, and K. Maskell. Cambridge: Cambridge University Press.

———. 1996b. Climate Change 1995. *Impacts, Adaptations, and Mitigation of Climate Change: Scientific-Technical Analyses*. Contribution of Working Group II to the Second Assessment Report of the Intergovernmental Panel on Climate Change. Edited by R. T. Watson, M. C. Zinyowera, and R. H. Moss. Cambridge: Cambridge University Press.

———. 1996c. Climate Change 1995. *Economic and Social Dimensions of Climate Change*. Contribution of Working Group III to the Second Assessment Report of the Intergovernmental Panel on Climate Change. Edited by J. P. Bruce, H. Lee, and E. F. Haites. Cambridge: Cambridge University Press.

———. 1997. Workshop on Regional Climate Change Projections for Impact Assessment, Imperial College, London, 24–26 September 1996.

———. 1998. *The Regional Impacts of Climate Change: An Assessment of Vulnerability*. A Special Report of IPCC Working Group II. Edited by R. T. Watson, M. C. Zinyowera, and R. H. Moss. Cambridge: Cambridge University Press.

Intergovernmental Panel on Climatic Change (IPCC). 2001a. *Third Assessment Report of Working Group I: The Science of Climate Change*. Houghton, J. T., Y. Ding, D. J. Griggs, M. Noguer, P. J. van Der Linden, and D. Xiaosu, eds. Cambridge: Cambridge University Press.

Intergovernmental Panel on Climatic Change (IPCC). 2001b. *Third Assessment Report of Working Group II: Impacts, Adaptation and Vulnerability*. McCarthy, J. J., O. F. Canziani, N. A. Leary, D. J. Dokken, and K. S. White, eds. Cambridge: Cambridge University Press.

Intergovernmental Panel on Climatic Change (IPCC). 2001c. *Third Assessment Report of Working Group III: Climate Change 2001: Mitigation*. Mertz, B., O. Davidson, R. Swart, and J. Pan, eds. Cambridge: Cambridge University Press.

Jacobson, Mark Z. 2001. Strong Radiative Heating due to the Mixing State of Black Carbon in Atmospheric Aerosols, *Nature* 409: 695–697.

Kelly, D. L., and C. D. Kolstad. 1999. "Integrated Assessment Models for Climate Change Control." Update in *International Yearbook of Environmental and Resource Economics 1999/2000: A Survey of Current Issues*, ed. H. Folmer and T. Tietenberg. Cheltenham, United Kingdom: Edward Edgar.

Lempert, R. J., and M. E. Schlesinger. 2000. "Robust Strategies for Abating Climate Change." *Climatic Change* 45: 387–401.

Mann, M. E., R. S. Bradley, and M. K. Hughes. 1999. "Northern Hemisphere Temperatures During the Past Millennium: Inferences, Uncertainties, and Limitations." *Geophysical Research Letter* 26(6): 759.

Mass, C., and S. H. Schneider. 1977. "Influence of Sunspots and Volcanic Dust on Long-Term Temperature Records Inferred by Statistical Investigations." *Journal of Atmospheric Science* 34(12): 1995–2004.

Mastrandrea, M., and S. H. Schneider. 2001. "Integrated Assessment of Abrupt Climatic Changes." *Climate Policy* (submitted).

Mearns, L. O. 1997. "Transforming the Results of Climate Models to the Scales of Impacts." Paper presented at the IPCC Workshop on Regional Climate Change Projections for Impact Assessment, Imperial College London.

Mendelsohn, R., W. Morrison, M. Schlesinger, and N. Andronova. 2000. "Country-Specific Market Impacts of Climate Change." *Climatic Change* 45(3–4): 553–569.

Morgan, M. G., and H. Dowlatabadi. 1996. "Learning from Integrated Assessment of Climate Change." *Climatic Change* 34(3–4): 337–368.

Morgan, M. G., and D. W. Keith. 1995. "Subjective Judgments by Climate Experts." *Environmental Science and Technology* 29: 468A–476A.

Moss, R. H., and S. H. Schneider. 2000. "Uncertainties in the IPCC TAR: Recommendations to Lead Authors for More Consistent Assessment and Reporting." Pp. 33–51 in *The Third Assessment Report: Cross Cutting Issues Guidance Papers (Geneva, Switzerland: World Meteorological Organization)*, ed. R. Pachauri, T. Taniguchi, and K. Tanaka. Available on request from the Global Industrial and Social Progress Institute at http://www.gispri.or.jp

Nakicenovic, N., and R. Swart. 2000. *Special Report of the Intergovernmental Panel on Climatic Change (IPCC) on Emissions Scenarios (SRES)*. Cambridge: Cambridge University Press. Summary for Policymakers available online at http://www.ipcc.ch/

National Academy of Sciences. 1991. *Policy Implications of Greenhouse Warming*. Washington, D.C.: National Academy Press.

Nordhaus, W. D. 1992. "An Optimal Transition Path for Controlling Greenhouse Gases." *Science* 258: 1315–1319.

Nordhaus, W. D. 1994a. "Expert Opinion on Climate Change." *American Scientist* 82: 45–51.

Nordhaus, W. D. 1994b. *Managing the Global Commons*. Cambridge: MIT Press.

Overpeck, J. T., R. S. Webb, and T. Webb III. 1992. "Mapping Eastern North American Vegetation Change over the Past 18,000 Years: No Analogs and the Future." *Geology* 20: 1071–1074.

Rahmstorf, S. 1997. "Risk of Sea-Change in the Atlantic." *Nature* 388: 825–826.

Rahmstorf, S., and A. Ganopolski. 1999. "Long-Term Global Warming Scenarios Computed with an Efficient Coupled Climate." *Climatic Change* 43(2): 353–367.

Ramanathan, V. 1981. "The Role of Ocean-Atmospheric Interactions in the CO_2 Climate Problem." *Journal of Atmospheric Science* 38: 918–930.

Raval, A., and V. Ramanathan. 1989. "Observational Determination of the Greenhouse Effect." *Nature* 342: 758.

Ravetz, J. R. 1986. "Usable Knowledge, Usable Ignorance: Incomplete Science with Policy Implications." Pp. 415–432 in *Sustainable Development of the Biosphere*, ed. William C. Clark and R. E. Munn. New York: Cambridge University Press.

Robinson, A. B., and Z. W. Robinson. 1997. "Science Has Spoken: Global Warming Is a Myth." *Wall Street Journal*, 4 December.

Root, T. L., and S. H. Schneider. 1995. "Ecology and Climate: Research Strategies and Implications." *Science* 269: 331–341.

Rotmans, J., and M. van Asselt. 1996. "Integrated Assessment: A Growing Child on Its Way to Maturity—An Editorial." *Climatic Change* 34(3–4): 327–336.

Roughgarden, T., and S. H. Schneider. 1999. "Climate Change Policy: Quantifying Uncertainties for Damages and Optimal Carbon Taxes." *Energy Policy* 27(7): 415–429.

Santer, B. D., et al. 1996. "A Search for Human Influences on the Thermal Structure of the Atmosphere." *Nature* 382: 39–46.

Schneider, S. H. 1993. "Can Paleoclimatic and Paleoecological Analyses Validate Future Global Climate and Ecological Change Projections?" Pp. 317–340 in *Global Changes in the Perspective of the Past*. ed. J. A. Eddy, and H. Oeschger. New York: John Wiley and Sons.

———. 1994. "Detecting Climatic Change Signals: Are There Any 'Fingerprints'?" *Science* 263: 341–347.

———. 1997a. *Laboratory Earth: The Planetary Gamble We Can't Afford to Lose*. New York: Basic Books.

———. 1997b. "Integrated Assessment Modeling of Global Climate Change: Transparent Rational Tool for Policy Making or Opaque Screen Hiding Value-Laden Assumptions?" *Environmental Modeling and Assessment* 2: 229–249.

Schneider, S. H., K. Kuntz-Duriseti, and C. Azar. 2000. "Costing Nonlinearities, Surprises, and Irreversible Events." *Pacific and Asian Journal of Energy* 10(1): 81–106.

Schneider, S. H., and R. Londer. 1984. *The Coevolution of Climate and Life*. San Francisco: Sierra Club Books.

Schneider, S. H., and L. E. Mesirow. 1976. *The Genesis Strategy: Climate and Global Survival*. New York: Plenum.

Schneider, S. H., and S. L. Thompson. 2000. "A Simple Climate Model Used in Economic Studies of Global Change." Pp. 59–80 in S. J. DeCanio, R. B. Howarth, A. H. Sanstad, S. H. Schneider, and S. L. Thompson, *New Directions in the Economics and Integrated Assessment of Global Climate Change*. The Pew Center on Global Climate Change.

Schneider, S. H. 2001. "What is 'Dangerous' Climate Change?" Commentary, *Nature*, 411, 17–19.

Shackley, S., J. Risbey, P. Stone, and B. Wynne. 1999. "Adjusting to Policy Expectations in Climate Change Modeling: An Interdisciplinary Study of Flux Adjustment in Coupled Atmosphere-Ocean General Circulation Models." *Climatic Change* 43(2): 413–454.

Singer, S. F. 1997. *Hot Talk, Cold Science: Global Warming's Unfinished Debate*. Oakland, California: Independent Institute.

Sorenson, L. G., R. Goldberg, T. L. Root, and M. G. Anderson. 1998. "Potential Effects of Global Warming on Waterfowl Populations Breeding in the Northern Great Plains." *Climatic Change* 40(2): 343–369.

Stocker, T. F., and A. Schmittner. 1997. "Influence of CO_2 Emission Rates on the Stability of the Thermohaline Circulation." *Nature* 388: 862–865.

Thompson, S. L., and S. H. Schneider. 1982. "CO_2 and Climate: The Importance of Realistic Geography in Estimating the Transient Response." *Science* 217: 1031–1033.

Titus, J., and V. Narayanan. 1996. "The Risk of Sea Level Rise: A Delphic Monte Carlo Analysis in which Twenty Researchers Specify Subjective Probability Distributions for Model Coefficients within their Respective Areas of Expertise." *Climatic Change* 33(2): 151–212.

Trenberth, K. E., ed. 1992. *Climate System Modeling*. Cambridge: Cambridge University Press.

Washington, W. M., and C. L. Parkinson. 1986. *An Introduction to Three-Dimensional Climate Modeling*. New York: Oxford University Press.

Wigley, T. M. L., and S. C. B. Raper. 2001. "Interpretation of High Projections for Global-Mean Warming." *Science* 293: 451–454.

Wigley, T. M. L., R. L. Smith, and B. D. Santer. 1998. "Anthropogenic Influence on the Auto Correlation Structure of Hemispheric-Mean Temperatures." *Science* 282: 1676–1679.

Wright, H. E., et al., eds. 1993. *Global Climates since the Last Glacial Maximum*. Minneapolis: University of Minnesota Press.

6

The World of Work in the New Millennium

Richard B. Freeman

The value of peering into the future is especially great in economics. There is money to be made by having a glimmer more knowledge about the future than the rest of society. You can beat the stock market if you know a bit beforehand what the newest report on the economy will say about employment, wages, and inflation. You can assure a better choice of careers if you know which fields will be hot and which will face a surplus of workers in the next decade. But economists disdain most future gazing. They know how hard it is to predict economic phenomena from one year to the next, much less what might happen over longer time periods.

Economics does not have a good track record in predicting the future over the short term or in the long run. In the 1970s, many leading economists viewed corporatist economies, based on peak level union and employer associations, as the most effective in dealing with inflation. That proved wrong. In the early 1990s, most business experts thought that Japan, with its lifetime jobs, was the future model for the world of work. That proved wrong. In 1996–1997 most economists believed that unemployment rates below 6 percent in the United States would generate accelerating inflation. That proved wrong at least through 2001, though at this writing no one knows whether the economy can maintain full employment without rising inflation much into the new millennium.

As for the long run, consider some famous prognostications. Malthus anticipated that a growing population would keep wages at subsistence level. Marx predicted the future of work under capitalism—the formation of a proletariat that would create socialism. During the Great Depression, the president of the American Economics Association pronounced unionism dead in the United States—just before the huge spurt in organizing associated with the CIO.

Given this performance, it is not surprising that economists shy away from predicting the future. Still, futurology is a thriving enterprise, filled with diverse analysts—Fortune Sellers, in William Sherden's terminology[1]—who earn a living in the competitive market, which is the ultimate test according to our discipline. Many prognosticators focus on the labor market. Jeremy Rifkind has announced the "end of work." Others proclaim the advent of the "virtual workplace" where workers put in brief stints for companies that form for particular tasks, then dissolve. In the 1970s the Club of Rome forecast a Malthusian environmental disaster that would reduce real wages to subsistence level (Meadows). James Goldsmith and Ross Perot have predicted that free trade will suck jobs from advanced to less developed countries. Some futurologists proclaim that nanotechnology will create global abundance. And there is always someone who sees the next great depression on the horizon.

Econometricians generally distrust long-run forecasts more than short-run forecasts. Confidence bands around predictions widen the further one gets from the current state. But there is some reason to believe that economics might do a better job predicting the long- or medium-run future than the short run. Economic models are clearest about comparative statics, which assumes full adjustment of economic agents to change, surely a lengthy process. Transients—behavior off the equilibrium point or path—are harder to analyze than equilibria, both mathematically and behaviorally. For long-term prognostication we need only get trend lines right, not oscillations around trend.

Following this logic, I focus on the future of the labor market over the long run. I describe standard modes of projecting, offer an assessment of possible developments in the labor market, beginning with "easy," largely quantitative, patterns that follow from current trends, and then turn to more controversial and speculative possible futures in the qualitative dimensions of work. I exclude any discussion of short-run changes in employment, unemployment, or wages, though predicting these factors is a major part of the economic forecasting business, critical in the policy decisions of central banks, in particular.

Standard Projections of Labor Supply and Demand

Virtually all governments in advanced countries and international agencies concerned with the world of work forecast the future labor force and the distribution of employment among industries and occupations. The methodology for these projections is twofold.

On the supply side, forecasts take demographic projections of the size of the population and of labor force participation rates (usually based on some judgmental extrapolation) to estimate the likely supply of labor in the future, by age and gender. Since the qualifications of workers is important in the labor market, many projections consider further the potential educational attainment of workers, usually through some form of extrapolation of trends in education. Because of the long training period and specificity of education, analysts and government agencies give more attention to projecting the demand and supply of highly educated workers than of less educated workers.

On the demand side, forecasters take estimates of the level of future GDP, project the composition of final demand among government, investment, and consumption and then apply these demand projections to an input-output table to project the level of output in different industries. Then forecasters estimate productivity trends by sector, usually on the basis of some extrapolation of past trends, to determine employment by industry. The final step is to multiply the projected industry employment by an industry-occupation employment matrix to obtain projections of employment by occupation.

Fixed Coefficient Projection Models

The most rigorous part of any standard projection model focuses on the demand for labor in different sectors within the framework of an input-output model. This model links projected changes in employment patterns to changes in final demands and technologies. In the United States the Department of Labor undertakes the main analysis and publishes its projections in the *Occupational Outlook Handbook*, a biennial publication to which guidance counselors newspapers and magazines give great attention.

The projections are based on the relation between four pieces of information:

1. Projections of the level and final demands of GDP

2. Projections of industry level output from input-output tables, conditional on the level and final demand for GDP projections

3. Projections of industry level employment based on projections of industry level output and estimated productivity

4. Projections of employment by occupation using a national industry-occupation matrix that gives the expected occupational distribution of workers by industry

The main equation for making the projections is:

$$O = [M]T[IO]X \tag{26}$$

where O is the column vector of projected employment for each of m occupations; [M] is the m by n matrix of employment by occupation and industry, with each coefficient giving the proportion of workers in industry n who work in the mth occupation; T is an n by 1 vector of employment per unit of output; [IO] is an $n \times n$ input-output matrix showing the purchase of goods in industries; and X is an n by 1 vector of final demands.

The multiplication of IO and X gives the projected output by sector. The T vector transforms outputs into employment. The M matrix transforms employment by industry into employment by occupation.

In a base period (1) is an accounting identity, so that the modeling assumption is either that the matrices and vectors have constant coefficients or that changes in their coefficients can be readily extrapolated. This framework works best when industries differ greatly in their occupational distribution (which is invariably true); when the mix of industries changes sharply over the period (sometimes true); and when the M matrix coefficients linking occupational employment to industrial employment do not change much (which is roughly true for aggregate occupations).

What is most striking to an economist about this methodology is that it has no formal feedback or adjustment mechanism to equilibrate the anticipated supplies and demands. It is not that the analysts who make projections are unaware that markets equilibrate through wages or other quantitative rationing or signaling devices. They have simply chosen to apply a more mechanical (and easier) methodology. Neither the supply nor the demand forecasts explicitly consider wage developments or rely on estimates of supply or demand elasticities of responses to market conditions on the part of individuals or firms. In this sense, the standard projections are essentially extrapolations of current patterns—more sophisticated than straight line extrapolations—but without any behavioral content that allows for changing behavior under changing conditions.

The cost of this mechanical methodology is that the standard forecasts invariably fail to capture turning point changes that result from changes in market conditions—for instance, slowdowns in the growth of Ph.D. production (Breneman and Freeman) and fall short of projecting supply changes for groups whose behavior is changing—such as women going into the workforce. Perhaps the best way to view standard forecasts is to know that they provide a benchmark or baseline for developing more interesting and insightful looks into the future.

Consistent with this view, the standard projection methodology does a good job in predicting changes in employment in major occupations during periods of economic stability, when it correctly captures the overall trend in employment, but falls short in periods when the economy diverges from consensus patterns of change (see table 6.1). In addition, when demands shift sharply toward or against particular occupations, such as for professionals versus production workers in the 1980s, the projections miss this key change. As table 6.1 shows, the standard projections understated the growth of professional employment in that period while overstating the growth of production labor. At the detailed occupation level, the projections have an error rate on the order of 20–24 percent, which is sufficiently wide given the normal level of changes to provide only the crudest guide to policy decisions. Still, the standard model gives a first-order approximation to actual changes in the sense that there is a sizable positive correlation between predicted and actual changes in employment (Freeman 1980; 1977). Because employment by occupation differs greatly by industry, knowing that a given sector will grow conveys useful information about the likely trend in employment in the occupations that are concentrated there. If we expect the manufacturing sector to lose jobs, we can be reasonably assured that employment in largely manufacturing production occupations such as assembling will fall. If we expect defense spending to decline in the vector of final demands, we can be reasonably assured that demand for certain kinds of engineers will drop as well.

But the purpose of projections is not so much to forecast the future but to influence, guide, or justify policies designed to affect the future. If the government projects a future shortage of workers in a given field under current policies, it may choose policies so that the shortage does not in fact occur, for instance, by giving incentives to schools and students to enter the field. Similarly, if it expects a surplus, it may design policies to reduce supplies in the future.

Table 6.1
The Accuracy of Standard Projections of Occupational Employment

A. Percentage difference between projected and actual employment by major occupation

	1960– 1975	1968– 1980	1980– 1990	1984– 1995
Total employment	3.2	−4.4	−0.9	−5.6
Executive and managerial	0.3	−17.2	4.4	−9.9
Professional and technical	−5.9	−3.0	−14.4*	−11.3*
Sales	6.4	−5.1	−21.8	−7.4
Clerical	−3.8	−6.8	6.0	−8.3
Service	7.4	6.7	0.9	−6.6
Agriculture, et al.	11.8	−5.4	−6.0	−3.6
Precision production (craft-skilled)	2.2	−4.8	16.3**	6.2
Operators and laborers	7.2	1.2	16.3**	−1.7

B. Average percentage error in projected employment in detailed occupations

	1960– 1975	1970– 1980	1980– 1990	1984– 1995
Number of occupations				
76	20.8			
64		22.4		
132			21.1	
348				24.0

Source: Neal Rosenthal, "The Quality of BLS Projections: A Historical Account," *Monthly Labor Review*, May 1999, tables 2 and 3.
A negative difference implies that the projected employment fell short of the actual employment; a positive sign implies that the projection exceeded the actual employment.
* For professional specialty only
** Projection for the two groups together

Depending on how people respond to projections, the very fact that a responsible agency has projected a surplus or shortage might itself affect outcomes. In some situations, projections can be self-fulfilling. Tell investors that the share price of Madness.com will rise, and perhaps it will, creating a financial bubble as investors try to make money on this information. Tell students that there will be a shortage of scientists, and many may decide to obtain science degrees, perhaps averting a shortage and generating a surplus.

The area where projections have the greatest potential for affecting policy is in science and engineering where the period of production requires educational institutions, young persons, and government funding agencies to make long-term investments in training. Absent immigration, shortages are likely to produce large wage increases without generating much additional flow of skills into the field. Not surprisingly given this issue, the National Science Foundation of the United States has for many years made its own detailed projections of the demand and supply of scientific labor. Sadly, however, in the 1980s the NSF publicized a set of projections that created what might seem an impossibility in a world of tabloid journalism: a scandal in the business of scientific projections. This episode highlights the use and misuse of projections of the world of work.

The Disingenuous NSF Projections

In the mid-1980s the U.S. National Science Foundation developed a set of projections that indicated that the United States faced a huge shortage of scientists and engineers.[2] The NSF based its claim largely on one demographic fact: that the number of twenty-two-year-olds was falling, which would reduce the number of young scientists. The NSF study projected a shortage of 675,000 scientists over the 1990s–2000s, which would drive up the wages and costs of science and thus make it hard for U.S. business to compete in high-tech sectors in the world market and for senior scientists to put together research teams with their current or anticipated budgets. In a key document, the NSF analyst argued that the United States should therefore adopt policies to encourage foreign students into the country with the promise of obtaining citizenship and should offer more fellowships and trainee-ships to "lure" Americans into graduate studies on the notion that students were myopic and would not realize (until it was too late) that generous fellowships did not foretell good career prospects.

The head of NSF used the projections to convince Congress to increase the agency budget. Some members of the scientific establishment represented these projections as fact and used them and related NSF projections to try to convince Congress to undertake specific policies regarding immigration, funding of science, and science education:

Simply stated, we face a severe and growing shortage of scientists and engineers.... By the year 2010, it is estimated that there will be 60,000 more engineering jobs than there will be engineers to fill them. We anticipate annual shortages of 7,500 natural science and engineering Ph.D.s in the next decade....

It is projected that by 1997 and beyond the demand for mathematics faculty alone will outstrip the supply. (Philip Griffiths, 31 July 1990, House Subcommittee on Science, Research and Technology)

Others used the projections to mount a publicity campaign to encourage large numbers of young persons to enroll in science and engineering.

But the NSF analysis was fundamentally flawed. It did not examine demand factors per the standard projection methodology but rather implicitly assumed that demand would grow at its historic rates. Under this assumption, any slowdown in the growth of supply would generate a shortage of workers at then existing salaries. Like the standard methodology, the NSF report gave no consideration to the likelihood that if a shortage were to develop and earnings and employment opportunities improved, more young persons would choose to enter the sciences. Even its demographically based supply projections were off-base, by failing to allow for the changing propensity of women to enter the scientific workforce. Internal agency analysts were aware of some of these weaknesses, but the NSF leadership ignored them, seemingly because it viewed the projections as a tool to help attain a particular policy agenda: guaranteeing U.S. industry and the senior scientists an ample supply of low-paid scientific workers.

On 8 April 1992, the House Committee on Science, Space, and Technology's Subcommittee on Investigations and Oversight held hearings on the projections. Many young scientists (including, in particular, mathematicians) were having serious problems in the job market, and it was becoming increasingly clear that the great shortage that the NSF had publicized was nowhere in sight. The hearing brought the problems with the NSF projections into public scrutiny. Analysts from various scientific associations, the Office of Technology Assessment, and the Bureau of Labor Statistics pointed out the flaws. Internal NSF documents showed that the agency's science studies division had raised problems with the projections that the agency leadership had swept under the rug. *Nature* ran an editorial on the issue that summarized the result: "The U.S. National Science Foundation should apply to its own studies the rigour it expects of grants-applicants. NSF made a sorry mess of its defense last week of a poorly done forecast that the United States will be short of 675,000 scientists two decades hence ... NSF's fuzzy thinking on manpower (was) encouraged by the inclination of elders in the research community ... seemingly indifferent to the hundreds of Ph.D.s competing for each academic vacancy (*Nature* 356, April 1992: 548). Reports in other scientific journals told a similar tale. Several years later, the new NSF head, Neal Lane, disavowed the study.

There are three lessons from this experience.

First, clunky though they may be, the standard mechanical projections of demand and supply, with minimal judgmental adjustments in parameters, are invaluable as a benchmark for any serious look into the future. There is a virtue to such an exercise, although it invariably fails to project the changes that are really important. They help flush out bogus projection methodologies.

Second, however, projections that do not take serious account of prices and market feedbacks are seriously flawed. If there is one lesson researchers have learned from the inability of even the best standard forecasts it is that market incentives and career choices in response to those incentives have a greater impact on changes in supply than demographic developments. Pay scientists as much as Wall Street analysts and the most talented Americans will choose science over finance rather than the reverse.

Third, analysts must either make projections with a firewall separating them from the goals of decision makers in the same way that national economic statisticians produce measures of the economy independently of the political process; or more bravely, assess the benefits or costs of the decisions that might follow from the projections. Ideally, projections and other statistical analyses to guide decisions should be put into a decision-theoretic model that includes loss functions: if this projection is right, and nothing is done, here are the costs; if this projection is right and we change policies, here are the consequences; if this projection is wrong, and we change policies, here are the consequences, and so on.

Future Developments in the Workforce and Employment

Behind formal projections of changes in employment by occupation or industry are a set of beliefs about ongoing trends or changes in economic patterns. It is the expectations about trends or changes, rather than the input-output framework, that are the critical component in the projections. Accordingly, in figure 6.1, I give the major quantitative trends or

Feminization of work in West

Aging more educated workforce in West

Younger less educated workforce in world

Decline of manufacturing production jobs in West

Increased employment in health and personal care

Figure 6.1
The future by extrapolations.

changes in the workplace that seem most likely to affect the future world of work. Some of these trends are widely recognized, though many economic forecasts have not fully recognized their magnitudes and implications for the future.

The first trend is the *feminization of work*, by which I mean the increased employment of women at relatively higher wages than in the past compared to men. In the past two decades U.S. women have made sizable inroads into better-paying jobs, and have obtained the education needed for those jobs even more rapidly. Substantially more women than men gain bachelor's and master's degrees, and the gender gap in law degrees, M.B.A.s, M.D.s, and Ph.D.s is closing rapidly. At the same time, the male edge in pay has diminished at all skill levels. As a result upward of 20 percent of women make more than their husbands while 40 percent of college graduate women make more than their husbands. The new millennium will see an increased number of women working as primary breadwinners in advanced countries, with potentially important consequences for families.

The second trend is for an *increase in the age/skill structure* of work-forces. In advanced countries, workers will become older and more skilled because an increased proportion of Western populations will be in the older age group and because more persons are going on to higher education. In addition, the time between completion of schooling and obtaining a regular job has risen due to the increased investments in post-school training, working as a temporary employee, or youth joblessness. The aging of populations may also possibly reverse the trend toward early retirement by older workers.

The third trend is for a *shift in the world labor force to less developed countries* where the typical worker is less educated and younger than in advanced countries and where he or she works with less capital and under very different rules of work than employees in advanced capitalist countries. From 1965 to 1990 the share of the world labor force in LDCs rose from 69 percent to 75 percent. By 2050 the share of world population in LDCs will rise above 85 percent as world population will approach 9–10 billion. That the world workforce will shift to LDCs does not, however, mean that the workforce will get younger or less skilled. It won't, since birth and death rates in developing countries have fallen enough to give most of those countries aging populations, and their workforces are increasing their education. What will happen is that an increasing proportion of workers will work under the labor market rules and regulations of current less developed countries.

The fourth trend is for a *continued decline in manufacturing production and employment in advanced countries and shift in the locus of this activity to less developed countries.* Part of the fall in employment in manufacturing may be illusory, as the service sector undertakes work currently done in manufacturing. But while manufacturing may not disappear as a source of employment in advanced countries as agriculture has done, the huge production lines of the twentieth century will certainly be absent in advanced economies.

The fifth trend is for *employment growth in the health sector and personal services in advanced countries.* Some parts of the education sector are also likely to expand, particularly higher education which can train increasing numbers of students from less developed countries. Overall, labor demand will continue to shift away from work based on physical attributes to work based on knowledge and personal relations, consistent with the feminization of work.

The sixth trend is for *near universal use of computers and modern information-communication technology* in all forms of work and in all forms of market transactions. Already in the United States the majority of the population works with computers, much as it works with the telephone. Delivery persons have computers, store clerks use computers, even CEOs use computers, and there are rumours that the British prime minister would like to learn a bit as well. The computerization of work lives will continue unabated. In addition, demand and supply for labor will increasingly make use of the Internet to clear markets (of which more momentarily).

In short, the next several decades will see a workforce in advanced countries increasingly made up of educated older women using com-

End of job or contingent compensation?

Increased leisure or greater work effort?

Worker participation or employer control?

Dominant firms or niche producers?

Frictionless economy or renaissance of institutions?

Apartheid economy or shared capitalism?

Figure 6.2
Conflicting scenarios.

puters in service sector jobs. Call it the grandma economy, though at current fertility trends, many of these workers, men as well as women, will in fact be childless.

Debating the Future World of Work

The standard projection methodology is solely concerned with numbers employed in different activities. As noted, it does not consider future earnings or rewards from different forms of work. Perhaps more importantly it makes no effort to foresee the way people are likely to work in the future—their job security, attachment to firms, locus of work, and so on. Here, individual analysts offer a wide spectrum of views. In this section I examine these issues in terms of six conflicting scenarios (see figure 6.2).

Changes in the Employment Contract
Capitalism has traditionally organized work through two types of contracts (Simon). The first is the sales contract, whereby purchasers or employers buy specified goods or services from workers, and pay them piece rates—an exchange of money for goods/services. The second is the employment contract, whereby employers buy *the authority* to assign workers to different tasks depending upon business need. Under an employment contract, firms pay workers on a time basis—an exchange of money for time/willingness to undertake activities that the employer designates. Employment contracts often involve long-term commitments between firms and workers—permanent jobs. Throughout the twentieth century most workers in advanced countries have received employment contracts and have been more or less permanently attached to particular firms.

In the United States and the United Kingdom the employment contract has begun to change. An increasing number of firms outsource parts of their production and/or use temporary help agencies to fill short-term demands for labor. An increasing number of firms are raising the variable component of their compensation, paying workers with companywide profit-sharing, gain-sharing (a more workplace form of sharing), company stock or stock options, employee stock ownership schemes based on pension funds, and defined contribution pensions, which place the risk of changes in the value of the assets that fund the pensions onto workers rather than firms.

These changes seem likely to continue into the next century. Rapid shifts in product demands resulting from global production and new information communication technologies require firms to be "lighter" on their feet in meeting volatile market demands than in the past. In a world of just-in-time niche-oriented production, firms with flexible employment practices and labor costs will have a competitive advantage.

Some analysts believe that this pressure will bring about the "death of the job" and the security that the employment contract brought to many workers, leading to more sales contracts. In this vision, large firms will hire virtual employees for particular tasks and outsource work to smaller firms with high turnover and low wages and benefits. The downsizing of large U.S. firms and growth of temporary help agencies in the United States in the 1990s seemed to fit these expectations. But if we are moving to the end of the job, tenure—defined as number of years with the same employer—should drop. It hasn't. On average, tenure with a firm in the United States has been relatively constant, falling a bit for less educated young men and rising for women. Most employees still seek long-term jobs, and many temporary workers and agencies operate in part as a means for training and testing future permanent workers. I do not see these relations changing any more rapidly in the next several decades than they have in the past.

But how then will firms obtain the greater flexibility that they arguably need in the labor area? If they do not shift from employment to sales contract by outsourcing work and hiring temporary employees, how will they survive?

My answer is that they will gain flexibility by altering the compensation package toward contingent pay as opposed to fixed wages or salaries. These methods of compensation simultaneously tie workers' financial well-being to that of the firm and create labor costs that vary with the performance of the firm. Many employees—especially the young owners of the intellectual capital critical in the new world of work—want ownership shares in their firms. They will not work for a firm that pays standard wages or that fails to give them a piece of the action. In turn, companies want to keep these workers and increasingly use share ownership to motivate them.

I believe that flexibility based on contingent compensation will prove to be more efficient than flexibility based on virtual employees and that we will see stronger links between workers and firms rather than the end of the job. An increasingly educated and aging workforce will not accept a life of virtual employment, at least not without a huge welfare state or insurance apparatus to maintain living standards in the intervals between jobs. The less educated and skilled may fall into a low-level contingent status; and some part of the educated and skilled workforce may find self-employment and independent contracting more lucrative than working for pay but the majority will find their interests more permanently aligned with their employer through contingent shared capitalist contracts.

The Work/Jobs/Leisure Debate
But will there be much work for anyone to do in the next century?

In the mid-1990s, with unemployment high in many advanced countries and the newspapers full of stories of layoffs, Jeremy Rifkind argued that the advanced world was entering a new era marked not by the end of the permanent job but by "the end of work," at least for those who did not fit into the information elite.[3] His solution: job creation in nonprofit or government-sponsored cultural activities. Other analysts such as Juliet Schor have called for reduced work time to allow for a less harried and more bucolic life.[4]

On a world scale, the idea that we have reached a point where a vast majority of people can do away with work is lunacy. Most people live in less developed countries where the prime need is for increased GDP, not increased leisure. In the most advanced capitalist country, the United States, the end-of-work vision also seems far off the mark. The employment-population rate in the United States in the 1990s rose to historic highs; the prevalence of dual earner families working more hours to achieve middle class living standards; the decision of most women with children less than five years old to work full-time all show that people want more rather than less work. And the consumption-based/consumer-debt-based U.S. boom shows no sign of a surfeit of demand for goods or services. As for business, American firms have convinced Congress to grant special visas to foreign high-tech workers to deal with alleged shortages while the economy absorbs hundreds of thousands of less skilled immigrants. Some U.S. commentators even claim that the nation has developed "a new economy" with perpetual full employment and low inflation.

To Europeans, stuck with high unemployment rates, the notion of the end of work or, perhaps more properly, a shortage of jobs, has some appeal. In their analysis of computerized technical change, Chris Freeman and Luc Soete worry that the new information/communication technology will create mass unemployment for a long time, as the economic system struggles to adapt.[5] Many European unions and governments endorse worksharing as a cure to joblessness—reductions in hours worked of the employed to create jobs for the unemployed. Unlike Americans, Europeans generally seek greater leisure, with unions taking a lead in trading off potential wage increases for reduced working hours. The historical trend for time worked to fall with rising incomes would also seem to work in favor of reduced time worked over the next century, if not of the end of work.

So what is more likely in the future? More work or less work? A shortage of jobs or a shortage of workers?

The key labor supply parameters for answering this question are the income elasticity of leisure and the substitution effect of wages on work. Unfortunately, there are no fully accepted estimates of these parameters, and even if there were, no surety that today's parameters will hold in the future. Income and substitution effects are behavioral parameters, not universal constants. They are likely to change as the nature or type of work changes, as the availability of goods changes, and as the technology for leisure changes. Even perfect knowledge of these parameters, moreover, will not give forecasts of whether demand for leisure or work will dominate the future. We need also to know future income levels and the incentive to work—the difference in lifetime incomes between persons who work more or less. In economies with large welfare states and egalitarian income distributions, people work fewer hours than in the United States or United Kingdom for the simple reason that work pays off less on the margin in those settings. Any prediction about whether work time will increase or decrease is intrinsically linked to predictions about the incentive structure and the pattern of inequality in the economy.

If I am correct about the greater role of contingent compensation in firms and greater employee participation in the revenue stream of firms, then the incentive for work will increase. It may balance out or even overpower the effect of rising incomes on the demand for leisure. Not every society may decide that the American workaholic model is the right one, but the notion that work will come to an end for the bulk of the population even in the most advanced countries seems wrong.

Working Virtual or Traditional

But how will people work in the future? In their homes or at cafes or in offices? Independently with a big say in their firm or as flunkies under the control of the masters of the new information technology? For huge multinationals or for smaller niche producing firms?

The answers to these questions depend critically on how society manages the information and communication technological revolution —"the biggest technological juggernaut that ever rolled."[6] The computer has already altered most work sites in advanced countries. At one point, people thought that the computer would create a paperless office, but this seems wrong in two ways. Workers and firms want paper records, and the increased efficiency of processing information has created demand for more information. Some observers think that the computer and the Internet will move the locus of production from workplaces to homes, but this also seems wrong in two ways. People want face-to-face interactions with their co-workers, and they often need the tacit knowledge of others to proceed with their work. While work could shift from workplaces to other sites over the next century— working in a cafe may meet the social needs, and the Internet might offer sufficient outside knowledge to assist workers—the current trend is in the other direction, with more firms providing child-care facilities to workers, moving household activities into the work area. Perhaps the correct forecast is that the new information technologies will simply reduce the space barrier between work and home.

Workers today want greater participation in workplace decisions, and managers, lacking the technical information or skills, increasingly empower workers or teams of workers to make key decisions. But if decisions are decentralized, firms must align the worker interests with those of the firm. This underlies the growth of several forms of shared capitalist contingent pay—giving all employees rather than just top managers stock options, shares of profits, and so on. New information/communication technologies that differentiate the skills of workers from managers will strengthen this trend. But the new technology also raises a very different possibility. It increases the ability of management to monitor workers more closely, raising the danger of Big Brother-oversight of workers. Privacy at workplaces will be contested terrain in the next century. My bet here is that the forces leading to increased incentives and employee participation in decisions will dominate 1984-style monitoring in the next century just as decentralized market decision making dominated centralized planning in the past century.

Information-technology offers opportunities for individual entrepreneurs and small businesses to compete with established firms in the marketplace, but it also offers opportunities for monopolization of production by large multinationals. Will the size of firms increase or decrease as a result?

The issue hinges on economies of scale in production of physical goods and in e-commerce, and to a lesser extent, on the mergers and acquisitions by which existing firms seek to eliminate new competitors. Windows or Linux? One big Internet store or a world of small specialists? Walmart.com or mom-and-pop.com? At this writing, not even the Delphic Oracle could give an answer to these questions.

Finally, the Internet is affecting the way people find employment. The flow of information on jobs through the Web is huge and certain to grow. An increasing number of persons know about opportunities and make their availability known to employers through the Internet. An increasing proportion of job transactions are likely to be initiated and eventually take place over the Internet. The job market of the future will begin with e-commerce.

An Apartheid Economy?

In the 1980s, the distribution of income in the United States and the United Kingdom grew increasingly unequal. In other advanced countries, inequality in employment grew. As centralized wage-setting systems retreated in various countries—Sweden and Italy, in particular—

wage inequality began growing there as well. Analysts have given many reasons for rising inequality: globalization, technological change associated with the computer, deceleration of the growth of the educated workforce, immigration of less skilled workers to the West, weakened labor market institutions; falls in the minimum wage (U.S. case). Most analysts stress technological change as the prime driving force for the rise of inequality, though the evidence is far from compelling. Most analysts, myself included, believe that globalization has not been the critical factor that protectionists fear, but we could be wrong. In any case, the standard analysis predicts that inequality will continue to increase: technology is not going away, and more workers in LDCs will join the global economy.

The 1990s full employment boom in the United States raises questions, however, about whether this analysis is on target. During this boom full employment arrested the growth of inequality and raised the wages and employment of less skilled workers, suggesting that analysts may have overplayed the strength of the structural forces producing inequality. If the United States can maintain full employment and if other Western economies reattain it, perhaps the income distribution in the future will narrow rather than widen. If not? A return to 6–7 percent unemployment in the United States will raise inequality, bringing the United States closer to an apartheid economy (Freeman 1998) where the distribution of income is highly bifurcated between the super-wealthy— the upper 1 percent or so of the income distribution who have gained the most from recent economic progress—and the rest of society, with a socially excluded segment made up disproportionately of minorities, single parents, and children at the bottom. Squeezed in between the super-wealthy and the poor are the middle class—the key group in representative democracies. Some analysts view a highly unequal apartheid economy as economically or socially nonviable. But I believe that modern capitalism can survive and thrive with such inequality, so that this is one possible future for advanced countries.

Frictionless Economy or Renaissance of Institutions?

Some observers believe that the new information-communication technology, the Internet, will create the economists' dream general equilibrium world—an essentially frictionless market where a single price rules, determined by supply and demand with little institutional intervention.

Since information will be freely available at the click of a mouse, economic decisions will at long last be based on full information. Such a world has little place for traditional labor market institutions. Trade unions? Once they had a useful role to play in society, but no more. The decline of union density in the private sector in the United States, the United Kingdom, and some other countries and the loss of union influence even in countries where density has remained high provides some empirical backing for this view. Perhaps the invisible hand will finally find its home on the Internet. Perhaps the economic world of the next century will more closely resemble our models than our models resemble the world they were meant to depict. Truth being stranger than fiction, or life copying art, or something like that.

Are we moving into a frictionless and institutionless economy and labor market?

Surprisingly, there is no empirical evidence that the low search cost on the Internet is producing the single price. The major study of the issue has found that the dispersion of prices for books and CDs sold on the Internet is greater than the dispersion of identical products in conventional retail stores.[7] The evidence from behavioral finance that even in the financial market, which does establish a single price, there are numerous anomalies in the variation of prices over time does not bode well for the Internet's validating the simplest invisible hand model.

Even if the new information/communication produces a single price for goods and brings the real world more in line with economic models, I doubt that we will see the end of institutions. The tendency for workers to organize to improve their lot, by providing collective goods or by lobbying/bargaining for a greater share of economic rents, is not some anomaly due to market imperfections. It is a universal pattern—a natural part of economic activity. And when workers lack the wherewithal to look after their own interests, other concerned citizens—pro bono lawyers, nongovernment organizations—take up their cause. Historically, unions have grown in spurts, with surprising similarity in timing across countries. These spurts usually involve organizing traditionally nonunion workers and altering the institution to fit those workers. In the United States today doctors whose power at workplaces has been limited by HMOs are unionizing rapidly. Finally, modern information/technology strengthens the power of social groups, as much or arguably more than it strengthens market forces. The immediate access of information on the Internet creates a global social activist community and widens the scope for these groups to "make trouble" for the establishment.

In short, I expect that rather than seeing a withering away of unions or related worker-based institutions, we will see a new burst of labor organization in the future—probably in the form of occupational or craft style unions or guilds or more aggressive professional associations and in the form of social activist groups using the new technologies to enhance their powers.

Wildcards

There are potentially more dramatic changes in technology that could massively alter the world of work and even human life as we know it in the next century. Potential changes in the physical sciences include:

• Discovery of new forms of energy that greatly reduce the cost of energy. Cold fusion was a pipe dream, but nuclear fusion, superconductors, and other forms of new technology that will reduce energy costs are likely to come on board in the next century.

• Nanotechnology. The miniaturization of all sorts of things will increase our control over the natural world and affect productivity and work, possibly along the dimensions that nano-afficianados expect.[8] As we learn how to manipulate matter at the level of atoms, the possibilities for creating new materials, curing diseases, producing whatever commodities we wish—manna from heaven, gold from iron, and so forth—will be immense.

• Space travel and production in an environment without gravity. Science fiction comes to economics.

• Biotechnology. Every day the science journals and shortly thereafter (or sometimes before) the media reports on remarkable new findings and breakthroughs in biological sciences. The cloning of Dolly the sheep in the United Kingdom. New neurons forming in monkey brains. The rapid success of the human genome project. Genetic engineering, which ultimately will create the possibility of developing people or animals for specialized work. Genetic modification of food that could increase the productivity of agriculture. In the life sciences progress has the potential for transforming humans into something different, with powerful consequences for the world of work.

If there is one constant in the advance of science and technology, it is that scientists and engineers almost invariably make progress much faster than they themselves would ever have predicted. Barring social disaster, these advances should raise productivity and living standards—perhaps by enough to make the "end of work" scenario less unrealistic than it appears to me at this point.

All told, my substantive prognostication from the wild cards is a positive one. I expect modern information communication technology to create productive opportunities that will require firms to incentivize and empower workers and that will increase the opportunities for workplace democracy, decentralizing decision making and labor market institutions. However, I am near certain that there will be some major development or event that has utterly escaped my imagination that will shake up our economies and working lives. Any honest seer knows that in peering into the future the only certainty is that the future will surprise us. Chaos and power laws and nonlinear dynamics as well as our own ignorance guarantee as much.

Notes

1. William Sherden, *The Fortune Sellers.*

2. For a detailed discussion see Eric Weinstein.

3. Jeremy Rifkind, *The End of Work.*

4. Juliet B. Schor, *The Overworked American.*

5. Chris Freeman and Luc Soete, *Work for All or Mass Unemployment?*

6. Freeman and Soete, 39.

7. Erik Brynolfsson and Michael Smith "Frictionless Commerce?"

8. B. C. Crandall, *Nanotechnology*; K. Eric Drexler, *Nanosystems*; Edward Regis and Mark Chimsky, eds., *Nano: The Emerging Science of Nanotechnology.*

References

Breneman, David, and Richard Freeman. 1974. "Forecasting the Ph.D. Labor Market: Pitfalls for Policy." *National Board of Graduate Education.*

Brynolfsson, Erik, and Michael Smith. 1999. "Frictionless Commerce? A Comparison of Internet and Conventional Retailers." http://e-commerce.mit.edu/papers/

Chimsky, Mark, and Edward Regis, eds. 1996. *Nano: The Emerging Science of Nanotechnology.* Boston: Little Brown and Co.

Crandall, B. C. 1996. *Nanotechnology: Molecular Speculations on Global Abundance.* Cambridge: MIT Press.

Drexler, K. Eric. 1992. *Nanosystems: Molecular Machinery, Manufacturing, and Computation.* New York: John Wiley.

Freeman, Chris, and Luc Soete. 1994. *Work for All or Mass Unemployment?* Greenwich: JAI Press.

Freeman, Richard. 1977. "Manpower Requirements and Substitution Analysis of Labor Skills: A Synthesis." In *Research in Labor Economics*, edited by R. Ehrenberg. Greenwich: JAI Press.

————. 1980. "An Empirical Analysis of the Fixed Coefficient Manpower Requirements Model, 1960–1970." *Journal of Human Resources* 15, no. 2 (Spring): 176–199.

————. 1996. "Toward an Apartheid Economy." *Harvard Business Review*, September–October: 114–126.

Goldsmith, James. 1994. *The Trap.* New York: Carroll & Graf.

Rifkind, Jeremy. 1995. *The End of Work.* New York: Putnam.

Rosenthal, Neal. 1999. "The Quality of BLS Projections: A Historical Account." *Monthly Labor Review* (May), tables 2 and 3.

Schor, Juliet B. 1993. *The Overworked American: The Unexpected Decline of Leisure.* New York: Basic Books.

Sherden, William. 1995. *The Fortune Sellers.* New York: John Wiley.

Meadows, Dennis, and Donella Meadows. *The Limits to Growth: A Report for the Club of Rome's Project on the Predicament of Mankind.*

Nature. 1992. Editorial comment. No. 356 (16 April): 548.

Simon, H. 1957. "A Formal Theory of the Employment Relation." In *Models of Man: Social and Rational.* New York: John Wiley.

Weinstein, Eric. 1999. "How and Why Government, Universities, and Industry Create Domestic Labor Shortages of Scientists and High-Tech Workers." http://www.nber.org/~peat/Papersfolder/Papers/SG/NSF.html

7

Threats to Future Effectiveness of Monetary Policy

Benjamin M. Friedman

The mid-1960s Henry Levin film *Genghis Khan* featured a rugged-looking Omar Sharif in the title role playing opposite Robert Morley, at his plump and pompous best as the Chin emperor Wang Wei-shao. One of the film's early scenes shows the exquisitely attired Morley, calligraphy brush in hand, elegantly composing a poem. With an ethereal self-assurance born of unquestioning confidence in the divinely ordained course of worldly affairs, Morley explains that the poem's purpose is to express his displeasure at the Mongol barbarians who have lately been creating a disturbance on the Chin empire's western frontier, and, by so doing, cause them to desist.

Today expressions of intentions by leaders of the world's major central banks typically have immediate repercussions in financial markets, and perhaps more broadly as well. Does Chairman Greenspan believe that the U.S. business expansion has advanced to the point where a new round of wage inflation may be imminent? Did President Duisenberg imply that because Article 103 of the Maastricht Treaty refers to Article 102a, and both Article 102a and Article 105 refer to Article 2, Europe's chronic high unemployment may be a proper object of policy concern for the European Central Bank after all? Is Governor Hayami content to allow Japan to languish in a slump for yet another half-decade? Central bankers' public utterances and other, more subtle signals on such questions regularly move prices and yields in the financial markets, and these financial variables in turn affect nonfinancial economic activity in a variety of ways. Indeed, a widely shared opinion today is that central banks need not actually *do* anything. With a clear enough statement of intentions, "the markets will do the work for them."

In truth, the ability of central banks to affect the evolution of prices and output in the nonfinancial economy has always been something of a mystery. It is not that there are no good accounts of how this influence might arise. There are many. The problem is rather that each such story, while plausible enough at first or even second thought, turns out to depend on one or another of a series of by now familiar fictions: households and firms need currency to purchase goods and services. Banks can issue only reserve-bearing liabilities. No nonbank financial institutions create credit. And so on.

This central mystery notwithstanding, at the practical level there is today little doubt that a country's monetary policy not only can but does largely determine the evolution of its general price level over the medium to longer run, and almost as little doubt that monetary policy exerts significant influence over aspects of real economic activity, like output and employment, over the short to medium run. The assumptions necessary to explain in simple terms how this happens are fictions, but they are useful fictions. Apart from purely empirical matters of magnitude and timing, the live question today is which set of fictions (that is, which model) provides the most useful description of the underlying causal process.

Circumstances change over time, however, and when they do the fictions that once described matters adequately may no longer do so. A later scene in Levin's film shows Morley still magnificently clothed but now lying in the mud, face blackened by gunpowder, in the wake of a Mongol attack on the Chin capital. There may well have been an earlier time when the might of the Chin empire was such that the mere suggestion of willingness to use it was sufficient to make potential invaders reconsider and withdraw. But by Wang Wei-shao's day that time had evidently passed.

The object of this paper is to consider the possible future of central banks' monetary policy making—say, over the next quarter-century—in light of several significant aspects of how the circumstances that bear on this process have been changing over the past quarter-century. Simply extrapolating in this way the recent development of financial market institutions and practices is, of course, no substitute for actually knowing what lies ahead, but doing so at least provides some observationally grounded basis for thinking about the future. The point is to work out the implications for central banks' ability to carry out monetary policy. The question of what to do in response to those implications, should they indeed materialize, lies beyond the scope of this paper.

In keeping with the structure and themes of this conference on "Social Science and the Future," the first section pauses to consider the major issues on which monetary economists have, in the past, made predictions about what then represented the future. In retrospect, what is striking about the field in this regard has been not the record of success or failure but rather the inability to achieve agreement, even on first-magnitude issues of public import within this area of economics.

The second section then sets the stage for the main inquiry undertaken in this paper by asking just how a central bank's monetary policy actions influence financial markets (and, in turn, nonfinancial economic activity) in the first place. The answer to this question turns on the central bank's role as a legally maintained monopolist—in particular, a monopolist over the supply of bank reserves.

The third section sets forth the paper's main concern for the future of monetary policy: the possibility that the further progress of any or all of several trends, already visible in the financial markets of many countries today, may weaken or even undermine the relevance of the central bank's monopoly. The concern is that if this were to occur, then except for sheer self-fulfilling expectations analogous to what Wang Wei-shao mistakenly thought his poems would engender, the central bank would be powerless to move interest rates and hence also unable to affect either prices or real outcomes (like output and employment) in the nonfinancial economy.

The fourth section extends this line of argument to consider several aspects of these potential developments that arise in an explicitly international context.

The final section concludes with brief remarks on what to make of all this from a normative policy perspective.

Some Past Predictions from Monetary Economics

What can individual disciplines within the social sciences say now about prospects for the intermediate-term future—roughly a quarter-century ahead? A useful preliminary to that inquiry is to look back on what success or failure these same disciplines have had, in the past, in assessing prospects for what is now the present.

Anyone at all familiar with the field of monetary economics knows that the researchers and policy makers engaged in this particular line of

economic inquiry often fail to display unanimity on important questions. This tendency toward disagreement has been strikingly evident
within the past quarter-century. It has also been characteristic of views
on issues with fairly immediate implications for what lay ahead no less
than issues that are more narrowly analytical in the descriptive sense.
As a result, it is difficult to represent the field as a whole as either successful or unsuccessful, right or wrong, in anticipating the major trends
that have emerged in recent years. In short, on any given question experience has shown some views (and some economists) right, others
wrong.

Among the issues of the last twenty-five years that have especially
lent themselves to drawing inferences about the future, three stand out as
having not only generated widespread attention within monetary economics but also borne on issues of sufficient public import to reach the
attention of economists and noneconomists alike.

Money Growth Targets for Monetary Policy

The live issue on which monetary economics achieved the greatest degree of consensus (among the three considered here) is the extent to
which the growth of one or another measure of "money" is reliably related to the growth of income and prices and hence provides a useful
operating guide by which central banks can and should steer their
monetary policy. As the financial systems of one country after another
recovered from the dislocations and stringent regulation associated with
World War II, central banks in countries that ran independent monetary
policies (as opposed to, for example, simply pegging the value of their
currency against some other currency) mostly did so by setting interest
rates. By the 1960s, however—and especially by the mid-1970s—this
procedure displayed clear shortcomings.

At the simplest level, the emergence of price inflation meant that
the "nominal" interest rates observed in financial markets did not correspond closely to the corresponding "real" interest rates that presumably affect nonfinancial economic activity. More fundamentally, however,
because an interest rate is merely a *relative* price—it is the price of dollars
or yen or marks today versus dollars or yen or marks at some specified
date later on—a fixed interest rate meant that there was nothing to an-
chor the economy's price level. In principle, a central bank that was
simply fixing an interest rate stood ready to see *any* amount of money in

the public's hands, and by extension any level of prices in the economy, as long as the interest rate remained at the chosen level.

At the same time, economists also observed that in many countries some quantitative measure of "money," however defined for practical purposes, appeared to move closely with fluctuations of either income or prices or both. The suggestion therefore followed that by fixing the growth of money, a country's central bank could more closely influence its rate of business expansion or price inflation or both. In time, widely understood analysis of these ideas showed that whether choosing an interest rate or choosing a money growth rate (or attempting some compromise procedure) gave the central bank better control over such matters as inflation and employment depended not on first principles but rather on quantitative relationships that could only be assessed empirically. Because monetary economics is not a laboratory science capable of generating replicable experiments, the evidence available from actual experience is often incapable of clearly resolving such questions. Hence much disagreement persisted on the "money growth versus interest rates" debate. But it is fair to say that as of twenty-five years ago a clear majority of active monetary economists thought choosing money growth was the better procedure.

As a result of this line of thinking, in the 1970s many central banks around the world adopted formal targets for the growth of one or another measure of money. In the United States the Federal Reserve System did so halfheartedly in 1970, more seriously in 1975 under the prodding of a mandate legislated by Congress, and with still greater commitment beginning in 1979. The Deutsche Bundesbank adopted a money growth target in 1974. The Bank of England did so in 1976. (Beginning in 1975, and more so after 1978, the Bank of Japan often referred to a "money focused" policy and even used explicit money growth forecasts, but it is doubtful that Japan ever had genuine money growth targets.) In each case, procedural issues remained to be addressed —which measure of money? over what horizon? how to respond when actual money growth deviated from the target?—but the majority opinion among monetary economists was that these problems were resolvable and that money growth targets should be the centerpiece of formulating and conducting monetary policy.

Today few central banks still carry out monetary policy in this way. The conversation is instead—once again—almost entirely in terms of what (short-term) interest rate to choose. The Federal Reserve System began to de-emphasize money growth targets in the mid-1980s and finally made clear their unimportance to U.S. monetary policy in 1993. The Bank of England reduced money growth targets to a secondary status in 1988 and abandoned them in 1990. The Bundesbank never acknowledge any reduced importance of its money growth target, but over the years its policy choices increasingly resulted in actual money growth either faster or slower than the designated range. The new European Central Bank has formally stated that it regards money growth as one of the two "pillars" of its approach to conducting monetary policy (the other is the bank's inflation forecast), but it remains unclear how the two fit together and thus far actual E.C.B. policy making seems mostly to consist of choosing an interest rate anyway. Only the Swiss National Bank continues to rely on money growth targets as if nothing had changed. (Note: At the end of 1999 the Swiss National Bank too abandoned its monetary targets.)

And what did change? Put quite simply, the observed relationships connecting money growth to the movement of income and prices either deteriorated or collapsed outright in most countries. Plausible explanations for this phenomenon include the introduction of new financial technologies (both in the hardware used for data processing and communications and in the product designs offered by issuers of deposits), changing government or central bank regulations, increased interconnections among the respective financial systems in different countries, and even new attitudes among investors, businesspeople, and consumers as a consequence of their having lived through a period of rapid inflation. But for whatever reason, money-income and money-price relationships broke down. (As Bank of Canada Governor John Crow put it, "We didn't abandon the monetary aggregates. They abandoned us.")

But it was these empirical relationships that had stood behind the (near) consensus on the usefulness of money growth targets. Most monetary economists overestimated the durability of these relationships over time. As a result, they advocated a policymaking framework that most central banks have since had to abandon.

Costs of Disinflation
A pervasive problem among the world's industrialized economies a quarter-century ago—indeed, part of the motivation for adopting money

growth targets for monetary policy—was high inflation. Economists and central bankers widely believed that they knew how to solve this problem: simply reduce the pace of economic activity to the point at which excess supplies (of labor for hire, finished products for sale, raw materials, investment goods, and so on) slowed the upward spiral of wages and prices. But they also widely believed that along with slowing inflation, this kind of policy would impose large costs in terms of foregone output, jobs, incomes, and profits. Hence the dilemma that led many countries to do little or nothing about inflation at all, and others to resort to intrusive (and often ineffective) controls on wages and prices.

A new line of thinking advanced in the 1970s disagreed, arguing instead that *foreknowledge* of a disinflationary policy would reduce—in the limit, eliminate altogether—such a policy's real costs. The basic claim was that, in making decisions about real economic activities like how much to work, or what and how much to produce, workers and firms would be indifferent to their economy's overall inflation rate (or, equivalently, its overall price level) as long as they knew in advance what it would be. What sometimes led them to make decisions that took the economy away from full employment was being surprised by inflation that was either faster or slower (and therefore prices that were either higher or lower) than they had expected. Under this view disinflationary policy depressed economic activity only because the disinflation took people by surprise. A fully anticipated disinflation would instead be, in principle, costless.

At an intuitive level what was novel in this line of thinking was its application in the short to intermediate run of economic principles that were familiar, indeed widely accepted, as a description of the long run. Nobody believes that the level of output and employment in the United States in the year 2100 will depend much on whether the evolution of prices over the next hundred years is such that the typical worker's weekly wage at the century's end is $1,000 or $2,000, or even $5,000. Fundamental forces of human desire, productivity, and capital accumulation (importantly including the accumulation of knowledge, skills, and organizational insights) will determine real outcomes like output and employment, as well as real wages, over this horizon. But the idea that one price level versus another would not matter for real outcomes *next year*, as long as whatever level price were to prevail was fully anticipated, was new. And because it bore directly on one of the most important policy issues of the day, it was not just new but interesting.

Here far more than on the question of money growth targets, opinion was divided. Not surprisingly, analysis showed that this argument for the potential costlessness of disinflationary policy hinged on several important conditions, and how closely the circumstances of any given economy approximated those conditions was an empirical question. But shifting the debate to focus on required conditions, rather than implied outcomes per se, did little to resolve it.

In the end experience was also mixed. The disinflation that most industrialized countries have achieved over the last two decades has come at heavy cost. Output declined, unemployment rose (temporarily in the United States, but to date without reversal in many European countries), and profits and investment lagged. Hence any simple rendering of the "disinflation is costless" argument proved plainly wrong.

But it was also true that, by some measures, disinflation was less costly than many of the more pessimistic assessments had warned. In the United States, for example, a significant part of this story was a shift in the relationship between output and labor input. Measured by the rise in unemployment, the U.S. disinflation of the 1980s turned out to be almost precisely as costly as the earlier, pessimistic estimates had indicated. But measured by the shortfall of output from the existing trend, it was distinctly less so. In retrospect, the persistent disagreement stands out more than the clarity of the experience.

Need for Institutional Change
A different reaction to the phenomenon of chronic high inflation in so many countries was the suggestion, among some monetary economists, that this problem was the natural consequence of policymaking institutions that impart an inflationary bias to decisions made under them. The focus of this line of argument was the leeway that most central banks had always had to use "discretion" in deciding how to conduct monetary policy. Under some conditions, central banks exercising that discretion on a year-to-year (or even more frequent) basis would seek to boost output and employment by choosing an easier monetary policy than what firms and workers expected, thereby also allowing faster-than-expected inflation. But once that faster inflation had occurred, people might expect it to continue. Then the only way to boost output and employment again would be to choose a sufficiently easy monetary policy that inflation would be faster still. Over time, the result implied by this argument was an inflation rate that ratcheted ever higher, and that

policymakers would be reluctant to reduce for fear of triggering declines in output and employment.

The positive suggestion that followed from this line of thinking was that the way to reduce inflation, and then keep it low, was to amend policymaking institutions so as to take away central banks' discretion. The most severe way to do so would be to adopt some form of constitutional provision (in those countries with written constitutions) mandating a specific noninflationary monetary policy. Less extreme measures toward this end might be a legislative mandate along the same lines, or perhaps even a fixed regimen that the central bank could impose on itself.

The link between this idea and the "costless disinflation" debate that had arisen only slightly earlier was the crucial role assigned to workers' and firms' expectations, and hence to the credibility of the central bank's commitment to an anti-inflation policy. Under one view, disinflation would be costless if everyone believed it was coming. Under the other, what mattered was knowing that the central bank would not—because it could not—try to stimulate the economy by an inflationary policy. The two were clearly related. But in the latter case the focus was on the institutional arrangements under which the central bank makes policy, rather than on the central bank's choices directly.

Here too opinion among monetary economists was sharply divided. Some called for institutional change of a variety of forms, mostly at either the legislative or the internal central bank level. Others rejected this entire line of thinking as having little bearing on the actual problem of inflation in economies where conditions differed from those assumed in the underlying theory.

Whatever the potential relevance of this idea, experience showed that formal institutional change was not a necessary element in a successful disinflation. Most of the industrialized countries that have achieved virtual price stability over the last two decades did so under monetary policymaking institutions no different than they had before, when inflation was such a problem. (The United States is an especially good example in this regard.) Even in countries that have recently changed their policymaking institutions, in most cases the change occurred *after* inflation had slowed. (The establishment of the European Central Bank, with its primary if not exclusive focus on price stability, is an apt example here.) Some elements emphasized in this line of thinking, like the importance of the central bank's "reputation," or of appointing central bankers whose personal policy preferences are highly averse to inflation, may well have been key to the success that occurred. But formal institutional change was not.

On this question as well, however, the more salient point is that opinion was divided. It is impossible to say whether "monetary economics" got the future right or not. Many monetary economists did, but many didn't.

The Central Bank as Monopolist

The influence of central banks, especially over nonfinancial economic activity but even over the financial markets, has always been something of a puzzle. The easiest way to see why this is so is to consider the small size of most central banks, and the even smaller size of their monetary policy operations, in relation to the economies that they supposedly influence. In the United States, for example, a year's production of final output is more than $8.5 *trillion*. Including the production and exchange of intermediate goods and services, the volume of nonfinancial transactions that take place in the course of a year is several times $8.5 trillion. Yet the total volume of reserves that banks and other financial institutions maintain with the Federal Reserve System is less than $50 *billion*. And the difference between 2 percent per annum growth of reserves (which most observers would consider a tight monetary policy, all else equal) and 10 percent per annum reserves growth (which most would think highly expansionary) is whether the Federal Reserve buys $1 billion or $5 billion of securities over an entire year.

The more typical way of looking at the central bank's influence over the nonfinancial economy sidesteps these quantitative disparities by focusing on market interest rates. Firms as well as households rely on borrowing to finance their spending for many purposes, from putting up factories and houses to buying new cars and refrigerators, to paying college tuitions or simply taking vacations. It is not surprising that the cost of financing these expenditures therefore affects the willingness to undertake them. Moreover, in many cases where spending does not rely on borrowing, interest rates and expected asset returns more generally represent the relevant opportunity cost. Hence the ability to affect interest rates and asset returns is in turn sufficient to enable the central bank to affect spending in nonfinancial markets.

But this line of thinking only pushes the anomaly to be explained into a different arena: how, exactly, does the central bank affect interest rates? Here again, even a quick glance at the relevant magnitudes highlights the problem. In the United States, for example, the outstanding volume of securities issued directly by the U.S. Treasury is $3.7 *trillion*. Including issues of U.S. government-sponsored and guaranteed agencies brings the overall size of the government securities market to $7.1 trillion. Further including privately issued but publicly traded debt instruments that are close substitutes for government securities of one maturity or other brings the total size of the U.S. fixed-income securities market to $13.6 trillion. In 1998 alone, insurance companies bought (on net) $101 billion of securities in this market, pension funds bought $186 billion, banks bought $82 billion, and households liquidated $57 billion of securities that they already owned. Gross trading volume is typically in the hundreds of billions of dollars *daily*, and it is not unusual for a single private firm to buy or sell more than $1 billion of securities in a single transaction. Yet it is somehow supposed to make a major difference, for the entire level and structure of prices and yields in this nearly $14 trillion market, whether the Federal Reserve buys or sells $1 billion or $5 billion of securities *over an entire year*.

As table 7.1 shows, a similar disparity between the magnitude of central banks' monetary policy operations and the size of the markets in which they operate is characteristic of other economies as well. Going on to consider currency substitution—in other words, the fact that for many investors a debt security denominated in a foreign currency is an actual or potential portfolio substitute for a comparable debt security denominated in the currency of the investor's country of residence—only makes the disparity all that much greater from the perspective of any individual central bank (though not for all central banks taken together, as if they acted in concert). Considering equity securities as actual or potential substitutes for debt securities makes the disparity greater still, from the perspective of either a single central bank or all taken together. (The volume of equity securities held in U.S. markets was $15.4 trillion at 1998 yearend market prices.)

The standard explanation for central banks' ability to affect such large markets through such small operations is that transactions by the central bank are fundamentally different from transactions by private market participants. When a central bank buys securities, it makes payment by increasing the reserve account of the seller's bank, thereby

Table 7.1
Comparisons of Financial Magnitudes

	Percent of GDP				
	Bank reserves	Monetary base	Broad money	Out- standing govern- ment debt	Total domestic debt securities
Canada	0.6%	4.0%	43.4%	71.8%	84.5%
Euro-11	1.8	8.8	80.6	n.a.	n.a.
France	0.6	4.0	66.0	47.6	81.9
Germany	2.5	6.8	67.5	38.2	85.4
Italy	4.5	10.0	47.7	101.4	132.8
Japan	1.8	12.2	73.7	79.8	113.6
Sweden	0.6	4.9	47.5	55.4	122.8
Switzerland	2.7	10.6	106.9	21.4	70.7
United Kingdom	1.1	4.0	91.7	35.8	59.8
United States	0.5	6.3	70.5	43.8	163.8

Notes: All figures are percentages of GDP.
U.S. data, as of yearend 1998, are from the Board of Governors of the Federal Reserve System.
Euro-11 data, as of yearend 1998, are from the European Central Bank.
All other data, as of yearend 1997, are from the IMF (for bank reserves, monetary base, and broad money) and the BIS (for government and total domestic debt securities).

increasing the total volume of reserves that the banking system collectively holds. When a central bank sells securities, it receives payment by reducing the reserve account of the buyer's bank, thereby reducing the total volume of reserves. No other market participant can either increase or reduce the total volume of reserves. The central bank is a monopoly supplier (and withdrawer) of reserves.

This monopoly position matters because, under any of a variety of conceptions of the monetary policy process, banks and other financial institutions must hold reserves with the central bank in order to carry out the economic functions that households and firms look to them to perform. The traditional "money view" of monetary policy begins with households' and firms' demand for bank-issued money, against which banks must, by law, hold reserves (usually specified as some set fraction of each bank's outstanding deposits). When the monopolist central bank reduces the supply of reserves, banks therefore must reduce the amount of money that they supply to households and firms. As households and firms compete with one another to hold the now shrunken supply of money, their individual efforts to sell securities for money cannot produce any more money but do, collectively, drive the price of securities down—that is, they drive interest rates up.

The "credit view" of monetary policy focuses on a different aspect of the relationship between the financial and nonfinancial worlds, but for this purpose it leads to the same conclusion. Households and firms look to banks to extend loans (credit). Banks can do so only to the extent that they simultaneously create money—in other words, the respective totals on the two sides of any bank's balance sheet must always remain equal. But if banks must create money in order to advance credit, and creating more money means requiring more reserves, the central bank's role as monopoly supplier of reserves is again crucial. When the central bank reduces the supply of reserves, banks have to cut back on their lending, and the loan market will clear at a higher interest rate.

Under either the "money" or the "credit" view, therefore, the process by which monetary policy affects interest rates begins when the central bank buys or sells securities. In the case of a sale, the central bank receives payment by reducing the amount shown in the account that some bank maintains with the central bank itself. That bank therefore has less reserves than it did beforehand. If before this transaction the bank's reserves were just sufficient to meet its reserve requirement, based on its outstanding deposits, its reserves will now be insufficient. This bank may try to recoup its lost reserves by selling securities to someone else, but doing so only shifts the reserve deficiency from one bank to another. The only way for no bank to have a deficiency after the central bank sells securities (if all banks were just meeting their respective requirements at the outset) is to reduce the reserves that some bank is required to hold.

But since required reserves are based on deposits outstanding, this means inducing some bank customer(s) to hold a smaller volume of re-servable deposits. Moreover, the amount by which deposits need to fall in order to bring the banking system back into reserve compliance after the central bank sells securities is a multiple of the central bank's transaction. (If the reserve requirement is 10 percent, then the needed fall in deposits is ten times the sale of securities by the central bank.) One possibility is that a bank could induce some of its customers to switch from reservable deposits to some other bank-issued instrument, like a savings account or a CD. In order to do so, the bank would presumably have to raise the interest rates it offered on those other instruments. Alternatively, a bank could induce some customer to repay a loan, presumably by raising the interest rate it charged on bank credit. Equivalently, the bank could decide not to extend a new loan that it otherwise would have made. In this case the would-be borrower would have to seek credit elsewhere.

Any one of these responses (or all in combination) would, in sufficient volume, enable the banking system to meet its reserve requirements following a sale of securities by the central bank. And what all of these responses have in common is that they exert upward pressure on interest rates—from reselling the securities, from inducing customers to switch to savings accounts or CDs, from seeking early repayment of loans, or from denying credit to would-be borrowers. In each case the reaction triggered by the central bank's sale of securities pushes interest rates higher. (Conversely, reaction to a purchase of securities by the central bank would drive interest rates lower.) And in each case banks' need to hold required reserves with the central bank is the fulcrum of the process. Further, because banks also need to hold reserves to settle interbank payments, the same process would still be at work even in the absence of formal reserve requirements (more on this aspect below).

Some observers of financial markets, mindful of the intertemporal arbitrage conditions that relate the pricing of short- and long-term securities, attempt to skirt this kind of reasoning and argue that the central bank can affect interest rates on all but the shortest-term instruments— and hence can influence nonfinancial economic activity—merely by signaling its intention to change the prevailing level of short-term rates in the future. Hence a signal of intentions is sufficient to influence nonfinancial activity as well. The basic idea underlying this argument is that, apart from whatever risk and liquidity premia the market assesses, the yield on a two-year bond should equal the (geometric) average of the currently prevailing one-year yield and the expected one-year yield a year in the future. If the central bank does or says something that changes expectations about next year's short-term rate, it thereby moves today's long-term rate. And since many if not most kinds of spending by households and firms are more sensitive to long- (or at least medium-) than short-term interest rates, doing so thereby affects the nonfinancial economy as well. It is just this kind of reasoning that people have in mind when they speak of letting the markets do the central bank's work for it.

But this logic makes sense only if the central bank can credibly affect widely shared expectations of future short-term interest rates, and unless most market participants are prepared to be fooled most of the time, that in turn makes sense only if the central bank can indeed affect actual short-term interest rates when the time comes. And that ability relies on some process like the ones described by the familiar "money view" and "credit view." At the end of the logical chain, the central bank's role as the monopoly supplier of reserves is essential.

Threats to the Relevance of the Central Bank's Monopoly

It may seem odd, at the close of the twentieth century, to suggest that the ability of central banks to control or at least shape the development of their respective economies stands at risk. Two decades ago chronic price inflation had reached levels that profoundly disturbed not only many economists and public policy mavens but also much of the general public in most of the world's industrialized countries. In some countries prices threatened to rise even faster, perhaps explosively. Today inflation is negligible in most industrialized countries, and almost everyone awards central banks primary responsibility for this dramatic reversal. Over just the last decade many large economies have also experienced reduced instability of output and employment, and many people credit central banks for this accomplishment too. In short, it has been a good era for monetary policy.

But financial institutions and financial practices are changing, and the direction of many of these changes spells trouble for the ability of central banks to carry out their monetary policy responsibilities effectively. The heart of the matter lies in the way central banks influence market interest rates. In most countries there is no challenge to the central bank's position as the monopolist controlling the supply of reserves. Rather, the question is whether that monopoly will remain relevant.

Erosion of the Demand for Bank Money

Being a monopolist is of little value if nobody needs, or even wants, to have whatever the monopoly consists of. The "money view" of monetary policy begins from the assumption that households and firms need money, for transactions purposes or portfolio purposes or both, and goes on to exploit the fact that banks can create money only if they have the reserves they are required to hold in parallel with their outstanding deposits. (In the United States today, for example, banks are required to hold reserves against forms of deposits used to settle transactions but not against other kinds of deposits, like savings accounts and CDs.) That is what makes the central bank's monopoly over the supply of reserves relevant.

In recent years, however, the development of new technologies has advanced to the point where there are a variety of visible alternatives to conventional bank money as a means of undertaking transactions, and in some cases even of settling transactions. Especially with the introduction of third-party credit cards in the 1960s, and increasingly so since then, economists' standard "cash in advance" models have no longer borne much relation to arrangements for purchasing goods and services in the modern economy. For most items, neither cash in one's pocket nor an adequate balance in one's checking account is necessary at the time of purchase. More recent improvements like electronic cash, and "smart cards" (which have now made significant inroads in such countries as Germany, France, and Japan and are just coming into use in the United States), have accentuated this trend.

The reason central banks' influence over interest rates has survived these developments is that money, in the conventional sense, has remained necessary for ultimate settlement of these transactions. The merchants who accept Visa or Mastercard need to be paid, and that still means having conventional money deposited into their bank accounts. And once a month individuals who use these credit cards must make a payment by transferring conventional money out of their bank accounts (unless they borrow the money that is due—about which more below). For reasons well described by familiar models of the "transactions" and "precautionary" demand for money, the ability to buy goods and services at will throughout the month but then settle all of the transactions together at month's end may well reduce the typical household's or firm's average need to hold money balances, but it does not eliminate this need. Hence banks' demand for reserves may be smaller, for a given fractional reserve requirement, but it remains as well. As is well known, the central bank's ability to carry out monetary policy depends not on the size but on the stability of the demand for reserves.

The future may be different, however, in either of two ways that bear on just this question. First, some types of "smart cards"—for example, the single-vendor advance-payment cards already put into circulation by many telephone service providers (this practice is now especially widespread in Japan), or by the New York subway system—could develop into genuine private monies. In New York, for example, the Metropolitan Transit Authority has made several attempts, to date largely unsuccessful, to persuade city-area merchants to accept MTA smart cards in payment for purchases. Even if such cards were to gain acceptance, as long as issuers like the MTA in turn settled with merchants by transferring balances at banks, then in effect these cards would be no different from today's Visa or Mastercard. But it is easy to imagine how—twenty-five years in the future, after acceptance of such cards had become sufficiently widespread—firms would simply accept, and swap, balances on *the MTA's* books. (Hence the form of "smart card" in question here also differs importantly from today's MONDEX card, in which the issuer is always a bank and the redeemer is always a bank.)

Such a system would still involve the use of bank money, but only as the initial base of the value chain. The customer who buys a "smart card" from a nonbank firm would presumably pay for it using a bank check or cash. But to the extent that third parties were willing to accept balances on the nonbank firm's books in payment for their own transactions, there would be no need for the firm that issues the card to maintain bank balances to back up in full its corresponding liability. At that point, nonfinancial transactions made by swapping balances on that firm's books would take place independently of any new, contemporary use of bank money (or cash), and hence independently of any need for reserves at the central bank.

Needless to say, not all nonfinancial firms are equally plausible candidates to undertake this activity. Nonfinancial firms typically do not have access to the safety net that central banks, deposit insurance funds, and other government agencies normally maintain for banks. Hence a customer who buys this kind of "smart card" would have to have confidence in the permanence and soundness of the firm issuing it. Moreover, telephone companies and other widely used utilities have the further advantage that nearly everyone buys services from them on an ongoing basis. Even if customers bought a telephone company's advance-payment card and then found that no merchants would accept it, they could always use the balance on it (which, to recall, represents the company's liability to them) to pay their telephone bills.

Such a development would involve advancing these card systems, or other forms of e-cash, to the point where they would provide not merely payment but also settlement. At the moment this prospect is hardly imminent. But with rapidly advancing data processing and encryption technology, and the gradual disappearance of the visible distinction between banks and other businesses (importantly including nonfinancial firms) in the public's perception, the prospect is far from inconceivable a quarter-century in the future. As long as taking deposits and providing payment services is a source of profit for banks, bank customers—like telephone companies, New York's MTA, or the merchants whom the MTA would like to induce to use its cards—have an incentive to recoup some of their costs by undertaking a form of this activity themselves. And to the extent that they can pass on some of what they recoup to their own customers, individuals will have an incentive to use these alternative payment vehicles just as nonbank firms will have an incentive to provide them.

How would central banks respond? One possibility would be to engage in a regulatory race, in which the monetary authorities in each country continually expanded the coverage of reserve requirements to blanket new issuers of what amounts to money, while the issuers of private monies responded by continually changing their product in order to evade each new set of expanded requirements. Experience—for example, that of the Federal Reserve System in the 1960s, when the new instruments in question were Eurodollar deposits and negotiable CDs— suggests that this is a race the central banks might well lose.

If so, what would then be left to the central bank would be its control over the remainder of the monetary base, the great majority of which in most countries is not bank reserves but circulating currency. Although monetary theorists frequently write as if control over "central bank money" were all there was to monetary policy, and sometimes point to empirical correlations between a country's monetary base and its income or prices, currency has become increasingly irrelevant to legal, domestic transactions. Moreover, the observed correlations between growth of currency and growth of either income or prices mostly reflect the fact that central banks normally just accommodate whatever the public's demand for currency happens to be. If advances in electronic technology facilitate the use of private nonbank monies outside the scope of the central bank's reserve requirements, neither the nickels and dimes used in vending machines nor the $100 bills used to pay drug dealers will be sufficient to preserve the efficacy of monetary policy.

Cooperation of a central bank's government can also be an important part of the story. Governments typically make payments, for purposes of income transfers as well as purchases of goods and services, using deposit accounts at banks. It is fair to assume that they will continue to do so. Governments can also easily require that all tax payments be in the form of bank money (or an equivalent that is settled in bank money). Hence one sector of the economy—a large one in many countries—is a potentially captive market for this purpose. But the government sector is not what most people have in mind when they worry about the central bank's ability to influence nonfinancial economic activity. If private monies not linked to the holding of reserves were to proliferate, the fact that the government pays by check and requires all tax payments to be by bank check would not be sufficient to maintain the effectiveness of monetary policy either.

Proliferation of Nonbank Credit

An entirely different trend, but one that likewise threatens the relevance of the central bank's position as monopoly supplier of reserves, is the declining role of banks (and other depository intermediaries) in advancing credit to the nonfinancial economy. Under the "credit view" of monetary policy, banks are important not because they create deposits but because they make loans. Money creation is merely what happens on the other side of the balance sheet when a bank extends credit. But because the deposits thus created are subject to reserve requirements, this process too generates a demand for the reserves over which the central bank has a monopoly on supply. If the lender is not a bank, however, so that the liabilities behind the loan are not deposits, then credit creation ordinarily implies no increase in the demand for reserves.

In the United States banks have been losing market share in the credit business ever since World War II. In 1950 the financial assets (mostly loans and securities investments) of U.S. commercial banks represented 51 percent of the total assets of all U.S. financial intermediaries. By 1975 banks' market share had fallen to 38 percent. Today it is just 24 percent. Including savings institutions and credit unions, which also come within the scope of the central bank's reserve requirements, the combined share of the U.S. credit market accounted for by depository institutions was 65 percent in 1950, but only 30 percent today. The difference over time primarily represents the rapid advance of pension funds, insurance companies, and mutual funds—none of which hold reserves (in the sense of balances with the central bank) against their liabilities. In consequence, economists' empirical research on questions pertaining to the "credit view" of monetary policy mostly focuses not on aggregate business need for credit but only on those firms that are "bank dependent" by virtue of being too small, or otherwise insufficiently known, to borrow from nonbank lenders via the securities market.

There are two reasons, apart from simple extrapolation of past experience, for thinking that the trend toward diminished importance of banks and other depository intermediaries is likely to continue. First, advances in data processing technology, and therefore in the availability of information, are continually reducing the prevalence of the informational asymmetries that give bank-type "relationship" lending an advantage over "arm's length" lending in securities markets. Individual households seeking home mortgage financing, for example, no longer have to sit through extensive interviews with bank loan officers. In uncomplicated cases, which represent the majority of home financings, supplying standard information on line—information that potential lenders can in turn readily verify on line—is sufficient to produce a competitive loan offer within twenty-four hours.

And second, even for those households and firms that remain "bank dependent," securities markets have now advanced to the point where the bank that investigates the borrower's creditworthiness, originates the loan, and services the credit relationship, no longer needs to hold the loan in its own portfolio. Instead, today most kinds of bank-originated loans are regularly sold to firms that package them into aggregated portfolios of similar credits, which in turn stand as collateral behind securities owned and traded by market investors—the pension funds and insurance companies and mutual funds that are taking over market share from banks, as well as households who buy these securities directly on their own account.

In the United States, home mortgage lending was the first sector of the credit markets to be securitized in this way, under government sponsorship, and by now more than half (by dollar volume) of all home mortgages outstanding are held by securities market investors rather than by the banks or savings institutions that made the loans. Similarly, nearly two-thirds of government-sponsored student loans, all originated by banks, are securitized. But securitization has only just begun to gain momentum in other sectors of what until recently was primarily the banks' market. Today 28 percent of consumer credit, 17 percent of commercial mortgages, and 11 percent of firms' trade credit is securitized. There is now even a small but rapidly growing market in which banks are securitizing their ordinary commercial and industrial loans.

The import of securitization in this context is simply that it severs even the bank-originated component of the economy's credit extension process from any direct relation to the central bank's system of required reserves. A loan extended by a bank and held on the bank's balance sheet is financed by deposits, which are subject to reserve requirements. (In many countries not all kinds of deposits, and not all forms of nondeposit bank liabilities, are subject to reserve requirements; but this only makes the existing linkage weaker.) The same loan extended by the same bank but securitized and sold to a nonbank investor is financed by that investor's liabilities or net worth, neither of which is subject to reserve requirements. From the perspective of the "credit view," therefore, the central bank's monopoly over the supply of reserves becomes irrelevant.

Private Bank Clearing Mechanisms

In some countries today—for example, in the United Kingdom and Canada, and increasingly so among small banks in the United States since required reserve ratios were reduced in 1990 and 1991—many banks' motivation for holding reserve balances with the central bank actually has little or nothing to do with reserve requirements. These reserves are, rather, a necessary means of settling interbank transactions through the central bank's clearing mechanism. On any given day, a bank may have more checks presented for payment than checks deposited. If its reserve balance is insufficient to cover the difference, its account at the central bank will be overdrawn at the end of the day, in which case most central banks will assess a penalty of one form or other. If the central bank does not allow "daylight overdrafts," the bank must similarly maintain an adequate reserve balance to cover such contingencies even on an intra-day basis.

The role played by the interbank clearing mechanism in creating a demand for reserves is far removed from either the "money view" or the "credit view" of monetary policy—or any other standard textbook story, for that matter. (There is some ultimate connection to the "money view," since the use of bank money in executing day-to-day transactions is what creates the need for a clearing mechanism in the first place.) But nonetheless, and in just the same way, it gives the central bank the leverage to move large markets with tiny operations. The main point is once again that these clearing needs impose on banks, and therefore indirectly on the economy as a whole, a need for what the central bank is a monopolist over.

But competition can threaten this monopoly too. Private clearing mechanisms like the CHIPS network, and other privately maintained interbank netting systems like those studied in the 1990 report of the ad hoc BIS committee (the Lamfalussy Report), potentially represent just such threats. In a way that is conceptually parallel to nonfinancial businesses' incentive to introduce private monies in order to capture for themselves some of the profit that otherwise accrues to the banks, private clearing mechanisms like CHIPS offer banks the ability to econ-omize on either charges paid or collateral required in central bank set-tlement systems, like the Federal Reserve System's "Fedwire" or the European countries' systems that are now linked by the European Union's TARGET system. The crucial question is who is best situated to be the provider of financial network services. Central banks have some advantages in this regard, but their superiority is not unambiguous. And, again by analogy to the use of private monies, private settlement systems can be (and are) used along with the systems provided by central banks.

Most of the discussion of private clearing mechanisms to date has focused on the risks that they present for a breakdown of the payments system in the event of default, and as of today that prospect is certainly the more serious concern. Moreover, so far even these private mecha-nisms for clearing interbank accounts rely, at the end of the process, on transfers of central bank money. CHIPS, for example, is a net settlement system in the sense that it nets participating banks' respective claims on one another *within the day*. But at the end of each day, remaining claims on CHIPS that have not netted out are settled using the Fedwire. Except for the intraday netting, therefore, banks participating in CHIPS still need reserves at the central bank to settle their payments.

But this need not be so. A private mechanism like CHIPS could evolve into a system of purely bilateral transfers among private banks analogous to the settlement method now used by European countries' central banks, which do not maintain clearing balances at the European Central Bank. Another possibility would be transfers of deposits at a single private bank that all the others agreed to use. A quarter-century or so into the future, therefore, it is also readily conceivable that one or more of these private clearing mechanisms may sufficiently erode banks' need for central bank reserves to undermine the relevance of the central bank's monopoly. If so, it would also undermine the central bank's ability to carry out an effective monetary policy.

Explicitly International Dimensions

One of the most consistent developments in the monetary sphere in the last quarter of the twentieth century has been the increasing irrelevance of nation-state boundaries. The easiest way to see that this is so is simply to note that the number of national currencies has not kept pace with the proliferation of independent countries. One of the few safe predictions about the world twenty-five years in the future is probably that there will be more countries but fewer currencies.

The disappearing relevance of national borders in this context also prompts several lines of speculation (and each is no more than that) about what the future may bring. Each stems from realizing that the wave of currency consolidation that is now in progress, and likely to continue for the foreseeable future, is mostly not an attempt to rearrange the world into "optimal currency areas" in economists' usual sense. In some settings, like Western Europe, the motivation is instead to exploit economic unification, in this instance monetary unification, as the leading edge of political unification. In other settings, especially among smaller countries and in the developing world, the motivation is to mitigate the speculative instabilities that many central banks increasingly face in a world where currencies are convertible, capital flows freely, and market participants in the aggregate (and even some individually) bulk large compared to the assets at the central bank's disposal.

Especially in the wake of the East Asian financial crisis of 1997–1998, much of the discussion of the implications of globalization of financial markets has emphasized the problems posed for a central bank of a small country that is trying to maintain a specific chosen value of its currency. But for this purpose currency policy and monetary policy are the same. Whether the central bank has the resources to withstand speculation against the exchange value of its currency is really the same question as whether the central bank has the ability to control the short-term interest rate on marketable obligations denominated in its currency.

Rapid advances in electronic technology, especially in communications, not only have brought many more investors into the international markets (some on their own account, some via mutual funds) but also have created a much greater degree of coherence in the attitudes and portfolio behavior of investors who remain physically dispersed. As a result, one central bank after another, among economies that are not large but not tiny either, has found itself overwhelmed. Thus far the central banks of the larger industrialized countries have not faced serious inability to control their short-term interest rates. But as financial globalization advances, this prospect too is hardly impossible. If so, the central banks of the large countries would, in all likelihood, seek to change the rules governing global financial markets in some way designed to maintain their ability to carry out monetary policy.

The tendency for central banks of the larger countries to resist surrendering their monetary policy powers to the forces of global market speculation is likely to be even greater because of some of the lessons learned from the East Asian crisis. Benign assumptions about the workings of speculative markets notwithstanding, it was simply not true that the countries that got into difficulty were exclusively those that were highly indebted, or were running large budget deficits or current account deficits, or had made other obvious policy mistakes, or where transparency of financial dealings and the rule of law more generally were especially weak. What was striking about the crisis as it rolled through one country and then another was the degree of apparent arbitrariness in investors' behavior. Even the explanations offered after the fact, for what had happened to any specific country, often tended to point to national vices that, only a few years before, the international investment community had largely hailed as virtues.

Small countries have little ability to alter the rules of international finance in order to protect themselves from arbitrarily destabilizing speculation. Their only choice is to participate in global markets or not. Large countries, however—and especially the large countries acting in concert—have broader latitude in this respect, and if they feel threatened they are likely to use it. Just what changes in the rules they would most likely seek is harder to say, although the surprising abruptness with which the idea of capital controls has gone from being a taboo subject in polite conversation to a focus of open-minded inquiry is perhaps suggestive. (Indeed, the sheer number of recently published books hailing the wisdom of the judgments made by unfettered capital markets may itself be a marker that the tide of informed opinion is beginning to turn in a different direction.)

Here too, the likely outcome in many cases is a continued race between regulators and innovators, with the advantage over time probably on the side of the innovators. To the extent that countries act in concert, however, they may gain an advantage in this regard. One of the reasons for the failure of many past attempts at the national level to bring certain classes of transactions with the central bank's regulatory (and reserve requirement) sphere is market participants' ability to move the endangered transactions "off shore." No doubt regulatory havens will always exist, but the more countries were to coordinate their efforts in this dimension the more isolated, and therefore subject to potential discrimination, the remaining unregulated domiciles would become.

Globalization of financial markets also has implications for the ability of central banks to maintain the relevance of their monopoly over the supply of reserves—and hence the effectiveness of their monetary policy actions—through their operation of the payments clearing mechanism. International markets magnify the potential ability of private clearing mechanisms to compete with public ones. Moreover, currency substitution opens the way for what amounts to competition among national clearing mechanisms, even if each is maintained by a different country's central bank in its own currency. As firms and households, and therefore banks, use currencies other than that of their own country, the country's geographical space becomes less relevant for indicating over what financial transactions and nonfinancial economic behavior the central bank's actions have efficacy. (A parallel process is the use of "units of account" other than a country's currency to denominate wages and other payments.) Hence individual central banks may have influence over geographically dispersed sectors of economic activity, and specific economic disturbances like productivity shocks or oil price shocks may likewise exert their effect on geographically dispersed sectors rather than recognizable national economies.

Finally, what implications follow from the trend toward currency consolidation per se? Living with a common currency means living under the same monetary policy, and hence the same interest rates and exchange rates. When different countries or different parts of the same country have a common currency, therefore, it is highly likely that from time to time the monetary policy that will be best for one will be quite unsuitable for the other. This phenomenon is thoroughly familiar among the disparate regional economies within the United States. (The most obvious example is what happened to Texas in the mid-1980s, when the regional economy was depressed because of falling oil prices but U.S. monetary policy remained highly restrictive as part of the continuing effort to restore nationwide price stability.) There is no reason not to expect the same kind of outcome from time to time among, for example, the member countries of the European Union.

As is well known from the standard theory of optimal currency areas, however, under the right conditions even countries or regions with highly dissimilar economies can happily share a common monetary policy. The usual list of such conditions includes price flexibility, labor mobility, and the ability and willingness to make cross-country, or cross-region, fiscal transfers. Of these, neither price flexibility nor labor mobility seems likely to increase sharply within the immediate future (although each is really the subject for another paper). What remains, therefore, is the possibility of fiscal transfers.

It is extremely doubtful that the countries that are now pursuing currency consolidation in reaction to financial or economic distress have any prospect of coupling it with any kind of serious international fiscal transfer system. If Argentina goes ahead and abandons the peso in favor of the U.S. dollar, for example, it presumably will not do so in the expectation of compensation from the United States any time the Federal Open Market Committee chooses a monetary policy that may be optimal for the U.S. economy but injurious to Argentina. Countries that are consolidating their currencies as an aspect of desired further political unification, however—like the European Union—are a different story.

Because of the substantial economic heterogeneity that prevails across the participating countries, Europe's new monetary union is very likely to prove unstable in its current form. Much speculation, recently diminished by the euphoria surrounding the Euro's successful introduction (to date only as a unit of account), has focused on whether some crisis or other may drive one or more of the union's eleven member countries to abandon the project, and if so, just what that would mean. A more likely outcome, however, is that the pressures of such a crisis—or of repeated crises—would trigger the creation of a deeper union, importantly encompassing coordination of fiscal policies across the member countries (beyond the existing obligation under the Maastricht Treaty to limit government deficits to 3 percent of national income) as well as fiscal transfers among them.

The logical starting place for such fiscal transfers would be lender-of-last-resort policy and deposit insurance, both of which arise as natural adjuncts of monetary policy even though they are essentially fiscal functions, and both of which (especially lender-of-last-resort actions) may be easier to introduce politically because they arise in the context of actual or threatened financial crises rather than as an aspect of ordinary ongoing circumstances. Beyond lies the entire range of intergovernmental revenue sharing schemes, as well as personal tax and transfer systems, that would enable a member country enjoying a monetary policy that is right for its economic needs to help ease the burden on another member country that is forced to accept the same monetary policy even if its needs are sharply different. Just how far the European Union will go along this route, if that is indeed the eventual outcome, is no doubt a matter of the specific time horizon in question. But the thought that monetary union may in time foster the evolution of a deeper, more fundamentally political level of unification is probably not inconsistent with what the Euro's original architects had in mind.

Concluding Remarks

It is important to be clear that the threat outlined here to central banks' ability to conduct monetary policy, arising from any or all of several ways in which their monopoly over the supply of reserves might become irrelevant, applies to central banks' ability to influence prices in the nonfinancial economy no less than production and employment. Hence even those who believe that central banks should not concern themselves with real outcomes anyway (as a stricter interpretation of the European Central Bank's mission than that given above would imply) cannot simply sweep the issue aside. If the central bank cannot affect interest rates—in other words, the prices of financial assets—in its country's financial markets, because borrowing and lending in those markets proceed independently of whatever amount of reserves it chooses to supply, it cannot affect the price level of goods and services in the nonfinancial economy either.

Whether, and to what extent, the appropriate response to this loss of monetary policy potency is to be regretted—and, where possible, resisted—depends on fundamental economic presumptions that lie well beyond the scope of this paper. At the most basic level, economic theory provides no clear answer to what would determine an economy's price level if what its inhabitants used as money depended entirely on their own ability and willingness to innovate, without effective restraint from the central bank or some other designated authority. Especially in light of many industrialized economies' success in achieving price stability over the last two decades, and the important role that most observers assign to these countries' central banks in bringing about this achievement, the prospect of diminished central bank effectiveness will not be reassuring.

Similar considerations arise with respect to output and employment. There is no lack of theories to describe how central bank actions can affect nonfinancial economic outcomes, but the quantitative importance of actual monetary policies in accounting for observed business fluctuations remains a subject of empirical debate. Those who discount that importance (in the limit, who believe that monetary policy is "neutral" with respect to nonfinancial outcomes) need not be apprehensive, at least on this ground, about the trends identified here. But for those who believe that monetary policy is a major influence underlying the movement of output and employment—for example, who credit the favorable economic performance in the United States in recent years in substantial part to the Federal Reserve System—the prospect of diminished central bank potency is a proper object of concern. Whether, and to what extent, to favor aggressive regulatory changes to preserve the economic relevance of the central bank's monopoly over the supply of reserves turns on the same set of issues.

Of course, central banks will still always be able to announce what they want interest rates, or inflation, or output and employment to be. Private economic agents, and especially participants in the financial markets, will continue to pay attention. But without the ability to implement a policy with some independent means of making those intentions come about, such pronouncements will be just that. With nothing behavioral to back them up, they will have about the same force over events as Wang Wei-shao's splendid poems.

Note

This paper was initially prepared for the conference on "Social Science and the Future" held at Oxford, United Kingdom, 7–8 July 1999. Parts of the paper subsequently appeared as "The Future of Monetary Policy: The Central Bank as an Army with only a Signal Corps?" (*International Finance*, vol. 2, no. 3). I am grateful to Kenneth Kuttner for helpful discussions, to Michael Klein, Adam Posen, Hal Scott, and participants in the conference for helpful comments on an earlier draft, to Stephen Weinberg for research assistance, and to the Harvard Program for Financial Research for financial support.

8

The Architecture of Government in the Twenty-First Century

Timothy Besley

Introduction

This chapter is about the future organization of government and the division of responsibility between national, supranational, and subnational units. While some might argue that all of economics is speculative, the task in hand is unusually so. These issues cut across traditional disciplinary boundaries into law and political science. Reflecting comparative advantage, the analysis takes a broadly economic perspective, even though it refers to writings in other branches of the social sciences.

Speculation in this area is made more relevant by the fact that questions of governmental responsibility are on the policy agenda all over the world. Examples abound of significant debates about the organization of government. The future of the European Union is a case in point where there are many important issues. There are debates about the appropriate structure of authority and whether veto rights for member states should be retained. There are also unresolved debates about subsidiarity and the domain in which this should apply. It is also unresolved whether the European Union should be granted powers to tax. The future complexion of the membership is under debate, with possible admission of states from the former Soviet block.

Supranational governance issues are also on many minds following the recent crises in the world economy that further illustrated the possibility for spillovers across national boundaries. This raises questions about the future of financial regulation and the role of supranational bodies such as the World Bank and IMF. Supranational authority is also a pressing issue in the regulation of e-commerce where changes in technology have significant implications for tax collection and regulation.

As a final illustration, consider the recent military intervention in the Balkans where NATO made the judgment that humanitarian concerns were more significant than respect for national sovereignty. This throws up a host of questions about the relative importance of national sovereignty relative to supranational authority the implications of which have yet to be fully explored.

Reorganization of government is also on the agenda at a subnational level, with calls in many countries for greater local self-determination. This can be seen in the case of the clamor for autonomy for ethnic groups in the wake of political upheavals such as the break-up of the Soviet Union. However, the current decentralization moves in the United Kingdom, which will see greater regional autonomy for Wales, Northern Ireland, and Scotland, are a further case in point.

Many of the key changes in the latter part of the twentieth century would not have seemed possible in an earlier era. While it is true that the European ideal has its roots in Napoleonic Europe, history had made force seem like a much more likely basis for integration than the kind that we observed in the post-war period. However, visionary social scientists, for example John Maynard Keynes, developed a view of the financial architecture of the post-Second World War period, which emphasized the importance of supranational governance. Thus, developments in this area over the past fifty years would certainly have seemed within the realm of possibility.

Virtually all contemporary debate about the role of nation-states concerns how their power (and hence relevance) is diminished by a host of recent developments. The most radical view sees the era, ushered in by the Treaty of Westphalia in 1648, in which nation-states are viewed as the dominant international force as all but over.[1] Here we will discuss dimensions of this and develop a framework for thinking about it. We use this framework to grasp the centripetal and centrifugal forces acting on nation-states. This will be the basis for speculating on the future.

The analysis developed here isolates some key forces that underpin a rational theory of the architecture of government. At the heart of the process is the nature of externalities between actors, that is the way in which actions affect the well-being of others. More global externalities imply a larger rationale for supranational action. Also relevant is the technology for organizing government—the transactions costs involved in organizing and making collective decisions. Particularly key here are costs of communication, enforcement technologies, and possible sources of scale economies in state action. Increasing economies of scale would predict larger jurisdictions. Finally, we should consider the extent of heterogeneity of individuals in their goals and outlooks. Given any technology for collective choices, it will be harder to organize collective decisions, the more diverse are the objectives of the relevant actors. Thus, a world community composed of intense feelings of nationalism will likely be much harder to organize collectively than one where these forces are weak. Overall, I will argue that contemporary and future organizational changes can usefully be understood in relation to these forces.

Principles of Governance

Predicting the future requires both theory and data. The analysis begins, therefore, by laying out a rudimentary theoretical approach to understanding the forces that shape the ideal governmental structure. There are three key forces that shape the ideal structure of government: (1) regulating (positive and negative) externalities, that is, activities by which one individual's action affects the well-being of others, (2) exploiting scale economies in provision of key public inputs, and (3) the available technology for organizing and implementing collective choices.[2] Developments in the structure of government should reflect the evolving nature of externalities, scale economies, and collective choice technologies. Below, we argue that technological and cultural change, coupled with a dynamic world economy have implications for all of these that ought to shape the future architecture of government.

Externalities between economic actors are at the heart of the need for collective action. In practice, there are a host of activities where individuals impose benefits and costs on others through their actions. Collective decisions to regulate these actions can improve the outcome for all concerned. Externalities range in scope from highly local effects where, for example, one individual dumps rubbish in his neighbor's backyard to global effects as when usage of fossil fuels in one country results in global warming.

An externality can arise because of either technology or values. For example, redistribution is a public good if one individual cares about the well-being of others whether or not they directly affect his or her own life. Cultural values are also an important source of externalities. Thus, the French may care about protecting their language, making this a national public good, but the importance of this good rests on how strongly preferences for this are felt within this country. Many common interests in nation-states stem from shared values creating what Anderson (1990) calls *imagined communities*. Most countries have important national symbols that they seek to protect.

Economic approaches to government intervention emphasize the importance of externalities in shaping government intervention. The insight that there is scope for taxes and regulations that curb harmful and promote beneficial actions is often attributed to Pigou (1928). The traditional view also emphasizes that governments will need coercive power to implement these solutions since those whose behavior is curbed will need to be compelled to pay taxes or comply with regulations.

However, in one of the most powerful papers of the past fifty years, Ronald Coase questioned this view in his "Problem of Social Cost" (Coase 1960). Coase argued that private negotiations between concerned parties could sometimes (albeit in extreme conditions) obviate the need for government. This is best not taken at face value, but rather as a challenge to the easy passage from the identification of external effects of actions to a prescription for *government* action. Moreover, as a positive theory, the Coasian perspective is valuable—there are many organizations in the world that seem to serve the purpose described. For example, lawyers and doctors regulate the reputational externalities that are involved if some individuals underperform. We will argue below that the sphere in which the Coasian perspective is most relevant is in understanding the kinds of agreements reached between sovereign states.

Coase's theory provides a notion of idealized governance based on voluntary agreements between interested parties to realize mutual gains. Whether it is one state whose pollution affects the forests of another, or one citizen whose radio disturbs a neighbor, voluntary negotiated settlement can, in principle, yield an efficient solution without recourse to coercive power.

There are, however, good reasons why this paradigm breaks down. First, there are many situations in which externalities affect many different individuals where multilateral negotiations are impossible. Second, there are situations where there is imperfect information between the negotiating parties concerning the effect of the externality and its benefits and costs. A third possible source of problems is where the legal framework defining responsibilities is not fully developed. This is often the case for negotiations between states when international courts have limited jurisdiction if one party violates agreements. It may also be difficult to detect whether a violation has occurred.

This explains why, in practice, government is not organized along Coasian lines. The kinds of town meetings that have taken place in small New England settlements could be presented as a (romanticized) version as might meetings of some professional bodies or even academic departments. However, as a predictive theory of government action it comes up short.

This helps to explain a key feature of real world governance structures that rely heavily on systems of *delegated authority*. This describes a situation where one or more members of a polity are charged with regulating externalities between its members. However, because power is delegated, it is necessary to design mechanisms by which the individuals to whom power is delegated are selected and are held accountable for their actions. In the case of government, some form of electoral process has become widely accepted as a basis for legitimate authority and underpins systems of representative democracy.

Delegated authority can be understood as a response to two important forces: the need for expertise in decision making and transactions costs involved in communicating policy preferences. As we already observed, the Coasian ideal breaks down in situations of multilateral externalities because of the difficulties for the concerned and interested parties to communicate with one another. Delegating decision making makes it unnecessary for such information flows to take place. Delegation is also important because it allows individuals to develop expertise in solving particular policy problems.

Delegated authority structures can be described in vertical and horizontal dimensions. A useful abstraction is to think in terms of three main tiers of government corresponding to levels at which externalities are occurring. The lowest level are local externalities, with obvious examples being street cleaning, flood defense, or fire protection. It makes sense to organize governmental responses to such problems at a local level with local delegated authority regulating the externalities involved. Individuals may have particular preferences and desires that can be reflected in local services and it is easiest for decision makers to be accountable for their performance at a local level. We see this type of arrangement in most societies. Such governments often have the power to tax citizens and to regulate certain kinds of externality producing behavior.

If individuals and factors of production are mobile across jurisdictional boundaries, then the likelihood of truly local externalities is much diminished. This is because individuals can move in response to the harm or benefit that they receive from others' actions. Thus, beneficial action in one jurisdiction will induce in-migration affecting the well-being (for good or ill) of that jurisdiction and those from which individuals move. This is precisely the logic behind the view that economic and political integration are closely allied. Once markets for goods and services are open, a host of policy choices within a jurisdiction affect others. Thus, increased mobility of people, goods, and resources increases the spillovers between jurisdictions and makes it more natural to organize governance at a higher level. Capital mobility within the European Union is already relatively free. In theory, labor mobility is free too. However, labor flows are relatively modest. Nonetheless, if this increases in the future (as surely it will), then this will have greater significance for all manner of social and labor market policies. For example, no longer would it be possible for individual states to choose their social safety net policy without taking into account their affects on migration, with the specter of a "race to bottom" looming. To students of U.S. social policy, such debates will already be familiar and provide the rationale for federal action in these areas.

The next tier in the vertical hierarchy concerns regulation of national externalities. Examples include the desire to preserve national cultures and the conduct of monetary policy. The latter is important since historically nation-states have monopolized a national currency that governs transactions in that economy as well as seignorage rights. This generates an important common interest problem for the citizens in having a well-managed currency. Equating nations with currencies in this way also brings home what kind of sacrifice is implicit in the Euro experiment. Delegated authority to manage national externalities has typically been through some form of national government.

The highest tier of externalities is supranational in character. These are increasingly prevalent in contemporary events whether through global warming or financial crises. They concern situations where activities in one country affect the citizens of another.

Treaties between nations to regulate supranational externalities are close to the Coasian ideal since they are the product of bargaining between nations. This form of supranational governance is perhaps the oldest. It is unsurprising that the externality created by the threat of military action between nations should be internalized this way given how costly it is to fight wars. However, treaties need not be solely about military conflict and numerous tax treaties are an example of supranational governance that have sprung up to deal with cross-border externalities in taxation (particularly of mobile factors of production). The Montreal protocol, regulating the use of chloro-fluoro carbons is also a good example of treaty-based governance.

While treaties may appear to be a natural solution to governance issues, they are severely limited in their scope and effectiveness. This is well illustrated in the history of the United States—see Inman and Rubinfeld 1997 who argue that the U.S. Constitution can be seen as a response to the failure of the Articles of Confederation to achieve agreement for the financing of defense between the newly independent states.[3] The increasing power of the U.S. federal government in relation to social insurance programs can also be traced to the fact that cooperative agreements between states became increasingly difficult in an era of rising unemployment.

Failures of the model of supranational governance can be met to some degree if a single large jurisdiction takes it upon itself to act as a policeman. This is the hegemonic model of international relations (see Gilpin 1987), and it is arguable that it describes the evolution of successful international governance rather better than a model of voluntary agreements. The success of the gold standard in the late nineteenth into the early part of this century relied on the power of the British government to enforce the standard in view of its position as a world power.[4] Postwar economic and political cooperation among capitalist countries from Bretton Woods to Kosovo has centered around the dominance of the United States as an economic and military force. However, this has clear limits, amply illustrated by the failure of the United States to promote tradable emissions permits after the Tokyo summit. This paints a picture of supranational governance that departs significantly from the Coasian ideal of voluntary negotiated settlements.

However, institution building is also important in international governance where supranational institutions gain real authority over nation-states. Here, we can contrast two basic models differentiated according to the way in which supranational bodies receive their authority. By far the most common model is *indirect* delegated authority where decision-making power resides with a supranational body, while sovereignty remains with nation-states. The United Nations and World Trade Organization work broadly on this basis. The European Union's commissioners are another example of delegated authority on this model.

This form of delegated authority may seem like the ideal structure for supranational governance, especially if one is committed to preserving the importance and authority of nation-states. However, there are weaknesses. First, the one-step-removed nature of authority may limit the scope for decisive action if it is needed. In the European Union, the national veto severely circumscribes major policy initiatives at the European level. However, weakening the influence of the nation-state's authority over policy outcomes raises the question of accountability. Appointment of authority at one remove without any kind of direct electoral test (or other test of accountability) appears undemocratic. Thus models of delegated authority, with the European Union being a prime example, are often under threat from those who regard it as too undemocratic and others who see it as lacking real authority.

Experience with the operation of the United Nations also illustrates the drawback of a system based on indirect delegated authority. The distribution of veto power in the Security Council have generated the need to find consensus between key players before actions are taken. However admirable this might be on other grounds (especially during the fraught Cold War era), the United Nations appears rarely to have been pro-active in solving global problems. Moreover, its ability to act decisively and quickly is often compromised. In this regard, it is instructive that the United Nations was more or less sidelined during the 1999 crisis in Kosovo.

Supranational government with direct delegated authority is the logical answer to the latter concerns with systems of indirect authority. However, to be effective at a supranational level, this would involve creating the means of accountability now applied to democratic processes in nation-states with delegation of authority over the heads of national governments. While some view this as the next logical step in the evolution of the European Union, it is far from uncontroversial.

It is also important to stress that the world's most powerful democratic federation (the United States of America) has been built around more than two centuries of political and economic integration. Moreover, the relative responsibility of states over key policy areas remains controversial. Indeed, the Republican's contract with America that saw them gain control of Congress in 1994 has resulted in a significant backlash against the power of the federal government. While the broad trend is toward centralization, the trend is not monotonic.

Deciding how far and how fast to proceed toward a United States of Europe will remain a major issue for debate in the future. The decision of the directly elected European parliament to fire the appointed European Commission in 1999 could signal the beginning of a new era in European integration with greater influence of directly delegated authority relative to appointees. However, the European Union falls a long way short of a true system of directly delegated authority. Moreover, the efforts to negotiate a Treaty of Nice in 2000 had only limited success.

The shape of supranational government also depends upon the set of nations who choose to form a coalition. The world currently comprises a patchwork of supranational institutions with different groups of members. To the extent that these correspond to the common concerns across national boundaries, this makes sense. However, it would be hard to argue that this is the only factor. Transactions costs in organizing cooperation rise as more nations are involved and it is easier to monitor and enforce arrangements with few members. Long-term relationships of trust are also important in the absence of international institutions for enforcing agreements.

The discussion so far has been mainly about the vertical structure of government. However, there are important issues concerning the horizontal division of responsibility. While most tiers of government (below the supranational level) have a core government (usually a directly elected legislature and/or executive), there are important questions about how broad the scope of government action should be within any tier. Somewhat unusually, the United States has separate elections for judges and regulators in many states. There is also scope for citizens' initiatives whereby voters place legislative proposals directly on the ballot—see Bowler, Donovan, and Tolbert (1998) for discussion.

In contrast to national and subnational government, supranational governance is typically functional with separate systems of governance dealing with particular types of issues. We have separate authorities dealing with trade policy, environmental policy, and coordination of economic policy. Each is accountable for its performance in that sphere alone.

One reason for this important difference between the horizontal structure of government is the possibility that are important spillovers between activities at the subnational level that are not present supranationally. This is undoubtedly true. The structure of government budget constraints means that more spending on one activity means less on another; a tragedy of the commons problem could easily arise if too many institutions were granted the power to tax a given set of citizens.

The main advantage of functionally specific government is the potential for improving accountability on the issue in question and with government policies that more closely reflect tastes of the majority. The danger is a form of populism that is ultimately self-defeating. For example, electing regulators may keep prices down, but could result in an electricity industry that is starved of the resources needed to innovate (see Besley and Coate 1999). Perhaps more menacing is the possibility of a return to public flogging or other forms of ritual punishment as a consequence of allowing popular sentiment to play more of a role in policy choices.[5] One is also concerned about democratic fatigue when nonexpert individuals are asked to decide on a host of specific issues. Nonetheless, innovations in information technology will surely have an impact on democratic process and may also enhance the scope for individuals to gain expertise in judging between policy proposals.

Economies of scale in government action are also an important force in shaping government action. There are certain spheres (defense being an obvious example) where larger states may need to spend less on a per capita basis when they coalesce with others. Indeed, any *pure* public good has the property that benefits do not diminish in larger jurisdictions whereas costs are spread over a larger population. In practice, most public goods are less than pure and, to this extent, the force of this argument is weaker. However, changes in technology that affect the extent to which this is true will change the argument for state action. A good example is the evolution of broadcasting technologies, once thought to typify a nonexcludable benefit, creating a strong rationale for state provision. Yet, modern technologies allow access to be restricted to those who pay. If exclusion is impossible, then the argument for large-scale media markets is also strong since benefits accrue to everyone and the costs are shared over the whole population. However, exclusion has brought the possibility of multiple specialized channels. Hence, the argument for even national (let alone supranational) television and radio channels on grounds of accessing scale economies is now much weaker as is the case for state provision.[6]

Most forms of government action create gainers and losers. Governance structures try to find a legitimate means by which collective choice may impose losses on certain groups in the population. The very essence of majority rule is the notion that this could be half the population. More generally, the congruence of objectives is an important factor in determining the scope for collective action through peaceful means as it diminishes the likely conflict that could arise under a system like majority rule.

More culturally diverse and unequal societies are less likely to find a consensual basis for action. Thus, the willingness of one nation to accept supranational authority will depend upon the degree to which objectives in this sphere of activity are congruent with one another. There are many examples where diversity holds up the process of political development. Nationalistic tendencies in Europe are the sand in the wheels of European integration. The difficulties in organizing wide-ranging deals on the environment are inhibited by the dramatic differences in per capita income across nations.

Thus, given a particular set of externalities and technology for collective choice, we would expect the resulting governmental structure that emerges to reflect the congruence of objectives. In situations where particular groups are willing to concede nothing, then effective collective action is typically impossible.[7]

Given a particular set of fundamentals, described by externalities and the policy and collective action technologies, the extent to which gains from collective action can be realized will therefore depend upon the degree to which there are heterogenous goals pursued. We would, therefore, predict a greater role for supranational government structures in spheres where nations perceive a common interest. This is behind the flurry of activity on international environmental agreements in recent years.

In a world with a plurality of interests and values there is no such thing as the ideal architecture of government—some structures will be better for some citizens. Which of these get adopted will depend upon on vested interests and the power of particular elite groups to make their own perspective dominant. Key powerful vested interests, particularly of a nationalistic variety, could potentially block moves toward a system of government that is in tune with the forces described above. Experience does however suggest that real changes are possible. We will return to the role of group identities below.

Forces Shaping the Future

Having laid out the principles of governance that shape the functions of government, the next step is to the major changes in the world that will have an impact on the structure of government. Perhaps the most important force shaping the future architecture of government will be the changing nature of externalities. There are broadly three ways in which this can happen. First, technology may change the extent to which one individual can affect the actions of another, as with the invention of nuclear weapons. Second, values may shift as individuals decide whether to support a particular issue of common interest. The extent to which individuals choose to identify with a nation or an ethnic group is a case in point. Third, new issues may emerge which lead to reclassification of a particular action, as when we develop the ability to detect global warming or the consequences of acid rain. Thus, pollution externalities, which were once thought to be local, become global.

The increasing importance of global externalities will likely remain a key challenge for the efficacy of nation-states in the future. In terms of technological change, these include the unavoidable effects arising from global climate change. This will strengthen the need for regulation of energy use and pollution at an international level. Collective action will have to go beyond the kinds of global summits that we have seen to date and will require the creation of supranational agencies on a permanent footing with delegated authority for policy design. It will be essential to bring the developing nations on board by strengthening the system of international aid as a compensation mechanism for the costs that will be imposed upon them by this process. This should be facilitated if the future brings better scientific evidence about the costs and benefits of global externalities. The difficulty of making reliable projections also makes it difficult to galvanize public action. The future will also need better cooperation between science and social science in this arena to understand policy response.

Another area where future supranational action is inevitable is the regulation of e-commerce. We should expect significant amounts of commerce to be conducted in this way. It is a technology that shows no respect for jurisdictional boundaries. Moreover, it is extremely difficult to define location in the case of many transactions. This has huge implications for regulation and taxation. Laws of libel and copyright are both threatened by the Internet and there is some evidence (Goolsbee 1998) that it is a source of tax evasion in the United States. The future will see the need for greater integration of regulatory structures to cope with this.

Externalities due to the changing nature of the world trade and payments regime are less clear-cut. Even now the backlash against the East Asian crisis is in the form of calls for more closed economies. Moreover, a glimpse in the last hundred years of world history provides convincing evidence that moves toward openness are not inexorable. The world trade and payments system was much more open in 1900 than it was in 1950 (see, for example, Obstfeld 1998). However, on the premise that contemporary gains in economic openness will remain, it is clear that nations will be increasingly susceptible to shocks that originate in other parts of the globe, as was vividly illustrated by crises in Russia and East Asia in the late 1990s. It is also clear that the trend toward openness is itself contingent on finding workable solutions for dealing with the international externalities that it creates.

If the future does consist of more openness to world events, we should expect to see international institutions being strengthened (as has been the case in Europe in recent years) and a corresponding decline in the importance of nation-states. The form that supranational governance might take is open to speculation. In spite of close to fifty years of economic integration, the European Union is still unwilling to create a sovereign body whose legitimacy is derived directly from the people of Europe. However, the drift in this direction seems clear.

Greater openness may threaten the ability of nation-states to operate effective safety nets. Rodrik (1998) argues that countries that are more open to trade have larger governments due to the need to protect their citizens against shocks generated by exposure to the world economy. However, openness also makes it more difficult to tax mobile factors. Hence, countries that are most needful of strong safety nets will find it hardest to sustain them. In the European Union this is compounded by the fact that, with mobile populations, there is the possibility of competitive downgrading of social protection. These arguments suggest that extending social protection will require collective action at an international level.

It seems unlikely that such actions will be possible at a global level, but it is likely that creating supranational cooperation over the design of social protection will be possible at the level of the European Union. However, the controversy surrounding the social chapter of the Maastricht Treaty suggests that the European Union has far to travel in developing an acceptable plan for integration of social protection. This will likely become a priority if institutions with direct delegated authority are strengthened. We might also expect to see such actions to regulate levels of social protection in other regional trading organizations (such as Nafta and Mercusor) even though neither seems very close to encouraging free mobility of labor among it members.

Many developments in supranational governance will continue to rely on the power of the United States for enforcement. If the next fifty years see a significant decline of U.S. economic power, without the rise of a power with similar willingness and resources to monitor and enforce international agreements, then this would be grounds for pessimism. The alternative is to develop supranational institutions with direct delegated authority. With the European Union as an important exception, there not good grounds to expect many such developments over the next twenty years. The current uneasy solution, which relies to such a degree on the clout of the United States, where necessary, provides only a halfway house. Progress on this front is only likely when it is clear that action centered around sovereign nation-states is no longer viable. However, there are areas, the World Trade Organization being an example, where there has been important progress. Moreover, it is clear that much can be achieved with such an institution compared to what could be achieved by independent states using only a threat of a trade war to sustain cooperation.

The forces described here will in time erode the power and influence of nation-states. In fact the era of nation-states could in time been seen as ephemeral. To see this, we need only remind ourselves that the idea of nations and nationalism are comparatively recent. In terms of the principles of governance laid out above, the logic of dominance by nation-states appears weak. Chief among national public goods are the cultural and national identities that are inculcated from history, literature, and mythology. While there is no doubt that these are extremely powerful movers in human motivation (witness the recent events in the former Yugoslavia) and they can dominate economic and other interests, there is also evidence that these forces can be weakened, as the history of the United States illustrates. A relatively small number of the activities of nation-states deals with externalities between citizens whose boundary is the nation.

The nation-state as an actor retains some strength from the fact that most citizens see their national government, acting in consort with other national governments, as the only satisfactory way of resolving supranational problems. Indeed the very notion of supranational presupposes the existence of nation-states. The hand of national governments will remain strong so long as national government is deemed essential to the effective solution of global problems.

The current experiment with a single currency in Europe is critical even though it remains half-hearted in key dimensions. The European Central Bank has well-defined authority, with a clearly defined structure of accountability. However, the current institutional setup also fails to centralize other key decisions about economic management between members of the Euro zone. Thus, the experiment is hardly being conducted under the most propitious circumstances—a compromise was even needed to select the head of the European Central Bank. It would be foolhardy to predict whether this experiment is ultimately viewed as successful. However, if it is, it will provide an important basis for further acts of supranational cooperation both within Europe and elsewhere.

Nation-states will also be under pressure from below, partly as a corollary of power being vested in supranational institutions. One key function for national governments is to regulate lower tiers of government and the externalities that arise between jurisdictions. One key example is the possibility of self-defeating forms of competition as in the case of taxing mobile capital, where there is a tendency for jurisdictions to bid down rates of taxation resulting in taxes being inefficiently tilted toward immobile goods and factors. While national governments have traditionally regulated such things,[8] there is a growing rationale for action by supranational bodies like the European Union. The logic behind this is clear. Any costs of tax competition are felt between as well as within nations, making the nation-state an unnatural level of government at which to regulate such behavior. A corollary of this is that efforts toward coordinating activities such as tax setting at the European Union level diminishes the rationale for government by nation-states as it exposes the fact that externalities from such competition are not at the level of nations. In fact, in areas such as state aids, the European Union has already demanded that national policy is subordinate to European Union policy. In light of such developments, we should expect to see greater calls for regional autonomy with existing nation states within regulation of externalities between jurisdictions handled at the appropriate suprajurisdictional level.

We might also expect calls for decentralization in the wake of increases in mobility of populations within the European Union. The logic of this was spelled out in a provocative, and much debated article, by Tiebout (1956) who observed that there are forces that should lead individuals with similar preferences to sort into self-governing jurisdictions. Were this true, it would be important to give the local jurisdictions the power to make the key local choices on the basis of which individuals choose to move. As cultural differences diminish across nations, and English language dominance progresses, it is less fanciful to imagine that such sorting will occur even though empirical support for the Tiebout hypothesis (even within in nation-states) to date is weak. Changes in information technology and transparency of government performance should also encourage this. It is now easier than ever in the United Kingdom for citizens to check the quality of schooling and public services in a neighborhood where they are planning to locate from the comfort of their own keyboards.

The logic behind European integration will increase further in the future. Solutions to pan-European issues of policy will require decisive centralized authority. In abolishing local currencies, the European Union has already swept away an important source of power of nation-states. Control over national debt in a newly powerful central administration is a logical next step and may even be necessary for the single currency experiment to work. Hence, there is some justification for the views of anti-Europeans when they speak of an inexorable move toward a European super state. The forces are in train (as they were two centuries ago in the United States) toward this model. The technological forces that are weakening the power of national government are largely unavoidable.

A further important source of change in the architecture of government will come through falling costs of communication and gaining access to information, particularly through the Internet. This will accelerate the kind of cultural diffusion that we have seen in the postwar period. Even relatively closed societies, such as China, are significantly influenced by Western (particularly American) cultural innovations. It will become more and more difficult for nations to defend their own cultural identity against the flow of culture across borders. To the extent that cultural homogeneity is a basis of nationhood, this will inevitably weaken the case for national governance.

Information flows make it close to impossible to give citizens a one-dimensional perspective on world events. The recent wars in the Gulf and in Kosovo both illustrated the difficulty of keeping citizens ignorant of the views disseminated through the international media. With luck, the Internet will be the final nail in the coffin of totalitarianism, which requires both monopolization of information flows in addition to monopolization of force.

Changes in technology will also make it easier for citizens to hold government accountable and to participate in democratic decision making. In effect, we can confidently predict that the transactions costs of collective decision making will be diminished. An optimistic view is that this should bring government closer to citizens, making it operate in a more open and transparent way. However, the possibility for misrepresentation in electronic communications is manifest and will require open societies to develop methods for counteracting fraud. All of this notwithstanding, there is strong evidence from the United Kingdom that citizens are willing to interact with governments using electronic means (see U.K. Government 1999).

Active communications act in the opposite direction to the forces toward decentralization that are described here, since traditionally, decentralization to local government has been the best way of achieving accountability. After all, transactions costs associated with information flows and contact between local people and providers of services were best organized at a local level. (The ideal of the New England town meeting, referred to above, typifies this.) Improvements in information flows and communication break the link between physical location and accountability. We should therefore expect externalities rather than transactions costs to become an even more significant factor in determining the location of government activity. In principal, it should be no more difficult for an individual in London to interface with a government in Brussels than one based in Westminster in the future.

This does raise the possibility of some gain in scale economies also pushing us toward a larger optimal size for governments. There may be less need in the future for many different governments to be keeping track of individuals tax or health records. This being so, there could be high efficiency gains from merging those activities that are replicated by different governments. This is especially true in a world where labor mobility across nation-states increases.

Technological changes in communication and information flows also open up further possibilities for functional rather than geographical notions of decentralized government to become more important. We are used to such ideas in the organization of professions where reputational externalities are important. Thus, lawyers in large parts of the world use functionally representative bodies that are accountable to their members to regulate themselves. However, the scope for regulatory decisions to be taken in consultation (and even voted upon) by those who are most affected by the activity in question would appear more possible in the future, and there is no reason to believe that nation-state boundaries should matter. One might, therefore, envisage a future in which citizens were more directly involved in an array of public decisions that were horizontally differentiated with a larger array of directly accountable single-issue authorities.

There is of course a danger that positive aspects of such changes alone are emphasized. The need for suitable means to validate information flows will be paramount. However, there is also scope for malign activity to be promoted through such terms. For better or worse, scope for direct collective action may also be altered, amply illustrated by the march on the City of London by protestors in 1999. The power of certain lobby groups to organize internationally will be enhanced by such developments, particularly if such groups are able to monopolize flows of information. This may constitute a threat to the more decentralized form of government that I envisage.[9] How functionally decentralized decision making can function without it being dominated by special interests on each issue is certainly an issue that will have to be dealt with.

The events in Seattle, Washington, and Prague in 2000 showed the potential for an unaccountable civil society to coordinate collective action on a global scale. The diminution of transport and information costs makes this kind of action increasingly possible and, hence, likely. It is as yet unclear whether this will be a catalyst or impediment to global governance. But it is clear that it is at least in part responding to a void in supranational governance.

Concluding Comments

The organization of government is shaped by a balance of three things: regulation of externalities, transactions costs, and vested interests. My main arguments have been that recent developments in technology, the economy, and social life have radically changed the nature of the technologies that we use for making collective decisions and public policies, and externalities between citizens. This implies significant shifts in governmental structures to reflect these changes.

The approach taken here places the forces of nationalism and ethnic identity firmly in the background. The forces to which we have appealed are defined with respect to interests, but not of this kind. These two forces are themselves somewhat in tension with one another since subnational ethnic identities tend to put pressure on the authority of nation-states. It is clear that some notions of group identity have significant implications for the future architecture of government. In the most extreme case, they place a binding constraint on the set of sustainable governmental structures.

Just because there are some circumstances in which nationalistic, religious or ethnic forces can gain primacy does not imply that they are binding in every case. It is also clear that the ebb and flow of particular group identities makes it difficult to regard these forces as a constant. There are a number of countries, the United States being the core example, where integration has been the norm.

It is clear that effective supranational democratic action does require the development of some notion of citizenship and civil society that transcends national boundaries. Dramatic changes in the communication of culture are evidence that important social norms can evolve internationally. Moreover, the scale and pace of evolutions across state

boundaries are proceeding apace. That is not to argue that human crav-
ing for group identity is unimportant. Loyalties to sports teams, clubs,
and families are perfectly consistent with the emergence of a core set of
values about the appropriate way to regulate externalities.[10]

It is not, therefore, unreasonable to look to a future where the
forces described above, rather than the forces of nationalism and religious
and ethnic identity, dominate the architecture of government. However,
there is evidently much uncertainty about the relative weights to be
placed on the reasons and the passions in shaping the world.

The aim of the project to which this paper contributed was to
speculate about the future. The forces described here suggest a future in
which international cooperation will inevitably be greater. The European Union is uniquely placed to establish an effective set of supranational democratic institutions with directly accountable supranational
institutions. This will not only be important in a European context, but
in providing a demonstration effect for other regions of the world where
there are potential gains for supranational cooperation. This could have
profound implications for the evolution of governance in other regions
of the world.

The forces described here also suggest a future with a greater degree
of functionalism in governance structures where particular issues are
taken out of the set of issues to be decided in general elections at the
national level and located at their appropriate national, supranational,
or subnational level within single issue authorities that are separately
accountable.

We have not discussed the appropriate time scale for the changes
envisaged here. While the argument suggests the need for an appropriate
organizational arrangement for government based on externalities, scale
economies, and the technology available for undertaking collective
action, this does not tell us how long the process of change might take.
Many economists had argued that the inefficiencies implicit in socialist
economic systems spelled inevitable doom, and yet the system lasted for
seventy-five years. Whether economists should be cheered by the success
of their logic or dismayed at the sluggishness of the adjustment process
depends very much on the time scale adopted.

In the case of changes in government structure, we are used to incremental change prefaced by long periods of debate. However, it is
reasonable to suppose that the European Union will have taken signifi-

cant steps toward directly accountable democratic institutions by 2020. This will create a rationale for locating other spheres of policy making, such as defense at the European level.[11] There should be a concomitant shift toward greater decentralized authority, already under way in the United Kingdom. The changes in communication costs over the next twenty years should also cement the development of a global civil society, albeit among elites. All such developments are prefaced on the recent period of unprecedented peace and prosperity (among developed nations) continuing. However, they are also part of the formula that makes this possible.

Notes

1. See the discussion in Hirst and Thompson (1996), chapter 8.

2. There are many contributions to the economics literature, beginning with Oates (1972) that develop aspects of these elements. Recent contributions include Alesina and Spolaore (1997), Bolton and Roland (1997), and Besley and Coate (1998).

3. See Coates and Munger (1985) for a specific illustration of how cooperative agreements can fail.

4. See the discussion in Gilpin (1987).

5. There is a long-standing debate on these issues going back to the dawn of modern representative democracy when many commentators were worried about the tyranny of the majority. In practice, the role of judiciary is critical in protecting violations of minority rights and property rights. Thus greater functional separation of government decisions may require stronger bills of rights to avoid the possible excesses of populism.

6. This not to say that there is not a strong case for government regulation for a host of reasons.

7. Bolton and Roland (1997) develop a theory of the disintegration of nations based on this idea.

8. However, this does not mean complete centralization in most cases. For example, U.S. states have agreed on a common base for levying capital taxes, with little effort at coordinating rate setting.

9. It parallels the traditional concern with geographically localized decision making that it panders to local elites.

10. Indeed there is an important self-enforcing logic here. In many circumstances, communities that function around a key set of common values create incentives for others to invest in those values so that they can enjoy the full benefits of membership in the community.

11. Indeed, specific proposals of this kind have been introduced since this paper was first drafted.

References

Alesina, Alberto, and Romain Wacziarg. 1999. "Is Europe Going Too Far?" Typescript.

Alesina, Alberto, and Enrico Spolaore. 1997. "On the Number and Size of Nations." *Quarterly Journal of Economics* 112(4): 1027–1056.

Anderson, Benedict. 1991. *Imagined Communities*. London: Verso.

Besley, Timothy, and Stephen Coate. 1998. "Centralized versus Decentralized Provision of Local Public Goods: A Political Economy Analysis." Typescript.

Bolton, Patrick, and Gerard Roland. 1997. "The Breakup of Nations: A Political Economy Analysis." *Quarterly Journal of Economics* CXII, 1057–1090.

Bowler, Shaun, Todd Donovan, and Caroline J. Tolbert. 1998. *Citizens as Legislators: Direct Democracy in the United States*. Columbus: Ohio State University Press.

Bull, Hedley. 1977. *The Anarchical Society: A Study of World Order in Politics*. London: MacMillan.

Coase, Ronald. 1960. "The Problem of Social Cost." *Journal of Law and Economics* 3: 1–44.

Coates, Dennis, and Michael Munger. 1995. "Strategizing in Small Group Decision Making: Host State Identification for Radioactive Waste Disposal Among Eight Southern States." *Public Choice* 82: 1–15.

Dixit, Avinash. 1996. *The Making of Economic Policy: A Transactions-Cost Politics Perspectives*. Cambridge: MIT Press.

Gilpin, Robert. 1987. *The Political Economy of International Relations*. Princeton: Princeton University Press.

Goolsbee, Austan. 1998. "In a World Without Borders: The Impact of Taxes on Internet Commerce." NBER Working Paper No. 6863. Cambridge, MA: NBER.

Hirst, Paul, and Grahame Thompson. 1996. *Globalization in Question*. Cambridge: Polity Press.

Inman, Robert, and Daniel Rubinfeld. 1997. "Rethinking Federalism." *Journal of Economic Perspectives* 11(4): 43–64.

Inman, Robert, and Daniel Rubinfeld. 1998. "Subsidiarity and the European Union." Pp. 98–109 in *The New Palgrave Dictionary of Economics and the Law*, ed. Peter Newman. Macmillan: London.

Oates, Wallace. 1972. *Fiscal Federalism*. Harcourt Brace: New York.

Obstfeld, Maurice. 1998. "The Global Capital Market: Benefactor or Menace." *Journal of Economic Perspectives* 12(4): 9–30.

Persson, Torsten, and Tabellini Guido. 1996. "Federal Fiscal Constitutions: Risk Sharing and Redistribution." *Journal of Political Economy* 104, 5.

Pigou, Arthur. 1928. *The Economics of Welfare*. London: MacMillan.

Rodrik, Dani. 1997. *Has Globalization Gone Too Far?* Washington D.C.: Institute for International Economics.

Streit, Manfred E., and Werner Mussler. 1998. "Evolution of the Economic Constitution of the European Union." Pp. 98–109 in *The New Palgrave Dictionary of Economics and the Law*, ed. Peter Newman. London: Macmillan.

Tiebout, Charles. 1956. "A Pure Theory of Local Expenditures." *Journal of Political Economy* 64: 416–424.

U.K. Government. 1999. *Modernizing Government.* http://www.cabinetoffice.gov.uk/moderngov/1999/whitepaper/whitepaper pdf.htm

Wallace, William. 1999. "Europe after the Cold War: Interstate Order or Post-Sovereign Regional System." *Review of International Studies* 25 (in press).

9

The Cybernetic Society: Western Future Studies of the 1960s and 1970s and Their Predictions for the Year 2000

Alexander Schmidt-Gernig

Introduction

Modern societies, due to their peculiar developmental dynamic, are in general future-oriented in the sense of being focused on progress. But because of this developmental dynamic, modern societies for their own stabilization are also dependent on prognoses, planning, and developmental visions, both positive and negative. Niklas Luhmann and others therefore correctly assert that particularly in modern societies, the continuity between the past and the future is "broken," creating a perception of the future as being primarily a risk that has to be planned and guided by *decisions*, instead of the rather traditional concept of the future as a contingently developing promise or danger that intrudes from the outside.[1]

In the historiography on the subject the Second World War is generally understood as a decisive break in the history of Western thought on the future because research on the topic increased quantitatively after 1945. More significantly however, dealing with the future achieved a new qualitative importance especially during the 1960s and 1970s because the future was discovered by academics in various disciplines as a field of genuine academic research to be approached with new interdisciplinary methods, combining *prognoses and projections*, the theory and practice of *programming and planning*, and finally, in the context of a "philosophy of the future," ethically based designs of *alternatives* to faulty developments.[2] Thus, due to a felt need for a "holistic" perspective in an era of unprecedented technological as well as social and economic transformation, beginning in the early 1960s an increasing number of not only economists and political or social scientists, but also engineers, system analysts, and physicists started to focus on the future of Western society as well as on the future of the entire globe.[3] In addition, an increasing number of think tanks with the specific task of establishing scientifically oriented future studies were founded: for example the Hudson Institute (1961), the World Future Society (1966) or the Institute for the Future (1967) in the United States and, in Western Europe the French Association Futuribles Internationale (in 1960), the German Berlin Zentrum für Zukunftsforschung (1968–1981), and the famous international Club of Rome, founded in 1967. Many of these institutions also edited their own periodicals such as *Futuribles* or *Analysen und Prognosen über die Welt von morgen* (1968–1981), or the still-existing British-American journal *Futures, The Journal of Forecasting and Planning* (in publication since 1968), as well as the more popular journal *The Futurist* (edited since 1967), or the more scientific periodical *Technological Forecasting and Social Change* (since 1969). Even many academic as well as private institutions that were not primarily dealing with future-related topics felt the need to focus on this new subject: for example, the European Cultural Foundation which, between 1967 and 1975, funded a wide-range, interdisciplinary attempt of more than sixty scholars to predict the social, economic, political, and cultural future of Europe in the year 2000.[4] International conferences of a new kind on the "future of mankind" were also held, for example, the conferences of the World Futures Studies Federation like Mankind 2000 in Oslo 1967, Challenge from the Future 1970 in Kyoto, the Third World Conference 1972 in Bucharest. Many others followed, creating international networks of forecasting and prediction as well as providing general knowledge for national and international policy making.[5] Moreover, the variety of the futurological research performed was remarkable in its geographical as well as temporal breadth, ranging from the region, the nation, and the supranational level to humankind as a whole. The research also included short-range prognoses (ten years) and long-term forecasting. The majority of this research, however, focused on the magical cipher of the turn of the century—the year 2000—and thus primarily comprised mainly medium-range prognoses and alternatives (twenty to thirty years). All these factors and especially the extraordinary organizational and ideological diversity of institutions and authors that performed research on the future (nongovernmental organizations [NGOs], governmental research institutes and those with close ties to governments, corporations, academies, independent research groups, individual authors) point to the fact that we are confronted with a special but influential form of a transnational public sphere, covering almost the entire spectrum of political interests and ideas rather than only several interest groups and lobbies.

Given this remarkable and unprecedented development of a collective effort to deal with the future of mankind, the historian wants to know more about the basic causes of its emergence and about the reasons for the nature of its predictions. What was predicted and what were the basic paradigms behind these predictions? Due to limited space, the focus here is only on some very characteristic, complex, and primarily American future studies of the late 1960s and early 1970s, which are intended to reveal some basic conceptions of the future in the year 2000 at that time. But, before describing these predictions in more detail, it is necessary to outline briefly the historical background to understand why "the future" became such a prominent topic in the public discourse at all.

Perhaps the most important motive to deal intensely with the future consisted in the perception of an unprecedented, sometimes even exponential growth in most important social and economic sectors such as GNP, mass consumerism, and technological innovations, but also in terms of global population and potential for destruction from the 1950s on—a dynamic development that seemed to change not only modern but all societies on the planet with a breathtaking speed, not least due to a dramatic growth of scientific knowledge. Just to give a purely quantitative idea of this growth, a few facts should be mentioned here: over 90 percent of the total worldwide scientific and technical information was produced in the twentieth century. Of this more than two-thirds was produced after the Second World War. Moreover, a telling indicator for this growth is the fact that the number of scientific journals doubled every fifteen years of the twentieth century and already by the mideighties the yearly output of scientific publications worldwide was over six million.[6]

However, it was the new emphasis on the paradigm of "information," triggered by the development of the first computers immediately after 1945, as well as the first insights into the basic biological structure of human DNA by Watson and Crick in 1953, that, along with the sheer quantitative multiplication of knowledge, gave this development a sort of revolutionary character.[7] Although the scientific basis for this revolution in information technology was already laid for the most part in the 1930s and 1940s, it was the war that drove its accelerated technological application in such forms as radar technology, new telecommunicatively guided artillery systems, and the development of nuclear weapons. Therefore one important driving force for the development of future studies may be seen in the general experience of World War II, with its intense and successful economic, military, and social planning. Especially in the United States this heritage of the war continued and was even intensified by the new rivalry of the superpowers after 1945. So it was no wonder that the first future studies were developed as a result of military operations research and systems analysis within the context of new institutions of the emerging military-industrial complex such as the RAND Corporation and were then soon applied to more comprehensive economic and social forecasts due to the spread of the systems approach during the 1960s.[8]

This dramatically accelerated application of pure scientific research on a large scale in the form of the development of high-capacity computers, satellites, rockets, and the like were to a large degree based on the development of a new kind of integrating Leitwissenschaft—cybernetics —which can, in the words of one of its founders Norbert Wiener, be defined generally as the "science of communication and control in animate and inanimate systems."[9] In this respect, after 1945 cybernetics became a new central model of natural-scientific thought and therefore also influenced strongly the application of natural-scientific explanatory models to the social sciences—an application that found significant expression particularly in the form of the newly emerging future studies. Cybernetics can be understood as the systematic recording of communication and control processes in systems or organizations of all kinds, of which primarily decision, regulation, and control mechanisms were the main foci of interest. The main epistemological presupposition consists particularly in the notion that biological, technological, and social systems are similar in certain basic characteristics and are held together first and foremost by communication in the sense of a transfer of information. Hence, the primary focus of cybernetics is on the *dynamic interactions* between certain structural parts of a biological, technical, social system as well as between the system as a whole toward its environment, based on channels of information flows by means of feedback loops. These feedback loops of information provide the theoretical basis for the observation that an open system can "learn" to organize and steer itself by reacting to new environmental challenges. Therefore, a system can intensify its "intelligence" or its problem-solving capacity because information about its own (past) performance is always reintroduced into the system in order to control its future conduct. This means that a cybernetic approach is *not* deterministic (although it focuses on the *rules* of communication within a system) because systems developments are contingent depending on the system's information about the environment, about its own "consciousness" (or memory), and about the relations between its own inner structural elements: the more information a system can receive and use, the better it will be able to adapt to changing environmental challenges.

This is why already in 1950 Norbert Wiener pleaded explicitly in his study "The Human Use of Human Beings"—directed at the social sciences—that societies, analogous to open biological systems, are best comprehended through the analysis of their communication channels and that the social sciences should therefore concentrate more strongly on these. Applied to the present this meant first and foremost for Wiener to examine more closely the networks between humans and cybernetic machines (primarily computers) and the networks amongst themselves, since these would determine the future to a decisive extent.[10] Therefore, Wiener as well as the famous biologist Ludwig von Bertalanffy, who himself had established a "general systems theory" which was supposed to be also applicable to the social sciences, can be seen as the founding fathers of a whole new paradigmatic approach that led to an increasing number of studies dealing with the influence of systems theory and cybernetics on society as well as on the social sciences from the 1950s on.[11]

Against this background, my main thesis is that especially the new future studies for the most part were strongly influenced by this cybernetic approach or even embodied this way of thinking on society in a very significant and influential way. A first group of studies directed its attention primarily to the influence of the new technologies on the change and continuity of social and economic structures in the highly industrialized countries (above all the United States), predicting the post-industrial society as a kind of *information* or *knowledge society* primarily based on the innovative potential of pure scientific knowledge as well as on the new information technologies. A second group of studies applied

the cybernetic approach to the level of global politics and global interactions, predicting the emergence of (or the hope for) a kind of *planetary
society*. A third group of authors tended to focus primarily on the role of
values and social norms as crucial factors of change, predicting (or hoping
for) the emergence of a *trans-industrial society*, which would bring the
dominance of a new collective consciousness of social integrity based on
a (spiritual) unity between man and nature. Despite their many differences, all three approaches had in common that they were based on some
kind of *evolutionary and historical stage theories*.[12] But this does not mean
that they only foresaw continuous developments and linear processes
without any possible turning points. At least the more comprehensive
and complex studies clearly were not based only on mere trend extrapolations but offered mixed pictures, carefully weighing the probabilities
of continuity and rupture. Therefore, with regard to the new field of
futurology, one can observe a very significant change from the traditional systems theory based on historical evolution in the tradition of
Herbert Spencer to a general systems theory inspired by biology and
mathematical models that consisted of a turning away from the idea
of strict historical or evolutionary determinism in a linear-causal sense
toward the idea of processes of interaction between social systems and
their environments following cybernetic mechanics of regulation. This
does not mean that more traditional historical or philosophical patterns
were given up completely. On the contrary, one often finds a kind of
mix of general historical-philosophical assumptions and those of systems
theory. And it is also clear that some of the forecasters rejected the idea
of analyzing the society as a kind of cybernetic system (the famous sociologist Daniel Bell for example), but in general, the trend toward a more
or less explicit scientific systems approach in the 1960s and 1970s (not
only in the field of futures studies) seems to be quite evident.[13]

Finally, one should add a fourth different and very influential group
of futures studies, the reports to the Club of Rome on global dynamics
and their "limits to growth" (as well as many comparable studies on
world models), but I will leave out this group in this context because
these (very intensely debated) studies primarily focused on more traditional patterns of the industrial society, such as limited natural resources,
capital investment, pollution, or urbanization but directed attention only
very implicitly and indirectly to the impact of the new cybernetic technologies on social change. Nevertheless, it is very important to notice

that these studies were strongly and even more explicitly committed to a cybernetic approach on the methodological level by for the most part using quantitative methods of computer simulation based on cybernetic mathematical models.[14]

Paradigms and Predictions

The Post-Industrial Society as Information Society

Perhaps the most important and influential paradigm, especially among futurists of the 1960s and early 1970s, was the model of the post-industrial society based on new technologies of communication and information.[15] The observed exponential growth of knowledge and technological innovations and the growing applications of cybernetics on society itself, according to these analyses, were about to create a "cybernetization" of society and therefore would change the character of the traditional industrial society profoundly, turning it into a society essentially based on "knowledge" and permanent learning, dominated by new intelligent information technologies. Despite the basic idea of accelerated change, the continuity of the process seemed to be assured by the enormous impact of scientific and technological innovations on other trends of modernization, driving them into the same continuous and irreversible direction—a trend that would reinforce itself just by the overlapping of the different trends of modernization and therefore would guarantee the developmental logic of the system. Herman Kahn, one of the most influential futurists of this paradigm, together with Anthony Wiener expressed this idea of a self-reinforcing modernization in one of the most prominent future studies of the late 1960s. He described a "long-term multifold trend," which seemed to have developed in Western societies since the Middle Ages. This trend of profound modernization consisted of some principal elements such as the centralization and concentration of economic and political power, an accumulation of scientific and technical knowledge due to increasing institutionalization of research and development, combined with a growing importance of the service sector as well as of literacy, education, and the "knowledge industry." These deep structural changes had brought the dominance of bourgeois, bureaucratic, and meritocratic elites as well as an increasingly secular, individualistic, pragmatic, utilitarian, and hedonistic culture in general. Moreover, this trend, according to Kahn and Wiener (and others), gained its tremendous developmental power by reinforcing itself and therefore started to spread increasingly all over the world with an accelerating speed particularly during the twentieth century.[16] These basic characteristics set the tone for many future studies that extrapolated this multifold trend into the future according to its assumed inner logic, conceptualizing modernity or modernization as a universal, irreversible, systemic, global, and goal-oriented (and therefore relatively predictable) change according to its inner system logic of increasing "information."

What did this mean for the concrete predictions of the Western societies in the year 2000? Kahn and Wiener in 1967 predicted the continuity of the multifold-trend as the very likely "surprise-free" projection to the year 2000: major technological progress is seen in the fields of nuclear power, electronics, computers, information processing, and automation as well as the increasing biological manipulation of man. Both authors give a list of 100 concrete technological achievements predicted to be very likely by the year 2000.[17] Looking back today, many of these predictions were amazingly realistic, for example, the general use of automation and cybernation in management and production, the pervasive business and other widespread use of computers for intellectual and professional assistance, including home computers communicating with the outside world as well as home education via video and computerized learning. Their predictions of direct broadcasts from satellites to home receivers, multiple applications of lasers, the emergence of new techniques for very cheap and reliable birth control, the increase in life expectancy, increasingly inexpensive worldwide transportation of humans and cargo, as well as new and possibly pervasive techniques for surveillance, monitoring, and control of individuals and organizations also sound quite familiar from today's perspective. On the other hand, many of their technological forecasts, especially in the field of space exploration and biological manipulation, look like mere science fiction, for instance, the construction of enormous artificial moons, (some) control of weather and climate, permanent inhabited undersea installations or colonies, permanent manned lunar installations and interplanetary travel to extraterrestrial cities, extensive use of robots and machines "slaved" to humans, the major reduction in hereditary defects, the extensive use of cyborg techniques, the practical use of direct electronic communication with and stimulation of the brain, the genetic control over the "basic constitution" of an individual, new improved plants and animals, and human hibernation for relatively extensive periods. Given these tremendous forms of scientific and technological progress, Kahn and Wiener expected an impressive acceleration of economic growth worldwide that at the same time would widen the GDP gap between the rich and poor countries significantly and therefore would increase the pressure for worldwide modernization.[18]

Although Kahn and Wiener also took "canonical variations" of this probable "standard world" into account (different forms of war, big famines, the rise of worldwide revolutionary movements, natural disasters, and the like), they clearly suggested the continuation of the multifold-trend as the most likely scenario for the year 2000 (although they admitted that a surprise-free world would be the biggest surprise). That this realm of predictions was not only a particular belief of two more or less prominent futurists but a widely shared set of expectations among many experts and forecasters during the 1960s becomes evident by also looking at one of the most prominent future studies based on the Delphi technique conducted by Theodore J. Gordon and Olaf Helmer at the RAND Corporation in 1963–1964. Roughly eighty experts from different fields were asked to answer a long list of questions in order to sketch their "most probable world" focusing on topics such as scientific breakthroughs, population control, automation, space progress, war prevention, and weapons systems. The characteristic elements of the world (and especially of the highly developed countries) in the year 2000 looked in many ways similar to those predicted by Kahn and Wiener (and many others): effective fertility control (reducing the population growth to 5 billion people by the year 2000), the wide acceptance of personality-control drugs, a universal satellite relay system and automatic translation machines, a permanent lunar base, and manned Mars and Venus flybys, as well as the operating of deep-space laboratories, but also automatic decision making at the management level (all already by 1984!), large-scale ocean farming, regional weather control, widespread use of molecular engineering, high IQ automatic machines, and the landing on Mars among many others.[19] Here again, only a major (nuclear) war seemed able to interrupt the continuous progress of information and biological technologies, whereas ecological problems, social resistance or costs, and the problem of the tremendous growth of world population were clearly underestimated or were not even taken into account. Predictions about the coming "biological revolution" especially tended to overestimate the impact of new technologies on Western societies by the year 2000. A good example is the British science writer Gordon R. Taylor who predicted a set of probable technical achievements in biotechnology such as extensive mind modification and personality reconstruction, the enhancement of intelligence in men and animals, memory injection and memory editing, perfected artificial placenta and true baby-factory, life-copying, and reconstructed organisms, hibernation and prolonged coma, the prolongation of youthful vigor, the first cloned animals, and man-animal chimeras among others.[20] Although Taylors' basic intention was to warn against the possible development of a "homo biologicus" who would become increasingly the master of his biological characteristics, these features describe the common expectations among experts and futurologists at that time quite precisely.

But not all of the future studies were blind to the social side and some focused more on the immediate consequences of such an accelerated technological progress on people's minds and behaviors. Perhaps one of the most prominent and widely perceived studies dealing with this aspect was Alvin Toffler's *Future Shock*. It was published for the first time in 1970 and soon became one of the landmarks of futurology, particularly due to its intense social analysis of current trends in American society.[21] Like many other futurist "colleagues" he considered the present as a revolutionary change comparable only to the Neolithic shift toward the agrarian society or the fundamental change of the industrial era from the end of the eigtheenth century on. But given the enormous acceleration of change within only a few decades, he reflected not only on the new forms of social mobility in all sectors of social life but especially on the mental consequences of this "super-industrialization." Using the analogy of the common term "culture shock," he predicted an intense general "future shock" of the entire American society, expressed by mass disorientation, neurosis, and free-floating violence. According to Toffler the post-industrial society would create enormous psychic pressures because the principle of "mobility" would become increasingly universal, forming every aspect of life, eroding all traditional forms of stability and custom. Therefore the society of the year 2000 would be a totally mobile society: people would build houses only for ten years or live in mobile homes; they would travel or move for most of their lives, following better and much more diverse job and consumer opportunities and therefore have only partial and superficial encounters and contacts with each other while being able to change their professional occupations rapidly. Moreover, this society would experience permanent revolutions such as youth, sexual, racial, or colonial revolutions, reinforced by an increasingly rapid flow-through of mental conceptions, images, and values dominated by the mass media and their newness-oriented logic. These turmoils of basic norms and values would lead to the emergence of many diverse subcultures, increasingly structured by peer groups rather than by traditional class lines. Toffler significantly did not see any possibility to escape these fundamental changes driven by the new communications technologies, but proposed measures of control and containment of the future shock with the help of a more future-oriented "anticipatory democracy," strengthening the importance and influence of individuals organized in many new "communities" designed to prepare people for accelerated social change. In this regard he (like many futurologists) recommended (and foresaw) the creation of new, more future-oriented types of education and of special groups to develop consistent social alternatives or utopias to be broadcast by the mass media.

The Post-Industrial Society as Planetary Society

Although many studies of the first group (especially the forecasts of the Hudson Institute) also dealt with the future of world politics more or less intensely, political power structures here were for the most part seen as dependent on economic and technological strength. In contrast to this assumption, the second group of future studies dealt primarily with the inner logic and dynamics of world politics in the nuclear age and therefore directed its attention primarily to the emergence of political networks and interactions on a global scale. This means that the basic structures and interconnections of political power played a central role in most of these forecasts, which pointed repeatedly to the problem of political stability on a national as well as on an international or global level. Given this focus, the cybernetic perspective of these future studies concentrated on the increasing significance of communication networks within states and above all between states and societies. Facing the global menace of a nuclear disaster, only increased flows of communication and information seemed able to increase the necessary learning capacity of political systems. Karl W. Deutsch expressed this new perspective in his pioneer study *The Nerves of Government* very clearly by pointing to the following crucial questions: "What is the tolerance of a given political system for contradictions and ambiguities within it? And what is the capacity of this political system for self-transformation with significant preservation of its own identity and continuity? Since the coming of nuclear weapons, societies depend for their survival on their political subsystems. The question of the life and death of nations, perhaps of mankind, has become politicized. Nations depend more than ever on the capacities of their political subsystems for tolerance, learning, and viable self-transformation."[22]

These questions of higher learning capacities by means of global communication and knowledge networks became the main focus of globally designed future studies, which looked for existing or possible trends but also obstacles of the development to a sort of "planetary society."[23] The idea of a fundamental overcoming of the industrial era therefore consisted not so much in technological and economic growth per se but in the assumption of a significant decline of the role of nation-state as an immediate consequence of the cybernetization of world society. Most of these studies therefore had in common that they addressed the future of humankind against the background of the existing structures and tensions of the international system, referring to macroproblems like the menace of a nuclear war, the growing economic gap between the so-called first and third worlds, the development of supranational institutions, the problem of human rights, the danger of environmental devastation and overpopulation, and the danger of individual alienation and social anomie within highly bureaucratized modern societies.

One of the most telling examples of this focus on the future of the international system inspired by cybernetics was the first big international future studies conference on "Mankind 2000" held in Oslo in 1967. In particular, one of the most important founders of peace research, the Norwegian political scientist Johan Galtung, in his contribution on the "future of the international system" referred explicitly to a cybernetic system analysis, based again on a stage theory of evolutionary development. The basic idea is that the scientific revolution and the emergence of new planetary means of communication and information tend to connect all parts of the world so that isolationist forms of politics become increasingly useless and even impossible. Even though Galtung assumes that the system of nation-states will still persist for quite a long time (he does not give precise indications but it seems evident that this system would persist still at least fifty years from the 1970s on), he argues that the character of this system has changed and will continue to change dramatically toward a system of intense mutual dependency where even the superpowers will depend strongly not only on each other but also on other minor actors in the global game. This increasing mutual dependency would make it less and less possible to isolate local or national conflicts. On the contrary, almost all bigger conflicts would tend to become international and in the long run global conflicts, thus creating a system of relatively high "entropy" in the sense of a high level of instability and disorder (in contrast to the classical system of the balance of powers in the nineteenth century, for instance). He therefore explicitly refers to a cybernetic model of information flows by arguing: "Since human beings have different capacities for the tolerance of ambiguity and storage and processing of information, we may assume pockets of low entropy (e.g., where there is homogeneity with regard to race), but that these pockets should be mixed and stirred in such way that the total system has very high entropy (low degree of order, high level of disorder, or 'messiness')."[24] According to Galtung, the degree of systemic complexity based on the intensity of communication and information flows is particularly crucial for the degree of the evolutionary development of a society. He therefore distinguishes between "primitive" (tribal), "traditional" (village), "modern" (national), and "neo-modern" (global) societies (corresponding roughly to the classical scheme of agrarian, pre-industrialized, industrialized, and post-industrial societies) depending on their state of (communications) technologies and therefore systemic complexity. Given the increasing interconnection between societies after 1945, according to Galtung, it is precisely the simultaneousness of all these stages of development on a global scale that creates a climate of growing tensions and disorder, especially among the less developed countries, because they are put under enormous pressure to modernize themselves to become part of the globalized society. Therefore the erosion of the nation-state first takes place in (smaller) highly developed countries, driven by new transnationally oriented elites whereas the less developed countries will first have to go through the stage of the highly developed nation-state before being able to reach the next step of a more transnational orientation. Thus Galtung predicts an increasing replacement of national identities by sub-, cross-, trans- and supranational identities in the highly and increasingly integrated part of the world—a tendency that, combined with intense economic and political interdependence, makes a major war quite unlikely in this part of the world, due to, in particular, an increasing significance of international nongovernmental (INGO's) as well as governmental (IGO's) institutions: "We predict a steady growth in the mutual interpenetration and intermeshing of all developed, industrialized nations with neomodern segments with each other; using INGO's and IGO's as building structures and individuals with cross-, trans- and supraloyalties as building blocks."[25]

Against the background of the Cold War and the fundamental change of the situation since the beginning of the 1990s, this prediction is quite amazing because it explicitly included the socialist countries, which also seemed to follow the logic of highly developed societies toward increasing communication and interaction. Although Galtung did not predict the collapse of the Soviet Empire before the end of the century, he was astonishingly right in forecasting a general rule of "peaceful coexistence" due to the increasing importance of (economic) transnational networks, driven by a fundamental de-ideologization as well as "technification" of the international political system. But it was clear that, on the other hand, this high level of integration and dependency made the international system increasingly fragile and vulnerable especially because the lower degree of integration in the less developed part of the world would cause constant crises and (civil) wars due to increasing pressures of rapid modernization. He (again correctly) foresaw the growing need to prevent the escalation of a global class conflict between the north and the south and predicted an intensified institutionalization of this conflict by means of supranational governmental as well as international nongovernmental organizations, including military interventions and the establishment of peace-keeping forces of the highly developed countries in areas of civil war within less developed countries.[26]

In his contribution to the conference, entitled "Looking Forward: 1999," the American historian Arthur I. Waskow pointed in the same direction.[27] Due to an increasing transnationalism (and criticism of the military-industrial complex) among the elites in the highly developed countries, he predicted the achievement of worldwide disarmament on the basis of secure mutual agreements of the superpowers, and therefore a broadened room for maneuver in international politics, but also a more destabilized and change-oriented world. Furthermore, he conceptualized an increasing importance of supranational institutions and the emergence of nonmilitary foreign policies of the major nation-states. Against this background of intensified communication and global integration, the elites of the less developed countries would also become aware of their situation and would force the developed nations to institutionalize industrial development and modernization in their countries. In this context, Waskow's hope focused primarily on the emergence of a kind of global public sphere and on the creation of many new transnational first world developmental institutions such as a "peace corps," a "farmer corps," an "engineer corps," and even a kind of international "peacekeepers academy," as well as future-oriented centers of public education to strengthen global conflict-solving capacities.

These are only very cursory examples of a general trend to predict the emergence of the post-industrial society as an economically and politically globalized society by the end of the twentieth century. Not surprisingly, within this general paradigm one finds many variations, reaching from rather sober analyses of the inner dynamics of the international political system (such as the cases presented above) to more enthusiastic and utopian ideas of a general evolutionary development of mankind toward a profound transformation of the human race toward a homogenous world society or—as in the works of famous architect Buckminster R. Fuller[28]—toward a kind of "spaceship earth," globally integrated and physically as well as spiritually liberated by the synergetic interaction of enormously advanced technologies of communication and automation. As physicist John R. Platt claimed emphatically in 1966: "We have been isolated human beings, selfish, combative, ignorant, helpless. But now for several hundred years the great evolutionary hormones of knowledge and technology have been pressing us, almost without understanding it, into power and prosperity and communication and interaction, and into increasing tolerance and vision and choice and planning—pressing us, whether we like it or not, into a single coordinated human kind. The scattered and competing parts are being bound together.... We have been men. We are emerging into man."[29]

But both the more sober as well as the emphatic designs of a coming world order and global integration clearly argued in terms of cybernetic system logic. By taking the new cybernetic and communicative technologies to be the main driving forces of the development in the future they would be able to guarantee the necessary "learning capacity" and evolutionary adaptability of the political system on the national as well as on the global level by means of top-down institutions such as the United Nations as well as by (perhaps even more important) bottom-up models of increased democratic participation.[30]

The Post-Industrial Society as Trans-Industrial Society

The third group of future studies began with this aspect of an expanding global consciousness of increasing interconnections and interdependencies. This group gained a strong influence in the course of the 1970s, not least in the context of the oil crises and the end of the long post-war economic boom. This is why the main focus of these studies was, on the one hand, the up to that point ignored ecological and, above all, social costs of the rapid scientific-technological change and, on the other hand, the notion of an ever clearer general dawning of consciousness of these costs and a resulting change in norms and values that seemed apparent in view of the new social movements such as the student movement, the civil-rights movement, feminism, and the hippies.[31] At the same time most of these studies (including those from a partly (neo-) Marxist perspective) were concerned with a critique of political power relations, especially those of the military-industrial complex.[32] Many of these studies therefore also took themselves to be an explicit critique of the futurology à la Kahn or RAND and attempted (with much more limited institutional and financial opportunities) to develop a sort of anti-futurology, which concentrated more strongly on the critique of existing power relations and the social costs of "progress" and, at the same time, were oriented toward a framework of "utopian" alternatives. Futurists such as, among others, Willis W. Harman, W. Warren Wagar, William Irwin Thompson, Gordon R. Taylor, Theodore Roszak, Ivan Illich, and Robert Theobald regarded the extensive "decentralization" of power structures on a national as well as global level as the decisive task and chance for development in the coming decades. The central focus of this critique was, above all, on the interconnections between industry, the military, science, and politics. Although one can trace this critique of corporations, bureaucracy, the military arms race, and the growing dependence of science on industry and the corresponding propagation of a "counterculture" of broken-up, "small," decentralized, and largely autonomous subsystems as a somewhat Rousseauian flight from modernity in the sense of a "new ruralism" (and so as a revival of the old Jefferson-Hamilton debate),[33] most of the authors were not primarily concerned with a return to agrarian societal forms, but rather with a fundamental change in the technological and scientific objectives to new modes of thought and behavior in the sense of a new unity of nature and man. The "limits to growth" predicted by the world-model studies and the transition to an economic form more strongly oriented toward scarcity and sustainability were to serve as the starting point for a new orientation that no longer saw nature purely as an object to be exploited, but rather as the highly fragile basis of humankind's survival. This seemed even more important given that the patterns of thought and action of the classic industrial society seemed to have led to central dilemmas and because of that into a global systems crisis. Willis W. Harman, the director of the Center for the Study of Social Policy at the Stanford Research Institute, acting for many voices, called this crisis situation a "growth dilemma" (growing social and ecological costs), a "control dilemma" (increasing uncontrollability of technological developments), a "distribution dilemma" (an ever-growing gap between rich and poor on a global level), and a "work-roles dilemma" (growing unemployment or "meaninglessness" of work due to automation and mechanization).[34] In view of the perceived crisis of industrial society, the transition to a "trans-industrial" society in the form of a fundamental renunciation of the traditional ways of thought of the industrial society seemed to be of central importance for the near and distant futures. Harman, who, characteristically enough, was a trained systems engineer well acquainted with the technical applications of cybernetics, carried over the idea of positive feedback processes to observed alternative lifestyles and new value orientations in society such as the growing interest in esoterica, meditation, and Asian religions and teachings as well as their concrete applications like yoga. In this sense the systems analyst Magoroh Maruyama spoke of a fundamental change from an industrial to a post-industrial logic, the beginnings of which could be observed not only in the arts and sciences, but also in the societal values and norms, in particular those of the younger generation. This new post-industrial logic would replace such principles of industrial thought as "standardization, homogeneity, competition, hierarchy, conquering nature, material satisfaction, efficiency and thinking in categories," with "de-standardization, heterogeneity, symbiosis, interaction, harmony with nature, cultural satisfaction, esthetics and ethics and thinking in social context."[35]

Other authors were more skeptical with regard to this presumed ability of systems for a sort of cybernetic self-transformation and were more likely to anticipate the collapse of the industrial world-system as a necessary requirement for a new trans-industrial or planetary era. In this respect, the historian W. Warren Wagar, supported by Immanuel Wallerstein's inspired world system analysis,[36] foresaw the collapse of the international system in the middle of the twenty-first century because the inner dynamics of the system, accelerated by the occurring cybernetization of society, seemed to overwhelm the system's abilities of self-regulation. Hence the system's inherent problems of exponential population growth, increasing poverty, and the growing devastation of the natural environment as well as the exponential depletion of natural resources in most (poorer) countries according to this prediction would sooner or later lead to the doom of "the golden age of capitalism."[37]

Thus the forecast for the year 2000 or the early decades of the twenty-first century in these studies looked like a comprehensive picture of all the world's problems already occurring in the 1970s: given the crisis or the lack of democratic rules in many countries except those in the West, limited nuclear wars and increasing (nuclear) terrorism organized by ideological fanatics, criminal gangs, or "insane nations" were foreseen as major features of the beginning decline of the industrial era. Furthermore, the continuity of the population explosion and its consequences like increasing violence, mass epidemics, growing hunger, and universal poverty would increase the crisis on a global scale also affecting the highly developed countries and leading to a significant decline of life and consumer standards particularly due to the excessive exploitation of natural resources. This exploitation would be accompanied by a fundamental and long-lasting economic depression caused by a breakdown of the monetary system as well as hyperinflation and the like. Moreover the collapse of the global biological environment revealed by excessive pollution of the oceans, climatic upheavals, and nuclear catastrophes would reinforce this profound economic crisis, followed by growing social anomie and loss of social cohesion within the industrialized as well as the developing societies—a development that would lead to the decline of intact family structures and to an increasing gap between the generations in terms of values and norms, followed by growing tensions and struggles between "races" and ethnic or religious groups especially in the United States, but also on an international level.

Conclusion—Looking Back from 2001

If one attempts to take stock of the three approaches presented, it hopefully becomes clear from the examples given just how strongly the future studies of the 1960s and early 1970s, in spite of their divergences in individual predictions or imagined alternatives, followed a common model that one could call the "cybernetic society." As we have seen, the basic idea consisted above all in seeing modern societies as integrated systems that obeyed certain (cybernetic) rules of communication and self-control in a manner analogous to complex biological and techno-logical systems. Due to the observed scientific and technological "revo-lution" the highly developed societies appeared to have entered a phase of intensified evolutionary dynamic on the basis of cybernetic systems logic in the sense of reinforced learning capacities that would lead toward a sort of learning society. Both elements—the dynamic as well as the system logic—seemed to make predictions not only necessary but above all possible, which partly explains the boom in futurological studies in the 1960s and 1970s. At the same time it has been shown that the various approaches are all in agreement about analyzing a change of enormous proportions, which seemed, at best, comparable with the transition to the Neolithic revolution. This assessment becomes espe-cially clear in that almost every study traced back its predictions and analyses more or less explicitly to a stage-theory of general evolutionary development. In this respect one cannot state that these studies argued completely ahistorically. However the techno-scientific bias in this thought is striking; it saw the "motor" of history primarily in techno-logical innovations and believed most of further social and cultural ele-ments could be deduced from them.

The point here cannot be to list in detail the "correctness" or fail-ure of the predictions made in relation to the technological and social change and compare them with the situation today. It is more inter-esting, in conclusion, to discuss some of the strengths and weaknesses of the sketched approaches and predictions from today's perspective. The *strengths* of the variations of the post-industrial society inspired by cybernetics lay above all in the area of technological predictions and their effect on economic and political development. Everywhere where systems logics were effective and could be observed, such as in the area of science, economics of (international) politics, the predictions were often right, sometimes amazingly so. Above all, the basic assessment that scientific knowledge was not only expanding massively but would also become the major force of economic productivity, proved to be accurate. That went also for the details: even if, for example, the enormously expanding Internet of the 1990s, which was still in its (military) infancy in the early 1970s, was not predicted in its present form, the general estimation of a forced worldwide, essentially computer and satellite-based communications network was correct and pointed the way. Even if, as we have seen above, the progress of biotechnology was certainly overestimated, there can be no doubt that most prognoses of the 1960s and 1970s are still on the agenda today and are, in part, already technically possible.[38] Above all, the studies focusing on the information society correctly predicted the trail, if not all details, of the synergy effects of innovation-technologies for instance with regard to the emergence of transdisciplinary networks between biological and computer technologies as well as with regard to the economic growth brought on by this emergence. Also in the area of political predictions, as we have seen, the sober and complex prognoses of a more or less intensive weakening of the East-West conflict, a continuation of the north-south problem, the growing importance of supranational and transnational organizations as well as economic and financial integration, and finally the emergence of a kind of world public sphere proved to be correct in general, although they did not predict spectacular events such as the collapse of the Soviet Union. Therefore, an essential strength of the future studies lay in the fact that they had already overcome the traditional fixation on the role of the nation-state alone and began to think in global dimensions, in the context of which the new technologies and their global economic effects, and international political developments as well as global ecological crises were the focuses of their observations.

The decisive *weakness* of the future studies appears with regard to the prognoses concerning social and cultural change whose scope and extent was, in most cases, considerably overestimated. This general tendency to overrate the effect of techno-scientific innovations on social and cultural change had above all to do with the fundamental conception of homogeneity and, more important, a simultaneity of modernizing processes due to their cybernetic feedback and corresponding mutual reinforcement. Because of this, the system logic of technological change appeared, through its enormous dynamic, to break into all areas of the society, thereby creating an irreversible standardizing effect. In the context of the idea of evolutionary-historical stages of a general pattern of development, this approach, in principle, had to lead to a kind of techno-scientific determinism that, at its core, tended to underestimate contingencies and contrary or paradoxical developmental tendencies, or simply the slowing of processes of change. Above all, the dimension of cultural change was certainly seen too linearly and as too dependent on technological structural changes, even if it must be emphasized that the area of societal values and orientations occupied a central status, especially in American futurology. But the weak points of this determinism are not only visible in the overestimation of the "future shock" within highly developed societies, as in Toffler's case (who made the newly emerging social movements a kind of standard for future development); they are also visible in the area of the predicted global integration. As correctly as the growing global integration through modern communications was, for the most part, seen, the notion of cultural homogenization linked to it appears all the more distorted, especially in light of contemporary research on globalization that ascertains a growing heterogeneity and splitting of (sub) cultures and, with it, the growing significance of the local, precisely because of increasing networking. It can only be mentioned here that the growing communications and economic networks just have not, as many sociological studies of globalization in the 1990s have shown, led to a worldwide alignment or, at the least, to a homogenization of lifestyles and value systems as the majority of the future studies expected in the 1960s and 1970s. Rather, it is precisely differences and distinguishing characteristics that have received a new significance for the molding of collective identities, as can be very clearly seen in the resurgence of diverse forms of regionalism and (ethnic) nationalism in many parts of the world in the last decade.[39] Moreover, the widespread idea of a "replacement" of values, norms, and lifestyles with new identities appears obsolete in view of diverse findings of a variety of identities that exist side by side. Therefore, instead of a replacement of traditional orientations, we can observe a striking alliance between values of self-realization *and* the market system, between individualistic lifestyles *and* the mass consumer culture, between hedonistic *and* altruistic values—in short the rise of the multicultural, eclectic, "postmodern" culture that combines "countercultural" as well as "affirmative" values and norms in many ways like a sort of patchwork of identities.

In addition, despite their pioneering orientation on globalization processes, most of the studies hardly took notice of those transnational integrative processes that could not be directly traced back to technological bases. This is why such central topics of the 1990s as (poverty-caused) migrations, mass tourism, the development of various international and supranational organizations, and multinational companies, as well as the internationalization of organized crime, were rarely recognized as the central problems of the future. The situation is similar at the national level where, for example, the integration of societal minorities, the formation and growing significance of individual and therefore heterogeneous lifestyles, and, above all, the role of women in the future, when not ignored, were relatively underestimated in their significance even in the 1980s.[40]

The most important reason for this misjudgment was certainly that the majority of the future studies generally thought too little about social actors and institutions and their "power of inertia" against too massive changes in the social environment. Similar to the leading sociological schools of the 1950s and 1960s, such as structuralism and functionalism, the future studies tended to overestimate the rule and system character of societies and so underestimate the relative autonomy of individual and collective actions. This is shown in the prognoses of the information society, among other things, in the overly low estimation of the influence of societal resistance to technological developments in the sense of a growing awareness of technological risks, as well as the possible reorientation of societal needs and priorities. In this regard the extent of the use of nuclear energy was, as we have seen, clearly overestimated because possible collapses, such as the Chernobyl reactor accident in 1986 and its far-reaching consequences for nuclear politics, were not taken enough into consideration. A comparable determinism, focused solely on technical feasibility, also holds for the prognosis of enormously expanding space exploration and the construction of extraterrestrial cities. Here also, only the euphoria of the first moon landing—realized under the very specific conditions of the Cold War in 1969—were extrapolated into the future and societal needs and their change (especially in light of the immense costs) were too little reckoned with.

But, paradoxically, such a determinism also holds for the studies of the "trans-industrial" society, which did concentrate on the social participants in the form of the new social movements and on the change in values in the highly developed societies, but were, due to a relatively high level of abstraction, again much too strongly focused on supposed determinants and system logics and far too little focused on the concrete, nondetermined patterns of social (and political) action. A consequence of this underestimation of the relative autonomy of participants and institutions with respect to the (cybernetic) system logics consisted in an often confused or latent "totalitarian" idea of social planning which, in most cases, hardly dealt with the complex conflicts among interest groups in modern societies and corresponded to either the idea of a "systemic" control by groups of experts or the generally equally confused idea of a "total" democratization of the controlling hierarchies and authorities "from below." Therefore, the relative decline of "holistic" systemically—and cybernetically—oriented futurology in the 1980s, despite the development of many innovative methods, had above all to do with the fundamental problem of the underestimation of social participants and the connected "contingencies" of the system. How highly this relative (political) autonomy of social participants should be estimated was made clear not least by the system-breaking revolutions in the Soviet Union and the East European states since 1989.

However, not only political events but also the inner scientific development caused the relative decline of the "holistic" variation of forecasting described above. Especially new results in applied systems theory in the 1980s and 1990s showed that the behavior of complex systems is much more complex and above all much more chaotic and therefore unpredictable than assumed before. Thus the new focus is on the patterns of self-organization of complex systems, concentrating more on the dialectics between chaos and systemic order rather than directing attention primarily to processes of self-stabilization. As sociologist Manuel Castells correctly points out: "Complexity thinking should be considered as a method for understanding diversity, rather than a unified meta-theory. Its epistemological value could come from acknowledging the serendipitous nature of Nature and of society. Not that there are no rules, but that rules are created, and changed, in a relentless process of deliberate actions and unique interactions. The information technology paradigm does not evolve toward its closure as a system, but toward its openness as a multi-edged network."[41]

Notes

1. Niklas Luhmann, *Beobachtungen der Moderne* (Opladen: Westdeutscher Verlag, 1992), 129–148, esp. 141–143. English translation: *Observations on Modernity* (Stanford: Stanford University Press, 1998).

2. Regarding the historical development of the futures studies after 1945 see among others Wendell Bell, *Foundations of Futures Studies: Human Science for a New Era* (New Brunswick, London: Transaction Publishers, 1997), 1: 1–68. For the general predictive aspects of the social sciences and the humanities see Bruce Mazlish, *The Uncertain Sciences* (New Haven, London: Yale University Press, 1998), 17–20.

3. Perhaps the best known of these "futurists"—some of whom published best-sellers, translated into many other languages—were Herman Kahn, Alvin Toffler, John McHale, Olaf Helmer, R. Buckminster Fuller, Daniel Bell, Kenneth E. Boulding, Dennis Meadows, and Peter F. Drucker in the United States, and Ossip K. Flechtheim, Robert Jungk, Karl Steinbuch, Bertrand de Jouvenel, Johan Galtung, Jean Meynaud, Fred L. Polak, Jean Fourastié, Dennis Gabor, Nigel Calder, and Gordon R. Taylor in Europe.

4. Plan Europe 2000, ed., *The Future Is Tomorrow: 17 Prospective Studies* (The Hague: Martinus Nijhoff, 1972). See also the final report: Peter Hall, ed., *Europe 2000* (New York: Columbia University Press, 1977).

5. See the listings in Peter Moll, *From Scarcity to Sustainability: Futures Studies and the Environment, The Role of the Club of Rome* (Frankfurt/M.: Peter Lang, 1991), 195–197.

6. See Rolf Kreibich, *Die Wissenschaftsgesellschaft. Von Galilei zur High-Tech-Revolution* (Frankfurt/M.: Suhrkamp, 1986), 26–28.

7. See the concise overview of the "information technology revolution" in Manuell Castells, *The Rise of the Network Society*, vol. 1 of *The Information Age: Economy, Society, and Culture* (Malden, Oxford: Blackwell, 1996), 29–65.

8. See, among others, John A. Hannigan, "Fragmentation in Science: The Case of Futurology," in *Sociological Review* 28, no. 2 (1980): 321–322. For the spread of the systems approach from the military to economic, urban, and social development analysis, see Thomas P. Hughes, *Rescuing Prometheus* (New York: Pantheon, 1998), 141–196.

9. See Norbert Wiener, *Cybernetics or Control and Communication in the Animal and the Machine* (Cambridge: MIT Press, 1948). See also the short overview of Wiener's life and his concept of cybernetics in Everett M. Rogers, *A History of Communication Study: A Biographical Approach* (New York: The Free Press, 1994), 386–410.

10. Norbert Wiener, *The Human Use of Human Beings: Cybernetics and Society* (Boston: Houghton Mifflin, 1989), 15–17.

11. See Felix Geyer and Johannes van der Zouwen, "Cybernetics and Social Science: Theories and Research in Sociocybernetics," *Kybernetes* 20, no. 6 (1991): 81–82, and Geof Bowker, "How to Be Universal: Some Cybernetic Strategies, 1943–1970," *Social Studies of Science* 23, no. 1 (1993): 108–115.

12. See the comprehensive overview in Michael Marien, *Societal Directions and Alternatives: A Critical Guide to the Literature* (New York: Lafayette, 1976), 391–393.

13. For the general wave of systems analysis in the 1960s see Howard Brick, *Age of Contradiction: American Thought and Culture in the 1960s* (New York: Twayne Publishers, 1998), 124–136.

14. For an overview of the most prominent studies and different point of views see Barry B. Hughes, *World Futures: A Critical Analysis of Alternatives* (Baltimore and London: The Johns Hopkins University Press, 1985), 12–25, and Sam Cole, "The Global Futures Debate 1965–1976," in Christopher Freeman and Marie Jahoda, eds., *World Futures: The Great Debate* (London: Martin Robinson, 1978), 9–49, as well as Larry D. Wilcox, "Futurology and the Social Sciences: Bloom and Boom or Gloom and Doom?" in *International Social Science Review* 58, no. 4 (1983): 202–210.

15. This paradigm, focusing primarily on the development of economic and social structures, was represented by such more or less prominent futurists like Herman Kahn (and co-workers), Stuart Chase, Peter F. Drucker, Olaf Helmer, John Naisbitt, Robert Ayres, Burnham P. Beckwith, Theodore Gordon, Daniel Bell, and Alvin Toffler in the United States, and Karl Steinbuch, Richard F. Behrendt, Frederic Vester, Jean Fourastié, Jean Meynaud, Pierre Piganiol, François Hetman, Arthur C. Clarke, and Christopher Freeman in Europe.

16. See Herman Kahn and Anthony J. Wiener, *The Year 2000: A Framework for Speculation on the Next Thirty-Three Years* (New York and London: Macmillan, 1967), 7, and in general the comprehensive interpretation of this book in Thomas E. Jones, *Options for the Future: A Comparative Analysis of Policy-Oriented Forecasts* (New York: Praeger, 1980), 85–110.

17. See Kahn and Wiener, *The Year 2000*, 51–55. See also the abridged version in Herman Kahn and Anthony J. Wiener, "The Next Thirty-Three Years: A Framework for Speculation," in Daniel Bell and Stephen S. Graubard, eds., *Toward the Year 2000: Work in Progress* (Cambridge: MIT Press, 1967), 73–100. See also the following studies of the Hudson Institute, which reinforced this basically optimistic outlook, such as Herman Kahn and B. Bruce-Briggs, *Things to Come* (New York: Macmillan, 1972) or Herman Kahn et al., *The Next Two Hundred Years. A Scenario for America and the World* (New York: William Morrow, 1976).

18. Ibid., 58 and 140–144. See also Jones, *Options*, 88–95. For instance, Kahn and Wiener expected average annual rates of growth of gross world product per capita of about 3 percent between 1965 and 2000 and then the doubling of the per capita world output until 2020, "reaching then about five times the world 1965 figure." But whereas the per capita product of the industrial world in 1965 exceeded that of the less developed world only by a factor of about twelve times, they predicted an

increase of this gap of about eighteen times by the year 2000, particularly due to the enormous increase of the population in the less developed countries. Given the rate of 2.2 percent of average annual growth of world per capita income between 1950 and 1990, these general expectations were quite correct (see Cooper in this volume). But also the growing discrepancy worldwide was foreseen correctly, given the fact that in the decade between 1980 and 1992 the annual growth rates reached from sometimes even more than 6 percent of GDP per capita in some booming (Asian) countries to negative growth rates of up to 4 percent in many African and some Latin American countries.

19. See Theodore J. Gordon and Olaf Helmer, *Report on a Long-Range Forecasting Study* in Olaf Helmer et al., *Social Technology* (New York: Basic Books, 1966), 44–95. See also Jones, *Options*, 44–67.

20. See Gorden R. Taylor, *The Biological Time Bomb* (London: Thames and Hudson, 1968) and the review with the same title in the *Futurist* 2, no. 6 (1968): 112–116. Taylor furthermore was quite realistic in saying that these predictions were primarily technical probabilities leaving the social and political considerations out of perspective.

21. See Alvin Toffler, *Future Shock* (New York: Random House, 1970).

22. Karl W. Deutsch, *The Nerves of Government: Models of Political Communication and Control* (New York, London: The Free Press, 1966), xiii. For a detailed analysis of the cybernetic impact on political science see ibid., especially 75–244.

23. See for instance (with different backgrounds and intentions) the works of authors such as Lester Brown, Richard A. Falk, Erwin Laszlo, John R. Platt, Erich Jantsch, Victor Ferkiss, Ossip K. Flechtheim, and Pierre Bertaux.

24. Johan Galtung, "On the Future of the International System," in Robert Jungk and Johan Galtung, eds., *Mankind 2000* (Oslo, London: Allen and Unwin, 1969), 14.

25. Ibid., 25 (italics in original). See also in general ibid., 19–41.

26. See ibid., 33–36, and also Richard F. Behrendt, "Some Structural Prerequisites for a Global Society Based on Non-Violent Conflict Solution," in Jungk and Galtung, *Mankind 2000*, 66–68.

27. See Arthur I. Waskow, "Looking Forward: 1999," in Jungk and Galtung, *Mankind 2000*, 78–98, especially 88–98.

28. See R. Buckminster Fuller, *Utopia of Oblivion: The Prospects for Humanity* (New York: Overlook Press, 1969), and regarding the development toward a planetary society see John McHale, *The Future of the Future* (New York: G. Braziller, 1969), particularly 267–300.

29. John R. Platt, *The Step to Man* (New York: Wiley, 1966), 202–203.

30. See among others Robert Jungk, *The Everyman Project: A World Report on the Resources for a Humane Society* (New York: Liveright, 1977).

31. One of the first descriptions of this new counterculture was Theodore Roszak's *The Making of a Counter Culture: Reflections on the Technocratic Society and Its Youthful Opposition* (Garden City: Doubleday, 1969).

32. As advocates of the radical paradigm in its different variations, see among others Gordon Rattray Taylor, *Rethink: A Paraprimitive Solution* (New York: Dutton, 1973); William E. Thompson, *At the Edge of History* (New York: Harper & Row, 1971); Theodore Roszak, *Where the Wasteland Ends: Politics and Transcendence in Postindustrial Society* (Garden City: Doubleday, 1972); Ivan Illich, *Tools for Conviviality* (New York: Harper & Row, 1973), and Robert Theobald, *An Alternative Future for America* (Chicago: Swallow Press, 1968).

33. This perspective is taken by Michael Marien, "The Two Visions of Post-Industrial Society," in Ralph Jones, ed., *Reading from "Futures": A Collection of Articles from the Journal* Futures, *1974–1980* (Guildford: Nestbury House, 1981), 21–39, esp. 27–32 regarding decentralization.

34. See Willis W. Harman, *Notes on the Coming Transformation* in Andrew A. Spekke, ed., *The Next 25 Years: Crisis and Opportunity* (Washington: The World Future Society, 1975), 12–14, and the critical comparison with Herman Kahn's model of the post-industrial society, ibid., 18–22. See also in more detail W. W. Harman, *An Incomplete Guide to the Future* (San Francisco: The San Francisco Book Company, 1976), esp. 39–88, and with regard to the emergence of a "transindustrial era," 113–145.

35. See Magoroh Maruyama, "The Post-Industrial Logic," in Spekke, ed., *The Next 25 Years*, 43. See also in more detail the comparing tables and explanations ibid., 44–50.

36. See Thomas R. Shannon, *An Introduction to the World-System Perspective* (Boulder: Westview, 1996).

37. See W. Warren Wagar, *Building the City of Man: Outlines of a World Civilization, A World Order Book* (New York: Grossman Publishers, 1971), and recently *A Short History of the Future* (Chicago: University of Chicago Press, 1992) as well as, among others, Gordon R. Taylor, *How to Avoid the Future* (London: Secker & Warburg, 1975), and Roberto Vacca, *The Coming Dark Age* (Garden City: Doubleday, 1973). For a collection of these doom prophecies see also the overview in Cornish et al., *The Study of the Future: An Introduction to the Art and Science of Understanding and Shaping Tomorrow's World* (Washington: The World Future Society, 1977), 21–34.

38. See Castells, *Rise of the Network Society*, 44–50.

39. See among others Roland Robertson, *Globalization: Social Theory and Global Culture* (London: Sage, 1992), and Stuart Hall, "The Question of Cultural Identity," in Stuart Hall et al., eds., *Modernity and Its Futures* (Cambridge, Oxford: Polity, 1992), 274–316, as well as the overview in Ulrich Beck, *Was ist Globalisierung?* (Frankfurt/M.: Suhrkamp, 1997), 80–149.

40. See Joseph F. Coates and Jennifer Jarratt, *What Futurists Believe* (Bethesda: Lomond, 1989), 24.

41. Castells, *The Rise of the Network Society*, 65. See also, for instance, Theodore J. Gordon, "Chaos in Social Systems," in *Technological Forecasting and Social Change* 42, no. 1(1992): 1–15.

Contributors

Clark C. Abt   Chairman, Abt Associates, Inc.; Associate, Belfer Center for Science and International Affairs, Harvard University

Timothy Besley   Professor of Economics and Director of the Suntory Toyota International Centres for Economics and Related Disciplines at the London School of Economics.

Joel E. Cohen   Laboratory of Populations, Rockefeller University and Columbia University

Richard N. Cooper   The Centre for International Affairs, Harvard University

Richard Freeman   Harvard University, NBER and Centre for Economic Performance, LSE

Benjamin L. Friedman   William Joseph Maier Professor of Political Economy, Harvard University

Richard Layard   Director, Centre for Economic Performance, London School of Economics

Alexander Schmidt-Gernig   Assistant Professor, History Department, Humboldt University, Berlin

Stephen H. Schneider   Professor of Biological Sciences; Senior Fellow, Institute for International Studies, Stanford University

Peter Schwartz   Global Business Network

Index

Abatement cost estimates, 144
Abt, Clark, 9–10
Accountability, of government
  authority, 213–214
Acid rain, and governance structures,
  220
Acquisitions, 173
Action
  supranational democratic, 227, 250
  and uncertainty, 26–27
Adriatic, decline of coal consumption in,
  109
Aerosols, "anthropogenic," 135
Africa
  coal consumption in, 109
  economic activity of women in, 42
  electrification projects in, 111
  energy consumption in, 103
  PGER in, 41
Age, and workforce, 166
Agriculture
  in advanced countries, 167
  intensification of, 65
  and population growth, 9, 48
AIDS epidemic, 56
Aiken, Howard, 53
Allard, H. A., 51
Amerindians, decimation of, 69
Ammonia, emissions of, 40
*Analysen und Prognosen über die Welt von
  morgen*, 234
Anderson, Benedict, 212
Anderson, James, 141
Anglo Pacific, PGER in, 41
Anthropogenic causation, 124

Anthropogenic radiative forcing, 135
Antibiotics
  discovery of, 52
  impact of, 49
  introduction of, 54
Anticipation
  methodologies of, 17
  useful, 27
Antigravity, discovering secret of, 24
Anti-inflation policy, of central banks,
  187
Antimalarials, impact of, 49
Appliances, impact of domestic, 49, 50
Aquaculture, and population growth, 9
Arable land, population and, 304
Argentina, monetary policy of, 204.
  See also Latin America
Arthur Andersen and Co., 88
Artillery systems, telecommunicatively
  guided, 236
Asia, East
  backlash against crisis in, 221
  financial crisis of, 201, 202
  PGER in, 41
Asia, economic activity of women in,
  42
Asia, Southeast
  electricity generation in, 107
  PGER in, 41
Atmosphere, earth's
  black-body radiation in, 134
  carbon dioxide in, 10
  during Ice Age, 125
  management of, 65, 66
Attitudes, and population growth, 9

Authority, delegated, 213–214, 216
Automation, predictions for, 240
Automobile. *See also* Electric vehicles
  gasoline costs for, 100
  invention of self-starter for, 51
Automobile manufacturers, EV
  prototypes produced by, 111

Baby boom, 47, 59
Bacteria, genetically engineered, 66
Balkans. *See also* Kosovo crisis
  hydroelectric potential of, 109
  military intervention in, 210
Bank money, erosion of demand for,
  193–197
Bank of Japan, money growth policy of,
  183–184
Banks
  clearing mechanisms of, 199–201
  diminished importance of, 198
Banks, central
  anti-inflation policy of, 187
  changing role of, 205–206
  and demand for currency, 196–197
  discretion of, 186, 187
  European, 184, 187, 201, 205, 223
  financial markets and, 179
  and inflation, 185
  monetary policies of, 180, 194
  money growth targets of, 183
  as monopolists, 188–193
  and nonbank credit, 197–199
  and "off shore" transactions, 203
  in regulatory race, 196
  reserve compliance of, 191–192
  as suppliers of reserves, 190
Batteries, lead-acid, 112
Behavior
  investor, 202
  and mathematical models, 19
Beliefs
  risk assessment in, 26
  specifications for, 19
Bell, Daniel, 238
Berlin Zentrum für Zukunftsforschung,
  234
Besley, Timothy, 13
Billiard balls, flow of time as, 17

Biological environment, collapse of,
  250. *See also* Atmosphere; Ecology;
  Oceans; Temperature
Biotechnology
  impact of, 25
  potential of, 176
  predictions for, 252
Biotic processes, human interventions
  in, 39
Birth control
  expanded availability of, 55
  forecasts on, 14
  predictions for, 240
Birth control pill, 54
Black-body radiation, 134
Black Death, in Europe, 43, 68, 69
Boeing, planning for future of, 1
Bonaparte, Napoleon, 3
Bongaarts, John, 43
Borlaug, Norman, 55
Borrowing, reliance on, 188. *See also*
  Credit
Bossel, Hartmut, 70
Bowler, Shaun, 217
Bradley, R. S., 127
Bretton Woods agreement, 53, 215
Britain, decline of coal consumption in,
  108. *See also* United Kingdom
British Petroleum
  investment in renewables of, 95
  solar investment of, 99
Broadcasting technologies, evolution of,
  218–219. *See also* Media
Broecker, W. S., 143
Brown, Harold, 94
Bucharest, Third World Conference
  1972 in, 234
Building-integrated photovoltaics
  (BIPV), 98
Buildings
  energy-independent, 111
  and energy transformations, 100–
  101
Bulatao, Rudolfo A., 43
Burtraw, 91
Bus, electric jitney, 111
"Business as usual" trends, 113
Businesses, planning for future of, 1

California
  deregulated energy market of, 93
  economic growth in, 84
  electricity deficit of, 115
  energy supply crisis in, 79
Cambridge Energy Research Associates,
  88
Cannan, Edward, 44
Capital
  accumulation of, 185
  controls, 203
  taxing mobile, 223
Capitalism
  employment contracts in, 168
  "golden age of," 250
Carbon, global cycle of, 39
Carbon dioxide (CO_2)
  in atmosphere, 10
  as greenhouse gas, 134
  impact of doubling of, 140
Carbon dioxide (CO_2) levels
  during ice ages, 126
  and investment in emissions controls,
    144
  since Industrial Revolution, 125
Carbon tax, 146
Career choices, market incentives and,
  165
Caribbean
  economic activity of women in, 42
  PGER in, 41
Carnegie Mellon group, 144
Castells, Manuel, 255
Census, U.S. Bureau of, 44
Central America, electrification projects
  in, 111. *See also* Latin America
Cereal crops, weed killers for, 53
Cess, Robert, 141
Change. *See also* Social change
  causes of, 3
  climate, 10–11 (see also Climate
    change)
  driven by technology, 14
  irreversible, 5
  key predictors of, 4
Chaos
  mathematics of, 18, 66
  theory, 6, 21

Chernobyl reactor accident, 254
Childbearing, in 21st century, 64
Children
  in developing countries, 59
  and family incomes, 174
  in 21st century, 60–61, 64
China
  coal consumption of, 106–107
  dependence on imported oil of, 93
  electrification projects in, 111
  energy consumption in, 103, 105
  energy policy options for, 94
  ICBM force of, 110
  oil consumption of, 90
  renewables in, 105
  scenarios for, 8
  U.S. DOE solar homes program in, 102
CHIPS network, 200
Chlorofluorocarbons, in greenhouse
  gases, 135
Choices
  future and, 70
  global integration of, 247
Cipolla, Carlo M., 69
Cities, in 21st century, 64. *See also*
  Urbanization
Citizens, and accountability of
  government, 225
Citizenship
  elements of, 42, 68
  rights of, 41
  and supranational democratic action,
    227
Citizens' initiatives, 217
Civil rights, 9, 42
Civil-rights movement, 248
Class conflict, north-south, 246
Climate
  human dependence on, 123
  human impact on, 138, 143
  predictions for control of, 240
  compared with weather, 131
Climate change, 10–11
  and carbon tax, 146
  dramatic, 139
  health impacts of, 147
  IAMs of, 143–144, 150
  modeling, 123, 128

Climate change (cont.)
  natural variability in, 129
  potential damage of, 149
  seasons and, 129
  societal value of, 149
  and volcanic dust, 128
Climate damage
  dimensions of, 149
  estimate of, 147
Climate forcing, radiative, 125
Climate science, policy implications of,
    140
Climate sensitivity
  elicited probability distributions of, 142
  equilibrium, 137
  IPCC range for, 136
  range for, 126
Climate signal, detecting, 127
Climatic impacts, regional projections
    for, 137
Climatic models, 129–130
  cause and effect in, 130–131
  fundamentals, 130–132
Cloning, 176, 258n.20
Cloudiness, 136
Club of Rome, 4, 158, 234, 238
Clubs, loyalties to, 228
Coal
  and carbon tax, 146
  decline in consumption of, 107
  environmental costs of, 107
  market share of, 106
  recoverable reserves of, 108
  U.S. DOE forecast on, 105–110
Coase, Ronald, 212
Coercive power, vs. negotiation, 212
Cohen, Joel, 6, 8, 43
Cohort-component projection, 43–44
Cold War
  end of, 22
  and first moon landing, 254
  and transactional networks, 246
Collective action, 219
Committee on Science, Space, and
    Technology, House
  Subcommittee on Investigations and
    Oversight of, 164
Common law, international, 68

Communication. *See also* Cybernetics;
    Media
  and energy transformations, 100
  falling costs of, 225
  and global integration, 247–248
  global TV, 81
  and post-industrial society, 239
  technology, 12
  20th-century changes in, 41–42
Competition, in trans-industrial society,
    249
Complex systems, behavior of, 255
Comprehensibility, 6
Computational technology, 12
Computers
  forecasts on, 14
  impact of, 172, 235
  and income inequality, 174
  invention of, 53
  predictions for, 240, 252
  universal use of, 167
Computer simulations
  based on cybernetic mathematical
    models, 239
  of climate, 10, 123, 131
  transient vs. equilibrium, 137
Conference on Social Science and
    Future, Oxford, 7, 181, 207
Congress, U.S.
  National Fuels and Energy Policy
    Study of, 84, 85
  and NSF projections, 163–164
  and Republican Contract with
    America, 217
Conservation movements, 66
Consumer credit, 199
Consumerism, mass, 235
Consumer preferences
  and energy consumption, 113
  for environment-conserving energy
    products, 81
Continental shelves, development of, 65
Continents, management of, 66
Contingent pay
  flexibility gained by, 169
  shared capitalist, 173
Contraception, expanded availability of,
    54, 55

Control processes, 236
Copernicus, 6
Copyright, and Internet, 221
Corporations, multinational, 68
Cortisone, synthesis of, 54
Cost-benefit optimization strategies, 149
Costs
  ecological, 248
  and Internet, 175
  social, 146
Credit
  consumer, 199
  proliferation of nonbank, 197–199
Credit business, banks' share in, 197
Credit cards, introduction of third-party,
  194
Crick, Francis, 235
Crime
  forecasting violent, 18
  organized, 254
Cultural change, predictions for, 252–
  253
Cultural satisfaction, in trans-industrial
  society, 250
Culture
  and human populations, 29
  in post-industrial society, 239
  quantitative indicators of, 31–32
  specifications for, 19
  and techno-scientific bias, 251
  20th-century changes in, 40–43
  in 21st century, 68–70
"Culture shock," 242
"Cumulus parameterization," 133
Currencies
  and monetary policies, 203–204
  and nation-state boundaries, 201
Cybernation, predictions for, 240
Cybernetics, 14. *See also*
    Communication
  defined, 236
  and global integration, 247–248
  influence on society of, 236, 237
Cytogenetics, 49

Dams
  mass of water redistributed by, 40
  Three Gorges, 87

Darmstadter, 91
Data collection and analysis,
  improvements in, 66. *See also*
  Information
"Daylight overdrafts," 199
DDT, synthesis of, 52
Decision making
  decentralized market, 173
  decentralizing, 177
  and uncertainty, 26–27
  and view of future, 6
Delegated authority
  dimensions of, 213–214
  indirect, 216
  for national externalities, 214
Delphi, Greek oracles of, 14
Delphi technique, 7, 18, 241
Demand, standard mechanical
    projections of, 165. *See also* Energy
  demand; Labor demand
Demand side, forecasts on, 159
Democracies
  and energy demand, 97
  future-oriented, 243
  and middle class, 174
  representative, 213
Democratic fatigue, 218
Democratic processes
  and global integration, 248
  means of accountability in, 216
Demographic approach, to predicting
  population growth, 43–45
Demographic developments, 8. *See also*
  Population growth
Denmark
  decline of coal consumption in, 108
  wind energy in, 80–81
Deposit insurance, in monetary policy,
  205
Depository intermediaries, 198. *See also*
  Banks
De-standardization, in trans-industrial
  society, 250
Deutsch, Karl W., 243–244
Deutsche Bundesbank, money growth
  policy of, 183–184
Developed countries
  cybernetic systems in, 251

Developed countries (cont.)
  defined, 62–63
  elites of, 246–247
  energy demand in, 96
  manufacturing in, 167
  peace and prosperity of, 229
  population density in, 63
  TFR in, 63
Developing countries, energy demand in,
  113. *See also* Less developed countries
Developing world. *See also* Less
  developed countries
  energy use estimates for, 101
  oil consumption of, 90
Dickinson, Robert, 141
Dictators, minor, 20
Disarmament, worldwide, 246
Disasters, forecasting of, 14
Disinflation
  costless, 187
  costs of, 184–186
"Distribution dilemma," 249
Diversity
  in complexity thinking, 255
  and political development, 219
Djerassi, Carl, 54
DNA structure, discovery of, 54, 235
Doctors, unionizing of, 175
Donovan, Todd, 217
Dowlatabadi, Hadi, 144
Drugs, predictions for, 241
Duisenberg, President, 179
Dynamic interactions, in cybernetics,
  236–237

Earth, rotation of, 40
Earth Day, 55
Earth system models (ESMs), 137, 138
Eastern Europe, system-breaking
  revolutions in, 255
East-West conflict, 252
E-cash, 196
Ecology
  lack of predictions for, 241
  and rapid scientific-technological
    change, 248
  terrestrial changes, 139
E-commerce

  multinationals and, 173
  regulation of, 221
Econometric models
  analysis of trends in, 158
  and long-term forecasting, 83
Economic analyses, 5, 116
Economic growth
  determining variables for, 6
  and environmental remediation, 106
  impact of, 19
  and oil consumption, 104
  solar-powered, 117
  during 20th century, 38
  world, 112
Economics
  politics and, 214
  predictions in, 157, 252
  of scarcity, 99, 248
  short-term forecasts in, 15
Economics, monetary
  and costs of disinflation, 184–186
  disagreements about, 182
  institutional change and, 186–188
  "money growth vs. interest rates"
    debate in, 183
  past predicitons from, 181–188
Economies. *See also* Financial markets
  apartheid, 173–174
  and CO_2 reduction costs, 146
  and energy demand, 96
  and human populations, 29
  institutionless, 175
  quantitative indicators of, 31
  in 21st century, 67
Economists
  environmental anxiety of, 147–148
  focus on future of, 233–234
  as forecasters, 79
  on technological change, 114–115
Ecosystems, managed, 65
Edison Electric Power Institute, 92
Education
  computerized learning in, 240
  and income inequality, 174
  opportunity for, 40
  and PGER, 41
  in post-industrial society, 239
  of women, 166

Efficiency, in trans-industrial society, 249
El Chichón, eruption of, 128
Elderly, in 21st century, 60–61
Electricity
  populations without, 101–102
  wind-generated, 91
Electric jitney bus, production of, 111
Electric utilities, EVs sponsored by, 111
Electric vehicles (EVs), 89, 90, 104
  politics of, 112
  production of, 111
  technology of, 95
Electrification
  LDC demand for, 81–82
  solar projects, 111
Electronic technology, and investor
    behavior, 202
Elites
  of LDCs, 247
  in post-industrial society, 239
Employment
  forecasting, 159
  future developments in, 165–168
  impact of Internet on, 173
  and income inequality, 174
  inflation and, 157
  and role of central banks, 193, 206
  standard projections of, 162
Employment contract, defined, 168
Employment-population rate, 170
Encryption technology, 196
Energy
  forecasting of, 115
  new forms of, 176 (*see also* Renewables)
  planning production of, 77
  renewable, 90–92 (*see also* Renewables)
  2020 forecasting for, 92–113
Energy, U.S. Dept. of (DOE)
  Annual Energy Review (1997) of, 84
  energy forecast of, 117
  forecasts of, 79–80
  International Energy Outlook 1999 of,
    89
  oil prices forecasted by, 103
  Performance of Past IEO report of, 85
  projections of, 113
  2020 forecast of, 101–111, 117

Energy consumption, 5, 9–10
  DOE estimates for, 101
  forecasting, 112–113
Energy demand, 77
  estimates for, 114
  forecasting, 112–113, 117
  growth in, 85, 97
  in LDCs, 81
  for oil, 89
  outpacing supply, 96–100
  predicting, 78, 79
  world, 97
Energy Economics, 94
Energy forecasts
  review of past, 82–86
  for world, 86
Energy industry
  markets in, 80
  restructuring of, 92
  world, 93
Energy prices
  forecasting, 87, 117
  predicting, 78
Energy shortages
  and building technology, 101
  impending, 97
Energy sources, new, 80. *See also*
  Renewables
Energy supplies, 77
  forecast for, 117
  growth of non-oil, 89
  political demand for, 95
  predicting, 78
  sustainable, 99
Energy transformations, technological
  changes driving, 100–101
"Engineer corps," 247
Engineering, projections in, 162–163
Engineers
  focus on future of, 234
  NSF projections for, 163–165
  progress and, 177
England, Bank of, 183–184
English language, dominance of, 224
Environment. *See also* Atmosphere;
    Oceans; Temperature
  and human populations, 29
  quantitative indicators of, 31

Environment (cont.)
  20th-century changes in, 39–40
  in 21st century, 65–67
Environmental Protection Agency, U.S.,
  sea levels study of, 144
Epidemics, predictions for, 250
Eskom, 90, 109
Esthetics, in trans-industrial society, 250
Ethics, in trans-industrial society, 250
Ethnic groups, autonomy for, 210
Ethnic identity, 227
Euro, 204–205
Europe
  coal consumption in, 108
  dependence on imported oil of, 93
  energy policy options for, 94
  PGER in, 41
  renewables in, 109
  rise of urban society in, 69
European Central Bank, 184, 187, 201,
  205, 223
European Cultural Foundation, 234
European Union (EU), 13, 204
  capital mobility within, 214
  delegated authority of, 216, 217
  future of, 209
  labor flows in, 214
  legitimacy of, 221
  national democratic institutions of,
  228–229
  national veto in, 216
  social protection afforded by, 221–222
  TARGET system of, 200
Evapotranspiration, 136
Events, interpretation of, 2
Evolutionary theories, 238
Exogenous approaches, to population
  projection, 45–46
Extrapolation
  for predictions, 6
  of technological trends, 12

Families, loyalties to, 228
"Farmer corps," 247
Farm machinery, solar-electric, 111
Federal Reserve System, U.S., 184
  and central bank potency, 206
  "Fedwire" of, 200

reserves maintained with, 188
  securities bought by, 189
Feminism, 248. *See also* Women
Feminization, of work, 166–167
Ferguson, Niall, 20
Fertility
  high, 35
  major changes in, 36
  predictions for, 241
  reduction in, 37, 47
  in 21st century, 61
Fertility rates, in LDCs, 35
Finance, international, 202
Financial crises
  in East Asia, 201, 202, 221
  supranational nature of, 214
Financial markets
  arbitrage conditions of, 192
  globalization of, 202, 203
  influence of central banks on, 188
Fisher, Ronald A., 49
"Five Numeraires," 149
Flight, air, 50
"Flux adjustment," 136
Food
  cereals, 49, 53, 55
  genetic modification of, 176
Ford, Henry, 50
Forecasters, types of, 19–20
Forecasting
  art of, 2
  conservative, 18
  elements of, 5
  failure of, 115
  measurement errors in, 82
  of oil prices, 88, 103
  purpose of, 15
  sources of error in, 83–84
Forecasting, energy, 77
  methods of, 116
  problems with, 83
  review of past, 82–86
  for 2020, 86–90
Forecasting errors, of demographic
  projections, 44–45
Forecasts
  demographic, 8 (see also Population
  growth)

exogenous, 45–46
usefulness of, 79
Foreign students, in U.S., 163
Forests, management of tropical, 65
Forrester's Industrial Dynamics, 82
Fortress Russia scenario, 23
Fortune sellers, 158
Fossil fuels
 dependence on, 9
 masking costs of, 99–100
 price increases of, 99
Freeman, Chris, 171
Freeman, Richard, 11
French Association Futuribles
 Internationale, 234
Friedman, Benjamin, 12
Friedman, Milton, 3
Fuel cell, development of, 25
Fuller, Buckminster R., 247
Fusion power, 111
Future
 perceptions of, 233
 planning for, 1
Futures, The Journal of Forecasting and Planning, 234
Future Shock (Toffler), 242, 243, 253
Future studies. *See also* Research
 cybernetics in, 236
 historical development of, 256n.2
 information society in, 239–243
 planetary society in, 243
 of 1960s and early 1970s, 251
 trans-industrial society in, 248–251
 weakness of, 252
Futuribles, 234
Futurist, The, 234
Futurists, 256n.3
Futurology
 enterprise of, 158
 evolution of theories in, 238
 mistakes in, 14
 modern, 13–15
 relative decline of "holistic," 255
 research in, 234–235

Gain-sharing, 169
Galtung, Johan, 244–246
Garden, global, 63

Garner, W. W., 51
Gas
 oil displaced by, 114
 unreliability of forecasts for, 104
 U.S. DOE forecast for, 104–105
Gas imports, U.S. dependence on, 110
Gasoline
 costs of, 100
 invention of, 51
 U.S. subsidies for, 112
Gates, Bill, 2
Gates, Lawrence, 141
Gender gap, in education, 166
General circulation models (GCMs),
 123, 131
 grids for, 132
 parametric representation in, 132–133,
 135
 validation of, 135–137, 138
General climate models (GCMs), 10
"General systems theory," 237
Generation gap, 250–251
Genetic engineering, 176, 240
Genetics, modern, 50
Genome, human, 23, 176
Genome sequence, first publishing of, 56
Geological processes, human
 interventions in, 39
Germany, decline of coal consumption
 in, 108
Globalization
 and CO_2 reduction costs, 146
 financial, 202, 203
 of futurological research, 238
 and income inequality, 174
 of political power, 243
Global summits, limits of, 220
Global warming
 collective action for, 211
 and development of renewables, 96
 and governance structures, 220
 "nonmarket" damages caused by, 148
 and solar-hydrogen energy economy,
 104
 supranational nature of, 214
Goldsmith, James, 158
Gold standard, success of, 215
Goodhart, Charles, 12

Gordon, Theodore J., 241
Governance. *See also* Delegated authority
  international, 215–216
  principles of, 211–220
  supranational, 215
  and technological innovation, 227–229
Governments. *See also* Nation-states
  accountability of, 213–214
  and central banks, 197
  decentralized, 225–226
  forecasting oil prices for, 87
  functionally specific, 218
  horizontal structure of, 217–218
  ideal structure of, 211, 219–220
  national, 223
  organization of, 209
  planning for future of, 1
  as policeman, 215
  representative, 39–41
  and technological change, 13
  technology for organizing, 210
  vertical structure of, 211–217
Grandma economy, 168
Great Depression, 46
Green energy revolution, 25
Greenhouse effect
  explained, 133–134
  human augmentation of, 135
  natural, 126
Greenhouse gases
  in atmosphere, 10
  during Ice Age, 125–126
Greening of Russia, 23
Green Revolution, 55
Greenspan, Alan, 19, 179
Gross Domestic Product (GDP), as measure of economic well-being, 38
Gross National Product (GNP)
  carbon taxes in, 146
  and futurological research, 235
  and income distribution, 38
  U.S., 148
Gross World Product (GWP)
  and energy consumption, 102
  predicitons for, 257–258n.18
Group identities, changing, 227–228
"Growth dilemma," 249

Guilds, 176
Gulf War, 114, 225

Haber-Bosch process for nitrogen fixation, 49, 51
Hadley Center, 137
Hajnal, J., 43
Hammond, Allen, 70
Harman, Willis W., 248, 249
Hayami, Gov., 179
Health records, government responsibility for, 226
Health sector, in advanced countries, 167
Helmer, Olaf, 241
Hemp, control of growth of, 51
Herbicides, 65
Herlihy, David, 68
Heterogeneity, in trans-industrial society, 250
Hierarchy, in trans-industrial society, 249
High-rise buildings, solar electricity-generating screening walls on, 98
Historical analysis, 116
Historical models, 20–21
Historical stage theories, 238
History
  as guide to future, 17
  and innovation, 26
  national identities from, 222–223
  study of, 2
  and techno-scientific bias, 251
Hitler, Adolph, 3
HMOs, 175
Holland, William, 141
Holocene Interglacial, 124
Holt, Benjamin, 50
Homogeneity, in trans-industrial society, 249
Hops, control of growth of, 51
Households
  in 21st century, 64
  U.S. securities bought by, 189
Hudson Institute, 234, 243
Hughes, M. K., 127
Human genome project, 176
Human settlement, infection and, 66–67

Humidity, computer simulations of, 131
Hunger, predictions for, 250
Hydrocarbons, as greenhouse gases, 135
Hydroelectric vehicles (HEVs), 104. *See also* Electric vehicles
Hydrogen
  distribution of, 105
  replacement of jet fuel by, 104
Hydrogen turbines, development of, 95

Iberian peninsula, decline of coal consumption in, 109
IBM, 2
Ice Age, 124–125
Illich, Ivan, 248
Illiteracy, 69
Imagined communities, 212
Immigrants, less skilled, 171
Immigration. *See also* Migration
  and Congressional policy, 163
  and income inequality, 174
Incomes, 5
  in apartheid economy, 173–174
  average annual, 69
  and energy consumption, 102
  global distribution of, 38
  improvement in average, 38
  and life expectancy, 45
  and monetary policy, 182–184
  rising inequality in, 174
India
  coal consumption of, 106–107
  energy consumption in, 103, 105
  oil consumption of, 90
  renewables in, 105
Indonesia
  energy consumption in, 103
  oil consumption of, 90
Industrial era, fundamental overcoming of, 244. *See also* Post-industrial society
Industrialized countries. *See also* Developed countries
  carbon emissions of, 106
  disinflation of, 186
  energy future of, 117
  price stability achieved by, 187

Industrial Revolution
  carbon dioxide levels since, 125
  inventions and, 3
Industry
  energy, 80, 92, 93
  forecasting oil prices for, 87
  knowledge, 239
  planning for future of, 1
  solar photovoltaic manufacturing, 111
Infectious diseases
  emerging new, 66
  impact of antibiotics on, 49, 52, 54
  threat of, 69
Inflation, 157
  high, 184–185
  and interest rates, 182
Information
  access to, 225
  decreasing costs of, 227
  and futurological research, 235
  value of, 67
Information-communication technology, 167
Information processing, increased efficiency of, 172
Information society
  post-industrial society as, 239
  predictions for, 252
Information technologies
  and democratic process, 218
  global growth of, 67
  impact on workplace of, 172
Inman, Robert, 215
Innovations
  energy, 80
  history and, 26
Institute for Future, 234
Insurance companies
  rapid advance of, 198
  U.S. securities bought by, 189
Integrated assessment analysts, 143
Integrated assessment (IA) activities, 140
Integrated assessment models (IAMs)
  of climate change, 143–144, 150
  uses for, 123
Integration, global
  impact on LDCs, 247
  through modern communications, 253

Intel, 2
Interaction, in trans-industrial society, 250
Interbank netting systems, 200
Interest rates
central banks' effect on, 189, 194
market, 188
Intergovernmental Panel on Climatic Change (IPCC)
mission of, 143
SAR, 141
and subjective probabilities, 150
Intergovernmental Panel on Climatic Change (IPCC) Working Group I
lead authors of, 140–141
Second Assessment Report of, 136, 143
Summary for Policy Makers of, 139, 141, 143
Intermarriages, 64
International Agricultural Research, Consultative Group on, 56
International aid, 220
International Centre for Maize and Wheat Improvement (CIMMYT), 55
International conventions, on status of women, 42
International cooperation, 228
International courts, 213
International Energy Outlook 1999 (DOE), 85, 101, 113
International governmental organizations (IGOs), 246
International Monetary Fund (IMF), 209
International nongovernmental organizations (INGOs), 246
International Rice Research Institute (IRRI), 55
Internet, 11, 175
and employment, 173
governments and, 225
impact of, 24
increasing use of, 167
law and, 221
predictions for, 252
Inventions, 20th-century, 49
Investors' behavior, in East Asia's financial crisis, 202
Invisible hand model, 175

Iranian revolution, 86
Iran oil crisis, 114
Italy, wage inequality in, 173–174

Japan
dependence on imported oil of, 93
as economic model, 157
energy policy options for, 94
money growth policy of, 183–184
Jobs, permanent, 168. *See also* Employment; Labor force
John Muir Woods, 65
Journals, scientific, 235
Judgment, expert, 17, 18
Just-in-time production, 169

Kahn, Herman, 14, 239, 240, 241, 248
Karl, Thomas, 141
Keegan, John, 20
Keilman, Nico, 43
Keith, D. W., 140, 147, 149
Kepler, Johannes, 6
Keynes, John Maynard, 210
Knowledge
global integration of, 247 (*See also* Information)
predictions for, 252
scientific, 235, 252
Knowledge industry, in post-industrial society, 239
Kosovo crisis
and access to information, 225
cooperation among capitalist countries and, 215
and United Nations, 216
Kyoto, Challenge from the Future 1970 in, 234
Kyoto Protocol, 105, 106

Labor, U.S. Dept. projections, 159–160
Labor demand
shifts in, 167
short-term, 169
standard projections of, 158–165, 165
Labor flows, in EU, 214

Labor force. *See also* Women
  forecasting, 159
  in LDCs, 166–167
  shift in world, 11
  and wage increases, 163
Labor markets, 64
Labor supply, standard projections for,
  158–165
Lamfalussy Report, 200
Lane, Neal, 165
Lasers, forecasts on, 14
Latin America
  economic activity of women in, 42
  energy consumption in, 103
  PGER in, 41
  Rockefeller Brothers'-financed Soluz
    in, 87
Law, international contract, 68
Learning, computerized, 240
Leisure
  demand for, 172
  income elasticity of, 171
Lender-of-last-resort policy, 205
Less developed countries (LDCs)
  accelerated change in, 99
  demand for energy-intensive consumer
    goods in, 81
  electrification of, 113
  elites of, 247
  energy demand in, 80, 94, 96
  energy future of, 117
  and global economy, 174
  indigenous energy supply in, 95
  manufacturing production in, 167
  nuclear power in, 110
  in planetary society, 245
  renewables in, 90
  shift in world labor force to, 166–167
Less developed regions. *See also*
  Developed countries
  growing demands of, 67–68
  growing populations in, 35–36
  TFR in, 63
Libel laws, and Internet, 221
Life expectancy
  and economic development, 45–46
  forecasts on, 14
  increases in, 36

predictions for, 240
Lifestyles
  heterogeneous, 254
  homogenization of, 253
"Limits to growth" theories, 45, 55, 238,
  249
Lindzen, Richard, 140, 141
Lippes, Jack, 55
Literacy, in post-industrial society, 239.
  See also Education
Literature, national identities from, 222–
  223
Living standards, progress and, 177
Lobby groups, international organization
  of, 226
London, 1999 march on, 226
Luhmann, Niklas, 233
Lutz, Wolfgang, 43

Maastricht Treaty, 179, 205, 222
MacCracken, Michael, 141
Macroeconometric modeling, 116
Maize
  CIMMYT, 55
  and cytogenetics, 49
Malthus, Thomas Robert, 47, 157
Manabe, Syukuro, 141
Mandela, Nelson, 81
Mann, M. E., 127
Manufacturing. *See also* Industry
  employment in, 11–12
  in LDCs, 167
Marconi, Guglielmo, 50
Market forces
  and career choices, 165
  and energy demand, 97
  and forecasting, 83
  self-realization and, 253
Market research, on energy-related
  consumer behaviors, 81
Markets
  frictionless, 174–175
  for urban residence, 64
Marshall, T. H., 42, 68
Maruyama, Magoroh, 249
Marx, Karl, 157
Mass consumerism, and futurological
  research, 235

Mass media
  power of, 41–42
  and social change, 243
  values dominated by, 243
Mastercard, 194
Material satisfaction, in trans-industrial
  society, 249
Max Planck Institute, 137
Measles vaccine, 54
Mechanization, and energy demand, 97
Media. See also Mass media
  access to, 218–219
  global TV, 81
  television in, 49, 52
Mendel, Gregor, 49, 50
Mergers, 173
Methane gases, during ice ages, 126
Methane production, agricultural, 66
Metric measures, international
  agreements on, 68
Microelectromechanical machines
  (mems), 25
Microscope
  electron, 52
  scanning tunneling, 24
Microsoft, 2
Migration
  and population growth, 9
  poverty-caused, 254
  rising pressures for, 64
  to urban areas, 36
Militarization, and energy demand,
  97
Military-industrial complex, 236, 246,
  248
Military technology, and energy
  transformations, 100
Minorities. See also Women
  income of, 174
  integration of, 254
Mitigation strategies, 149
Mobility
  of capital, 223
  social, 242
Modernization
  as predictable change, 240
  self-reinforcing, 239
Molecular biology, 23

Molecular engineering, predictions for,
  241
MONDEX card, 195
Monetary management, national, 12
Monetary policy
  "credit view" of, 191, 197, 198, 199
  inluence of, 180
  money growth targets for, 182–184
  "money view" of, 190–191, 193, 199–
  200
  and political level of unification, 205
"Monte Carlo" estimation technique,
  145
Montreal protocol, 215
Monynihan, Daniel Patrick, 18
Moons, artificial, 240
Morgan, M. G., 140, 147, 149
Mortality, childhood, in developing
  countries, 59
Mortgages
  commercial, 199
  home, 198
Motorization, and energy demand, 97
Mt. Agung, eruption of, 128
Mountain effects, 136
Mt. Krakatoa, eruption of, 128
Mt. Pinatubo, and climate change, 128
Movies, invention of talking, 52
Multifold-trend, 239, 240, 241
Mutual funds, 198
Mythology, national identities from,
  223

Nanotechnology, potential of, 25
Narayanan, V., 144
National Fuels and Energy Policy Study,
  Congressional, 84, 85
Nationalism, 227
  resurgence of, 253
  in world community, 211
National Research Council (NRC),
  U.S., on population predictions, 44
National Science Foundation (NSF),
  U.S., disingenuous projections of, 11,
  163–165
Nations
  and cultural homogeneity, 225
  political subsystems of, 244

Nation-states
  erosion of, 222–223, 245
  and global externalities, 220
  mobility across, 226
  in monetary sphere, 201
  role of, 210, 252
  safety nets of, 221
  and social change, 244–245
  sources of power of, 224
  values of, 212
  and WTO, 222
NATO (North Atlantic Treaty
  Organization)
  in Balkans, 210
  military power of, 94
Nature, 164–165
Nature, in trans-industrial society, 249,
  250
Navy, U.S., reasons for maintaining, 100
Neolithic revolution, 251
Nerves of Government, The (Deutsch), 244
Netherlands, decline of coal
  consumption in, 108
New Stalinism scenario, 23
Newton, Isaac, 6, 17
New York subway system's "smart
  cards," 195
Nice, Treaty of, 217
Niche-oriented production, 169
Nitrogen, global cycle of, 39, 40
Nitrogen oxides, as greenhouse gases,
  135
Nongovernmental organizations
  (NGOs)
  on renewable energy, 91–92
  and workers' causes, 175
Nordhaus, William D., 140, 146, 147,
  148, 149
Norms, social
  international evolution of, 227
  in trans-industrial society, 249
North, Douglas C., 68
North America, PGER in, 41
North Atlantic, rapid circulation changes
  in, 139
North-south conflict, 252
Norway, decline of coal consumption
  in, 109

Novelty, in forecasts, 21, 25
Nuclear disaster, 243
Nuclear fusion, 176
Nuclear power, 254
  buildup of, 94
  growth of, 98
  and political systems, 243–244
  safety of, 114
  U.S. DOE forecast for, 110–111
Nuclear wars, predictions for, 250

Occupational Outlook Handbook (DOL),
  159–160
Oceanic mixing processes, 136
Oceans
  development of food sources of, 65
  farming of, 241
  management of, 66
Ogilvey, James, 7
Oil
  access to foreign, 93
  forecasting demand for, 80
  market share of, 86–87
  unreliability of forecasts for, 104
Oil crises, 114, 248
Oil imports, U.S. dependence on,
  110
Oil prices
  failure to forecast, 114
  false expectations about, 115
  forecasting of, 88, 103
Oil shocks, 19, 21, 86, 114
OPEC (Organization of Petroleum
  Exporting Countries), 21, 89, 114
Optimal currency areas, standard theory
  of, 204
"Oracle bones," 13
Oslo, Mankind 2000 in, 234, 244–
  247
Outcomes
  achieving preferable, 9–10
  possible, 4
Output
  and central bank actions, 206
  and disinflation, 186
  and role of central banks, 193
Outsourcing work, 169
Ozone, as greenhouse gas, 135

Pacific countries
  economic activity of women in, 42
  PGER in, 41
Pakistan, oil consumption of, 90
Palmer, 91
Parents, single, 174
Peace, among developed nations, 229
"Peace corps," 247
"Peaceful coexistence," forecasting, 246
Peace-keeping forces, 246
Penicillin, discovery of, 52
Pension funds, 169
  rapid advance of, 198
  U.S. securities bought by, 189
Perot, Ross, 158
Personal services, and labor force, 167
PERT (Program Evaluation and Review
  Technique), 82
Pesticides, 52, 53, 65
Phillips curve, 19
Photovoltaic solar cells, 111
Physicists, focus on future of, 234
Pigou, Arthur, 212
Pincus, Gregory, 54
Planning
  global integration of, 247
  social, 255
  society's dependence on, 233
Platt, John R., 247
Polar drift, 40
Policeman, government role as, 215
Policy makers, insights vs. answers for,
  146
Polio vaccine, 54
Political rights, 9, 42
Political scientists
  focus on future of, 233–234
  as forecasters, 79
  on technological change, 114–115
Political systems, in nuclear world, 243–
  244. See also Nation-states
Political systems, international
  de-ideologization of, 246
  dynamics of, 247
  "technification" of, 246
Politics
  economics and, 214
  and EVs, 112

isolationist forms of, 244
predictions for, 252
and renewable energy, 92–93
"Polluter pays" principle, 146
Pollution
  and coal consumption, 86
  and governance structures, 220
  greenhouse effect, 10, 126, 133–134
  transboundary, 13
Population, human
  aging of, 166, 167
  densities, 63
  and futurological research, 235
  global, 61
  preventable ills of, 69
  projections for, 8
  quantitative indicators of, 30–31
  20th-century, 29
  in 21st century, 59–64
  widespread decline in, 68–69
Population Council, 54
Population estimates
  in 1950, 43
  fragility of, 8
  uncertainty of, 58
Population growth
  agriculture and, 48
  and arable land, 304
  and energy demand, 97
  failure to predict, 37, 241
  global rate, 35, 36, 37
  and per capita production, 257n.18
  predictions for, 43–46, 62, 250
  and social rights, 43
  in 21st century, 59
  and TFR, 37
  after World War II, 47
Post-industrial society, 237
  as information society, 239–243
  as planetary society, 243–248
  A. Toffler's view of, 242–243
  as trans-industrial society, 248–251
Poverty
  elimination of, 67
  global unelectrified, 96
  migration caused by, 254
  predictions for, 250
Power, global integration of, 247

Power plants, new, 90
Power relations
and future studies, 248
and workers' rights, 43
Prague, collective action in, 227
Precipitation, 136
Predictions. *See also* Projections
periodicity for, 6
point, 7
Prices. *See also* Oil prices
controls on, 185
effect of central banks on, 179–180
and Internet, 175
and monetary policy, 180, 182–184
Price shocks, impact of, 139. *See also* Oil
shocks
Primary gross enrollment ratio (PGER),
41
Prinn, Ronald, 141
Privacy, at workplace, 173
Prize, The (Yergin), 116
Production workers, shifting demands
for, 161. *See also* Labor force
Productivity, progress and, 177
Professional associations, 176
Professionals, shifting demands for,
161
Profit-sharing, 169
Prognoses, and projections, 233
Programming, planning and, 233. *See
also* Computers
Projections
expectations in, 165
fixed coefficient, 159–163
loss functions in, 165
methodology for standard, 161
prognoses and, 233
Prosperity
of developed nations, 229
and sustainable environment, 25
Public discussion, topic of future in, 4,
235
Public opinion
on energy industries, 115
for environment-conserving energy
products, 81
"green," 86
Punishment, ritual, 218

Quantum theory, 24
Quinine
impact of, 49
synthesis of, 52

Radar technology, 236
Radiative energy transport, 136
Radio, introduction of, 49, 50
Rahmstorf, S., 143
Rainfall, computer simulations of, 131
RAND Corp., 236, 241, 248
Regionalism, resurgence of, 253
Relativity, general, 23
Renewables. *See also* Energy
declining prices of, 99
in Europe, 109
forecasting for, 91, 92, 94
need for investment in, 96
private investment in, 95
self-financing of, 98
sources of, 97–98
in U.S., 110
Republicans in U.S., contract with
America of, 217
Research. *See also* Future studies;
Science
futurological, 234–235
in-depth, 26
market, 81
and uncertainty, 151
Research and development,
institutionalization of, 239
Research organizations, 82
Reserve ratios, required, 199
Reserves, central bank's monopoly over,
199
Reservoirs, impact of, 40
Resource depletion hypothesis, 82
Resources for Freedom Report of 1952, 84
Resources for Future (RFF) study, 91
Retirement, 166
Revolutions
industrial, 3, 125
Iranian, 86
permanent, 243
Rice
and cytogenetics, 49
IRRI, 55

Rifkind, Jeremy, 158, 170
Risk
  managing, 26
  useful anticipation for, 27
River, flow of time as, 17
Robots, predictions for, 240
Rock, John, 54
Rodrik, Dani, 221
Roszak, Theodore, 248
Rotmans, Jan, 146
Roughgarden, T., 148
Rubinfeld, Daniel, 215
Russia, crisis in, 221

Salaries, vs. contingent pay, 169. *See also*
  Labor force; Workforce
Sales contract, 168
Salvarsan, discovery of, 50
Sanderson, Warren C., 45
Satellites
  forecasting, 14
  introduction of, 54
  predictions for, 240, 241, 252
Scarcity, economics of, 99, 248
Scenario building, 3–4, 7, 15
Scenarios
  "competition," 70
  "end of the world," 150–151
  forces for change in, 24
  as forecasting tool, 22
  "it is good for business," 150–151
  "partnership," 70
  production of, 7
  range of emissions, 150
  Shell 1984, 22
  "surprise," 141
  as systemic tool, 26
  transient climate change, 137
  of 21st century, 58–59
  typical central tendency, 78
Schmidt-Gernig, Alexander, 13–15
Schmittner, A., 143
Schneider, Stephen H., 10–11, 141,
  148, 149
Schor, Juliet, 170
Schwartz, Peter, 3, 4, 7
Science
  funding of, 163

interaction with social science of, 5
  as oracle, 2
  and policy response, 220
  projections in, 162–163 (see also
    Projections)
  and uncertainty, 23
Scientific insight, major jumps in, 23–24
Scientific knowledge
  and futurological research, 235
  predictions for, 252
Scientists
  environmental anxiety of, 147–148
  NSF projections for, 163–165
  progress and, 177
Sea ice dynamics, 136
Sea levels, increase in. *See also* Oceans
  probability of, 145
  projections for, 144
Seasons, climate sensitivity to, 129
Seattle, collective action in, 227
Securities markets, 198
Securitization, of credit markets, 198–
  199
Security, energy, 93–94
Security Council, U.N., 216
Self-employment, 170
Self-realization, value of, 253
Semiconductors, 3
Sensitivity analysis, 22
Service sector
  labor force in, 167
  in post-industrial society, 239
Settlement, voluntary negotiated, 212,
  215
Sexually transmitted diseases, 49, 50
Shell
  investment in renewables of, 95
  solar investment of, 99
Shell-Eskom joint venture, 109
Simplicity, 6
Simulation. *See also* Computer
  simulations
  of climate, 10
  power of, 26
Single cells, regeneration of whole plants
  from, 55
Skyscrapers
  advent of, 101

electricity-generating screening walls
on, 101
Smallpox eradication campaign, 55
"Smart cards," 194–195
Smil, Vaclav, 84
Social activist groups, 176
Social analysis, 242
Social change
accelerated, 243
and impact of climate change, 11
predictions for, 252–253
and rapid scientific-technological
change, 248
and reproductive choices, 70
and role of nation-states, 244–245
Social insurance programs, U.S., 215
Socialist systems
early predictions for, 246
inefficiencies in, 228
Social mobility, 242
Social movements, 255
Social protection, supranational
cooperation for, 222
Social rights, 9, 42–43
Social science
and cybernetics, 236
interaction with science of, 5
as oracle, 2
and policy response, 220
Social Science and the Future, Oxford
Conference on, 7, 181, 207
Social scientists. *See also* Political
scientists
and energy forecasts, 78, 103
focus on future of, 233–234
forecasting of, 113–114
predictions of, 115–116
Social survey analyses, 116
Society
classification of, 245
"cybernetic," 251
"cybernetization" of, 239
planetary, 238, 243–248
post-industrial, 237
in 21st century, 59–64
and techno-scientific bias, 251
totally mobile, 242
trans-industrial, 238

Soete, Luc, 171
Solar energy, 89
cost performance of, 91
demand for, 112
forecasts for, 90
photovoltaic, 91
Solar energy age, 111–112
Solar flares, 66
Solar heating
home systems, 81
industry's support for, 98
Solar photovoltaic manufacturing
industry, 111
Solar systems, planetary, 24
Soot particles, 135
South Africa
electrification program of, 109
EVs in, 90
renewables in, 105
Shell/Escom's joint venture in, 98
Soviet Union
fall of, 22–23, 86
system-breaking revolution in, 255
Soybeans, control of growth of, 51
Space exploration
potential of
predictions for, 241, 254–255
"Spaceship earth," 247
Spectroscope, invention of mass, 51
Spencer, Herbert, 238
Sports teams, loyalties to, 228
Sputnik, 54
Stagflation, 19
Stainless steel, invention of, 50
Standardization, in trans-industrial
society, 249
Stanford Research Institute, 249
Stanislaw, Joseph, 88, 89
Statistical analyses, loss functions in, 165
Steam engine, 3
Stocker, T. F., 143
Stock options, 169
Stone, Peter, 141
Student loans, government-sponsored,
199
Student movement, 248
Subjective probability estimation, 140–
143

Superconductors, 176
Supernational bodies, 13
Superpowers
  rivalry of, 236
  and role of nation-states, 245
  U.S., 93
Super string theory, 24
Supply, standard mechanical projections
  of, 165. *See also* Energy supplies
Supply side, forecasts on, 159
Supranational governance
  delegated authority for, 216
  form of, 221
  after WWII, 210
Supranational organizations
  development of, 254
  role of, 209
  social protection offered by, 222
Survival, good scenarios for, 26
Sustainability, economics and, 248
Sweden
  decline of coal consumption in, 109
  wage inequality in, 173–174
Swiss National Bank, 184
Symbiosis, in trans-industrial society,
  250
Syphilis, 49, 50
System analysts, focus on future of,
  234
Systems theory
  influence on society of, 237
  and social forecasts, 236, 237

TAR, 141
Taxation
  carbon, 1473
  of mobile capital, 223
Tax records, government responsibility
  for, 226
Tax treaties, 215
Taylor, Gordon R., 242, 248
Technological change, 14
  impact on society of, 253
  and income inequality, 174
  societal resistance to, 254
  and sustainable energy supply, 99
Technological Forecasting and Social Change,
  234

Technological innovations
  and futurological research, 235
  and governance, 227
  and post-industrial society, 239
Technology
  global integration of, 247
  and governance structures, 220
  and national governments, 224
  new, 80
  and uncertainty, 23
Telecommunication, impact of, 49
Telecomputing, economic growth in,
  84. *See also* Computers
Telephone service providers' "smart
  cards," 195
Teletype, invention of, 52
Television
  impact of, 49
  invention of, 52
Temperature, earth's
  computer simulations of, 131
  determination of, 135
Temporary help agencies, 169
Tenure, defined, 169
Terrestrial ecosystem changes, feedbacks
  associated with, 139
Terrorism, predictions for, 250
Texas, and falling oil prices, 204
Thailand, coal-fired power plants in, 107
Theobald, Robert, 248
Think tanks, 82, 234
Thomas, Robert Paul, 68
Thompson, Starley, 141
Thompson, William Irwin, 248
Three Gorges hydroelectric dam project,
  87
Tiebout, Charles, 224
Time, flow of, 17
Titus, J., 144
Tobacco
  antibiotic resistance of, 56
  control of growth of, 51
Toffler, Alvin, 242–243, 253
Tolbert, Caroline J., 217
Tolerance, global integration of, 247
Total fertility rate (TFR)
  calculation of, 36
  world, 36–37, 47

Totalitarianism, impact of Internet on, 225
Tourism, mass, 254
Tournois, Julien, 51
Town meetings, New England, 213, 225
Toyota, Prius hybrid electric of, 89. *See also* Electric vehicles
Tractor, invention of, 50
Trade policy. *See also* Monetary policy
and globalization, 13
impact of changes in, 139
Trade unions, role of, 175. *See also* Labor force; Unions
Training, postschool, 166. *See also* Education
Trans-industrial society, 238, 248–251
Transistor, invention of, 53
Translation machines, 241
Transnationalism, 246
Transportation
decreasing costs of, 227
predictions for, 240
Transportation fuel
demand for, 89–90
forecasting demand for, 80
renewables for, 104
after 2020–2030, 96
Transportation technology, and energy transformations, 100
Treasury, U.S., securities issued by, 189
Treaties
Maastricht, 179, 205, 222
to regulate supranational externalities, 215
tax, 215
of Westphalia, 210
Tuberculosis
epidemiology of, 69
isoniazid for, 54
Turbulent convection, 136
Twentieth Century Fund, 4, 8

Uncertainty
classes of, 23
and range of probabilities, 150
research and, 151
scenarios based on, 24–25

Unemployment
and agreements between states, 215
and disinflation, 186
Europe's high, 179
in U.S., 174, 186
Unionism, 157
Unions
and demand for leisure, 171
for doctors, 175
United Kingdom
decentralized authority in, 210, 229
distribution of income in, 173–174
employment contracts in, 169
hours worked in, 171
United Nations
Commission on Status of Women of, 42
Conference on Human Environment, 55
delegated authority of, 216
Food and Agricultural Organization of, 53
inability to act of, 216
Population Division of, 44, 60, 61
Universal Declaration of Human Rights of, 53
United States
as democratic federation, 216–217
dependence on imported oil of, 93
distribution of income in, 173–174
dual earner families in, 170
employment contracts in, 169
energy policy options for, 94
hours worked in, 171
international reliance on, 222
military power of, 94
national ballistic missile defense of, 110
renewables in, 105
solar investment of, 99
status of women in, 41
"Units of account," 203
Urban areas, migration to, 36
Urbanization
and energy demand, 96
in 21st century, 59–60

Vaccination
impact of, 49
international agreements on, 68

Valery, Paul, 17
Validation protocols, 138
Value of people, rise in, 69–70
Values
  and generation gap, 251
  and governance structures, 220
  homogenization of, 253
  specifications for, 19
  in trans-industrial society, 249
Veto rights
  in EU, 209
  in U.N. Security Council, 216
Videos, predictions for, 240
Violence, predictions for, 250
Virtual reality, 26
Visa card, 194
Volcanic dust veils, 128, 138
Von Bertalanffy, Ludwig von, 237
Von Wassermann, August, 50

Wack, Pierre, 3
Wagar, W. Warren, 248, 250
Wages
  vs. contingent pay, 169
  controls on, 185
  and labor shortages, 163
Wallerstein, Immanuel, 250
Warming trend, of past century, 126–
  127. *See also* Global warming
Wars
  and forecasting errors, 2
  nuclear, 250
  Second World War, 182, 233, 236
Washington, collective action in,
  227
Washington, Warren, 141
Waskow, Arthur I., 246–247
Water, global cycle of, 39, 40
Water vapor, as greenhouse gas, 134
Watson, James, 235
Wealth, definition of, 67
Weapons, nuclear
  development of, 236
  and societies' survival, 244
  spread of, 114
Weather
  evolution of, 131
  prediction models for, 66

predictions for control of, 240, 241
  unpredictability of, 131–132
Welfare states, large, 171
Western societies, modernization in,
  239. *See also* Developed countries;
  Industrialized countries
Westphalia, Treaty of, 210
Wheat
  and cytogenetics, 49
  Mexican dwarf, 55
Wherden, William, 158
Wiener, Anthony, 239
Wiener, Norbert, 14, 236, 237, 240,
  241
Wigley, Tom, 141
Wind energy, 80, 89
  costs of, 91
  forecasts for, 90
  U.S. consumption of, 91
Winds
  computer simulations of, 131
  surface, 136
Women
  economic role of, 5
  education of, 166
  in labor force, 170–171
  and population growth, 9
  rights of, 53
  role of, 254
  in scientific workforce, 164
  status of, 41, 42
  in 21st century, 61, 64
  in workforce, 161, 167
Work
  computerization of, 167
  conflicting scenarios in, 168
  and demand for leisure, 170–172
  "end of," 170
  feminization of, 166–167
  incentive for, 172
  outsourcing, 169
Workaholic model, American, 172
Workers
  foreign high-tech, 171
  organizing, 175
  security for, 169
  shifting demands for, 161
  value of, 43

Workforce
  aging, 170
  educated, 170
  future developments in, 165–168
Working life, 5
Workplace
  changes in, 172–173
  democracy in, 177
  impact of computers on, 172
  privacy at, 173
  trends in, 11–12
  "virtual," 158
"Work-roles dilemma," 249
Worksharing, 171
World Bank, 209
  population projections of, 44
  solar investment of, 99
World Future Society, 234
World Futures Studies Federation
  conferences, 234
World modeling, 82
World Trade Organization (WTO)
  delegated authority of, 216
  and nation-states, 222
World War II, 182
  and information technology, 236
  and Western thought, 233
World Wide Web, 26. *See also* Internet
Wright brothers, 50
Wunsch, Carl, 141

Year 2000, futurological research on,
  234–235
Yergin, Daniel, 88, 89, 116
Yoga, 249
Young people, proportion of, 35–36
Yugoslavia, former, 223